W9-CTY-430

OFF
THE
DEEP
END

Nic Compton

OFF THE DEEP END

A HISTORY OF MADNESS AT SEA

ADLARD COLES NAUTICAL

BLOOMSBURY

LONDON · OXFORD · NEW YORK · NEW DELHI · SYDNEY

Adlard Coles Nautical
An imprint of Bloomsbury Publishing Plc

50 Bedford Square
London
WC1B 3DP
UK

1385 Broadway
New York
NY 10018
USA

www.bloomsbury.com
www.adlardcoles.com

ADLARD COLES, ADLARD COLES NAUTICAL and the Buoy logo
are trademarks of Bloomsbury Publishing Plc

First published 2017

© Nic Compton, 2017

British Library Cataloguing-in-Publication Data
A catalogue record for this book is available from the British Library.

Library of Congress Cataloguing-in-Publication data has been applied for.

ISBN: HB: 978-1-4729-4112-1
Trade PB: 978-1-4729-4113-8
ePDF: 978-1-4729-4111-4
ePub: 978-1-4729-4110-7

2 4 6 8 10 9 7 5 3 1

Text design by carrdesignstudio.com

Typeset in ITC Stone Serif Std by Deanta Global Publishing Services, Chennai, India
Printed and bound in Great Britain by CPI Group (UK) Ltd, Croydon CR0 4YY

MIX
Paper from
responsible sources
FSC® C020471

To find out more about our authors and books visit www.bloomsbury.com. Here you will
find extracts, author interviews, details of forthcoming events and the option to
sign up for our newsletters.

Chapter illustrations by pavila and IADA, Shutterstock.com

JAN - 8 2018

To Anna
who keeps me sane

'The wonder is always new that any sane man
can be a sailor'
Ralph Waldo Emerson

ARTWORK

This list refers to the illustrations in the plate section.

p1 (top) *Flying Dutchman*, Albert Pinkham Ryder, 1887

p2 (top) frontispiece from *The Voyage of the Beagle* by Charles Darwin, 1890

p2 (bottom) *The Mutineers turning Lieut Bligh and part of the officers and crew adrift from His Majesty's ship the Bounty*, Robert Dodd, 1790

p3 (top) *Critical position of HMS Investigator on the north coast of Baring Island*, engraving by William Simpson, original by Lieutenant SG Cresswell, 1854

p3 (bottom left) *Christopher Columbus*, by Sebastian del Piombo, 1519

p3 (bottom right) *Vice Admiral Robert FitzRoy* (1805–65), Samuel Lane

p4 (top) *Naval Hospital, Haslar, near Portsmouth: view from right*, coloured aquatint with etching by J Wells, 1799, after J Hall, 1799

p4 (bottom) *William Norris confined in Bethlem Hospital for 12 years*, from etching by G Cruikshank, circa 1820 after drawing from life by G Arnald, 1814

p5 (top) *The Raft of the Medusa*, by Théodore Géricault, 1819

CONTENTS

INTRODUCTION

Alexandria, 14 December 1941

On a moonless night, 56 kilometres (35 miles) north-west of Alexandria, my father is swimming for his life. The sea around him is pitch black but he can just make out the shape of various bits of ship's detritus and several dead bodies, covered in oil slick. Around him he can hear the cries of men injured in the carnage, though whenever he tries to swim towards them, the sound vanishes into the darkness. Eventually, the lights of a ship appear over the horizon and, as the vessel's white ensign looms into view, he realises rescue is at hand.

Lt Cmdr Charles Compton, to give him his full title, was serving on HMS *Galatea*, patrolling the north coast of Africa, when the 5,200-ton light cruiser was torpedoed by a German U-boat. The ship took just three minutes to sink – six times faster than the *Lusitania* – giving its crew almost no time to evacuate. Luckily for him, my father was in the bridge at the time and was able to scramble out and jump into the sea. The men working or sleeping deep in the bowels of the ship didn't stand a chance: those not killed by the explosions were trapped in the steel hull and drowned.

A total of 469 British sailors died off Alexandria that night: 447 ratings, 21 officers and the ship's commander, Captain EWB Sim. About 100 men ended up in the sea and were rescued by two British warships that were in the area – they were the lucky ones.

My father was doubly lucky. After being treated at a hospital in Alexandria, he was evacuated to Cape Town and then to London, where he became naval advisor on the Noël Coward film *In Which We Serve*. He never saw active service again, but instead was posted to the Foreign Office in London, and at war's end was transferred to the British embassy in Havana. He went on to enjoy a few years leading the high life in Hollywood, dining with Grace Kelly, dancing with Jackie Bouvier and having Christmases with the Kennedy family. For a couple of glorious summers, he hung out in Florida and went partying with JFK, long before the latter launched his presidential campaign.

Despite this, the events of that night in December 1941 would remain with him for the rest of his life. Years later, when I asked him about his wartime experiences, he described the excitement of setting off on his previous ship, HMS *Bulldog*, under the command of John 'Woozy' Wisden, who liked to crack open a bottle of champagne as they headed out to sea, and of dodging German bombers in the Channel thanks to a sudden fog.

However, when it came to talking about HMS *Galatea* he grew uncomfortable. He described the death of so many of his friends and colleagues, and his feelings of guilt that he and his fellow officers had not been able to save their ship – that they had somehow failed the rest of the crew. But quite quickly, he clammed up, and I realised it was time to change the subject. I later discovered that, even into his mid-nineties, he would sometimes wake up at night, shouting, apparently reliving the horrors of his wartime experiences of 70 years before.

Nowadays, like thousands of other survivors of war trauma, my father would probably be treated for post-traumatic stress disorder (PTSD), but in those days you were more likely to be given a slap on the back and told to get on with it – stiff upper lip, and all that. Like most men of his generation, he carried the psychological scars of his wartime experiences to his grave.

✴   ✴   ✴

Madness at sea is a largely hidden, unreported phenomenon. This is partly because, by definition, it takes place in an alien environment, away from society's gaze, and only the most dramatic examples make the news. Many people have heard of Donald Crowhurst, the singlehanded sailor who became delusional and jumped over the side after faking his position in a round-the-world race, but few know about the dozens of merchant seaman 'lost at sea' every year without explanation, half of whose deaths are thought to be suicides.

It's also a little-discussed subject because of the more general stigma attached to mental illness. Most people are quite happy to talk about their physical injuries in great detail, but rather more squeamish when something similar happens to their brain. Nowhere is this more the case than in the macho environment of a ship. Seamen are supposed to be tough, and it doesn't do to show any form of weakness at sea – physical or otherwise. They're typically a superstitious lot too, and in the past it was considered unlucky to have a madman on board – in the same way that it was unlucky to have a woman or a pig or a dead body on board. A sailor showing signs of mental illness was more likely to be thrown over the side than given a course of counselling.

Yet there are many reasons why seamen might be more-than-usually susceptible to mental illness. First, there's the physical environment. Living in a confined space with your fellow sailors for weeks or months on end with no chance of escape is likely to test the most acquiescent soul. And they certainly packed them in: 460 men slept in the lower gun deck of HMS *Victory*, their hammocks slung just 40cm (16in) apart, head to tail. It's not much better in a modern yacht, with the living space of some vessels taking part in one major round-the-world race calculated as being half the size stipulated by the EU as the lower limit for a multi-occupancy prison cell.

Then there's the stress of travelling to unknown lands, far away from family and friends, facing unpredictable hazards, with no support mechanism other than your fellow crewmates. If you're bonded within the group, then you'll do fine, but if you're on the periphery, then things are only going to get worse – much worse. Even on a huge cruise ship packed with 3,000 or more passengers, it's possible to feel claustrophobic, lonely and isolated – as testified by the hundreds of suicides on ocean liners.

As if that weren't enough, the sea has its very own smorgasbord of special, ocean-borne illnesses, guaranteed to eat away at your sanity. Top of the list during the Age of Sail was scurvy, which, in addition to horrendous physical symptoms, was often accompanied by extreme hypersensitivity, such that the scent of flowers could prove agonisingly painful and the sound of gunshot could kill a man. Then there was calenture, a type of heat stroke that turned men delirious and compelled them to jump over the side, usually to their deaths. Even today, many crews are affected by a modern version of calenture, which is thought to account for hundreds of cases of people unaccountably lost at sea – including, possibly, media tycoon Robert Maxwell.

The thousands of sailors who were shipwrecked during the Age of Sail faced their own conundrum. Surrounded by water, it was tempting to scoop up a mouthful of cool, blue sea and quench their thirst – but the certain outcome, as countless survivor accounts testify, was delirium and death. Others suffered an even worse fate. Take the whaleboat *Essex*, the original inspiration for *Moby Dick*. After their ship sank, the crew descended to cannibalism and were eventually found clutching the bones of their fellow crew, out of their minds with grief and hunger.

The scale of the problem was summed up by the Royal Navy's own Physician of the Fleet, who suggested that sailors were seven times more likely to go mad than the rest of the population. Surprisingly, given contemporary attitudes to mental illness, the Royal Navy was already on the case and had been sending its 'Naval Manicks' to a privately run asylum in London since 1755 or even earlier. When this facility was found wanting, it opened its own mental ward at the naval hospital in Haslar in 1818 – 10 years before the British Parliament got its own house in order with the first Madhouses Act.

Amazingly, the case studies and hospital journal for Block F at Haslar still survive, in musty boxes at the National Archives in Kew. Handwritten on thick parchment are the stories of hundreds of sailors, some injured in battle, others struck on the head by the ship's rigging or turned suicidal after picking up a nasty tropical disease. But many more were afflicted by more mundane concerns, such as the death of loved ones, unrequited love, uncontrollable jealousy, disputes with their work colleagues, and that old sailor's curse, alcoholism – or, as one doctor put it, 'an excess in the use of ardent spirits'.

It was a similar story during World War II. When a psychiatrist asked a group of 'psychotic' patients at an American naval hospital why they had gone AWOL, the replies were surprisingly ordinary, ranging from 'My train, bus or plane was late' to 'I wanted to see my wife and baby' and 'I can't keep away from girls'. Right down at the bottom of the list were most of the work-related issues, such as 'I was afraid of the sea', 'I didn't like the ship I was on' and 'I couldn't get on with the boatswain's mate'.

Whatever its cause, the stigma of mental illness remained. As recently as World War I, the number of sailors suffering from what was then commonly called 'shell shock' was buried in the official statistics under the more discreet term 'neurasthenia'. Around 20,000 naval staff were treated for this condition – or 5 per cent of the total force. By World War II, the condition had been reclassified as 'war neurosis', with nearly 25,000 personnel being treated. It wasn't just the name that had changed but the symptoms too. Whereas during World War I shell shock was typically characterised by shaking and tremors, by World War II the condition had been internalised and re-emerged in a variety of stomach complaints, earning the conflict the nickname of 'the gut war'.

Whether on land or at sea, some people are more predisposed to mental illness than others, including many of the world's most celebrated sailors. No less a figure than Christopher Columbus has been retrospectively diagnosed as suffering from bipolar disorder (aka manic depression), and the evidence suggests that at the very least he had delusions of grandeur. Charles Darwin's chum Robert FitzRoy, who was captain of HMS *Beagle* and later founder of Britain's

Met Office, had a history of depression in the family and ended up committing suicide – as did his predecessor on the 'cursed' little ship, Pringle Stokes. And there were few Royal Navy captains more wantonly sadistic than George Vancouver, who thought nothing of sentencing his uppity crew to five dozen lashes – ie five times the Admiralty recommendation – for a single misdemeanour. He was retrospectively diagnosed as having an untreated hyperthyroid condition, among other possible ailments, which would have explained his sudden mood swings.

More recently, there was the case of Paul Termann, a German sailor with a chip on his shoulder who embarked on a transatlantic voyage with a stranger he met on the quayside in the Canaries. During the crossing, what might have seemed like trivial disagreements on land grew so out of proportion under the distorting lens of the sea that he ended up killing the stranger – the yacht's owner – and his girlfriend and throwing them over the side. Then there was the ex-convict Bill Vincent who, during the final leg of a round-the-world race, took the extraordinary step of diving to his death from the back of the yacht he was sailing on. At the official inquiry, no one could explain his actions – though it was almost certainly to do with his own personal issues rather than anything that had happened during the voyage.

On a grander scale, it's easy to see why the sea might attract more than its fair share of misfits. Research into why Norwegian immigrants in the USA suffered from higher levels of schizophrenia than their counterparts back home concluded that people who were susceptible to mental illness were less likely to integrate into society and therefore more likely to emigrate in the first place. The logic can be extended to the sea: people on the margins of society are more likely to opt for an ocean-going life than those who are already successfully embedded within it. It's a point made in a recent report on the high level of suicides among Polish fishermen, which suggests: 'It is possible that persons with concealed social integration problems deliberately choose the employment on sea-going ships.'[1]

For what the sea does is magnify personality flaws, prodding and prying into a person's soul, until their true character is revealed. It's a cliché that the most convivial person, full of bonhomie and good cheer at the bar, can become a tyrant once at the helm of a yacht, and to some extent we are all affected in that way.

This is a theme picked up again and again in literature, be it in the traumatic voyage of self-discovery described in the *Odyssey*, the tortured guilt of the Ancient Mariner, the monomania of Captain Ahab in *Moby Dick*, or the destructive paranoia of Captain Queeg in the *Caine Mutiny*. The sea, far from being a benign and welcoming place, is an inhospitable environment where man's sanity is tested and often found wanting – and, as many authors have discovered, it provides a perfect setting in which to stage a psychological drama.

It's a rich area for psychologists too, and there are several case studies of long-distance yacht races as well as more general studies of the 'outlaw sea', where national laws don't apply. The philosopher Foucault described ships as 'not only the greatest instrument of economic development [...] but the greatest reservoir of imagination.'[2] And it's a thin line between the imagination and the fantastical; reason and madness.

But that's not the only view we have of the sea. Alongside this almost apocalyptic vision, there is a more benign interpretation of the sea – promoted in recent years by thalassotherapists and tour promoters alike – as a place of healing, both of the body and of the mind. Sail training is widely touted as being a means of improving the behaviour of young offenders, while organisations such as Turn to Starboard have shown how sailing can be used to help military veterans recover from PTSD.

In his own way, my father discovered this truth for himself. Despite his traumatic experiences in the navy during World War II, he was inexorably drawn back to the sea. First, he bought himself a small open boat, which he sailed around the Bahamas, and then, 20 years after being sunk on HMS *Galatea*, he returned to Europe and lived on, and raised a family on, boats – first an Essex smack, then a 60ft wooden ketch, and finally a classic motor yacht. For the next 15 years he taught people how to sail and took them on cruises around the Mediterranean, sharing with them the transformative, healing power of the sea.

CHAPTER 1

HERE BE DRAGONS

'The sea is as near as we come to another world.'[1]
Anne Stevenson

The moment you step on board a boat, the sea does its best to throw your mind into confusion. For a start, your highly developed sense of balance, which served you so well on land, is reduced to toddler status once you are afloat. Whereas on shore the earth's gravitational pull and the visual horizon provide reliable reference points for the vertical and the horizontal axes, that all goes out of the porthole when you're at sea. In rough weather, a boat will roll, pitch, heave, surge, yaw and sway – the aptly named 'six degrees of freedom'. What the body experiences as gravitational pull is a combination of all these factors, and almost certainly doesn't correspond to the actual vertical.

Your body sticks to its old habits, though, and insists the horizon must be at right angles to what it perceives as gravity – but the horizon won't play ball. In fact, the horizon seems to be jumping around all over the place, which it isn't supposed to do either. Meanwhile, your immediate surroundings seem to be standing still – particularly if you are looking down or are below decks – which contradicts the messages from your body that suggest you've accidentally wandered into a giant washing machine.

It is this disjunction between the various messages your body is receiving that is the main cause of seasickness. Your body is telling you one thing, while your eyes are telling you another. Our brain tends to prioritise visual data, but if it can't reconcile the different sources of information, it gets confused and the result is nausea. It's the body's way of saying: 'Stop, something's not right. Please resubmit information.'

Sea motion and seasickness aren't the only difficulties the sea throws at the unwary sailor to challenge his or her grasp on 'normality'. I remember when I was a child, as we were motoring off the coast of Italy on a particularly glassy calm day, a headland before us became strangely stratified. At first it looked as if it was just a strange rock formation, but as I stared at it the blobs of rock changed shape and the headland itself seemed to move. Had I been of a more susceptible nature, I might have thought I was going mad, or at least asked to see an optician. Instead, I dismissed it as heat haze, or a 'trick of the eye'.

In fact, it was a Fata Morgana. This is a mirage or, more accurately, a 'superior mirage', which takes place when the lower layers of air in the atmosphere are colder than the layers above it – rather than the other way round as is usual (also called a temperature inversion). Typically, this might happen on a clear winter's day, when the sun warms the upper layers of air while the lower layers are cooled by the sea. Under these conditions, the light rays from a distant object are bent (or refracted) so that it appears higher than it really is – or even upside down (known as looming).

It's not uncommon for objects on the other side of the horizon, which would usually be impossible to be see, to appear either on the horizon or even floating just above it – giving sailors the unique ability to see over the horizon! If the change of temperature is evenly spread, the object will look just the same as normal, but if the 'temperature gradient' is irregular it will be distorted and the object will appear taller (towering) or shorter (stooping). The latter is particularly dangerous when approaching land, when the coast may appear further away than it really is and lull a sailor into a fall sense of security.

In extreme cases, the object in the mirage will appear chopped up and distorted, and nothing like its original shape. In the Strait of Messina, between the toe of Italy and the island of Sicily, such mirages are so common that they have been given a special name: Fata Morgana, 'Fata' meaning fairy in Italian, and 'Morgana' after Morgan le Fay, a sorceress from Arthurian legend – so, literally, a 'fairy Morgana'. The phenomenon was first described 370 years ago by Father Ignazio Angelucci in a letter to his fellow priest Father Leone Sanzio:

'On the fifteenth of August, 1643, as I stood at my window, I was surprised with a most wonderful, delectable vision. The sea that washes the Sicilian shore swelled up, and became, for ten miles in length, like a chain of dark mountains; while the waters near our Calabrian coast grew quite smooth, and in an instant appeared as one clear polished mirror, reclining against the aforesaid ridge.

On this glass was depicted, in chiaroscuro, a string of several thousands of pilasters, all equal in altitude, distance, and degree of light and shade. In a moment they lost half their height, and bent into arcades, like Roman aqueducts. A long cornice was next formed on the top, and above it rose castles innumerable, all perfectly alike. These soon split into towers, which were shortly after lost in colonnades, then windows, and at last ended in pines, cypresses, and other trees, even and similar. This is the Fata Morgana, which, for twenty-six years, I had thought a mere fable.'[2]

This phenomenon is sometimes used to explain alleged UFO sightings, the idea being that the image of a car's headlight below the horizon might be deflected and look like a flying saucer skimming through the sky. It's also used to account for the many sightings of ghost ships at sea, something that has been a staple of sailors' yarns for almost as long as ships have sailed the oceans.

The most famous of these is the notorious *Flying Dutchman*. According to legend, the ship was trying to get around the Cape of Good Hope (or Cape Horn, depending on your source) during a terrible storm. Rather than pulling into harbour and awaiting better weather, the captain swore he would get around the cape come what may. For his arrogance, he and his crew were condemned to sail around the world forever. Another version has it that such heinous crimes were committed aboard the ship that the crew dared not return to port in case they were hanged as punishment. Either way, since its first recorded sighting in 1795, the ship has been regularly spotted by sailors the world over, and has inspired countless stories and books.

Among those who claim to have sighted the fabled ship was the future King George V, who was said to have seen the ship while sailing on HMS *Inconstant* off Australia in 1880. His tutor Dalton described the vision thus:

'At 4am the *Flying Dutchman* crossed our bows. A strange red light as of a phantom ship all aglow, in the midst of which light the masts, spars, and sails of a brig 200 yards distant stood out in strong relief as she came up on the port bow, where also the officer of the watch from the bridge clearly saw her, as did the quarterdeck midshipman, who was sent forward at once to the forecastle; but on arriving there was no vestige nor any sign whatever of any material ship was to be seen either near or right away to the horizon, the night being clear and the sea calm. Thirteen persons altogether saw her, including others from the other ships in the squadron, the *Cleopatra* and the *Tourmaline*.'[3]

Seeing the ship was supposed to portend terrible bad luck, and HMS *Inconstant* was no exception, as Dalton reported: 'At 10.45 am the ordinary seaman who had this morning reported the *Flying Dutchman* fell from the foretopmast crosstrees on to the topgallant forecastle and was smashed to atoms.'[4]

It would be churlish to dismiss the sighting of the *Flying Dutchman* by 13 sailors as an act of 'collective madness', and in most instances a Fata Morgana would explain the phenomenon. The image of a ship sailing below the horizon refracted as a 'looming' mirage would be visible to all on board, even though it might sail off in the opposite direction without ever actually coming over the horizon. Indeed, just such an explanation was offered to sailors by Frank Stockton in 1872, eight years before the sighting by King George and friends:

'The news soon spread through the vessel that a phantom-ship with a ghostly crew was sailing in the air over a phantom-ocean, and that it was a bad omen, and meant that not one of them should ever see land again. The captain was told the wonderful tale, and coming on deck, he explained to the sailors that this strange appearance was caused by the reflection of some ship that was sailing on the water below this image, but at such a distance they could not see it. There were certain conditions of the atmosphere, he said, when the sun's rays could form a perfect picture in the air of objects on the earth, like the images one sees in glass or water, but they were not generally upright, as in the case of this ship, but reversed – turned bottom upwards. This appearance in the air is called a mirage.

'He told a sailor to go up to the foretop and look beyond the phantom-ship. The man obeyed, and reported that he could see on the water, below the ship in the air, one precisely like it. Just then another ship was seen in the air, only this one was a steamship, and was bottom-upwards, as the captain had said these mirages generally appeared. Soon after, the steamship itself came in sight. The sailors were now convinced, and never afterwards believed in phantom-ships.'[5]

Here speaks the voice of reason, but the fact that Stockton makes his point in such a deliberate way smacks of someone out to persuade a credulous audience who were sceptical about there being a rational explanation for what they were seeing. Even in the late 19th century, belief in the supernatural was widespread and the tale of the *Flying Dutchman* was an alluring myth. In a world governed by religion and superstition, where science held little sway, it came naturally to explain strange phenomena in mystical or quasi-mystical terms. If saints could come back from the dead and walk on water, then why shouldn't ships sail forever and sailors turn into ghosts? It was simply the natural answer.

For others of a more sceptical nature, these descriptions of strange apparitions at sea were final proof that sailors who spent too long on the water were in danger of losing their marbles. It took another 100 years of meteorological science to prove that both these points of view were wrong. The *Flying Dutchman* was neither a ghost ship nor the product of madness, but a rather clever optical phenomenon devised by Mother Nature.

The reaction of 21st-century sailors to such experiences is rather more pragmatic. In a thread entitled 'Optical illusions at sea' on an online sailing forum, several sailors describe strange phenomena, including inverted images of ships hanging in the air (looming), distant lands appearing long before they should have been visible, and lighthouses that refuse to appear over the horizon (stooping). One contributor describes a scene that would have 18th-century sailors quaking in their sea boots: 'We once sailed through ourselves in fog. A faint image of our ship came out of the fog and straight through us. Quite a weird experience! Like sailing into a mirror. I beleive [*sic*] this may be the origin of the legend of the *Flying Dutchman*.'[6]

Despite such an extraordinary experience, there is no suggestion of magic or ghost ships, nor do the other forum users insinuate that the author might be deluded or suffering from mental illness. Everyone assumes the phenomenon is true and that there is a rational explanation for what is being described. It's a quantum leap from the position of King George's tutor 150 years before, and symbolic of the shift in consciousness over the centuries.

The sea plays host to so many natural phenomena and illusions, it's hardly surprising that, before the advent of science, sailors were a superstitious lot. How else could they explain the strange visions they were experiencing other than as supernatural occurrences? One of the most common of these visual 'deceptions' at sea is relative movement. We've all looked up at the moon on a cloudy evening and been startled to see it 'moving' from one side to another, only to realise it's the clouds that are moving and the moon is actually quite still. That's because our brain is used to seeing small things moving more quickly than big things – such as sheep across a field or cars across a road – so it momentarily concludes that the moon is moving behind the clouds, before more visual data is collected and it corrects itself. The principle can be applied to a navigational situation, with dangerous consequences, if the brain assumes a small boat in the background is moving, rather than the enormous container ship in the foreground.

Our brain will also make assumptions about the distance of objects, believing that dark, well-defined objects are nearer than pale, blurry ones, which can lead sailors to seriously miscalculate the distance and speed of an approaching vessel in certain conditions, such as in fog. Similarly, the brain makes suppositions about sound, believing that louder, higher-pitched sounds are nearer than softer, lower-pitched ones. The extra moisture in the air when it's foggy, however, means sound travels more efficiently, leading sailors to sometimes overestimate the distance of things, such as the whistle on a buoy. That might not sound like a bad thing, but if you're using the object to position yourself in a channel or to pass through a harbour entrance, then it could lead to a close encounter with a mud bank or a harbour wall.

At the other extreme, sailors exposed to the constant noise of wind and sea for a long time will sometimes hear 'voices' speaking to them. This is the 'white noise' phenomenon, whereby the ear is repeatedly subjected to a repetitive sound, in this case containing many different frequencies. The brain tries to filter out the background noise and to decipher the important sounds, such as someone calling out instructions, until eventually it 'finds' what it wants in the multiple sounds of the waves and the sea.

Professor Michael Stadler describes at least 30 such phenomena and illusions in his groundbreaking book *The Psychology of Sailing*, including hearing voices:

'It thus often happens that the sailor who has been exposed to this white noise for a long time, and who is also worn out from struggling against the storm, will succumb to the illusion that he is hearing voices or music even though he is quite alone. This is not a psycho-pathological symptom but an entirely normal occurrence which many people experience… In extreme cases, when one is tired and perhaps in a position where the sound of another voice would be welcome, it can quite easily happen that the acoustic system understands something from the stimuli which in reality does not exist.'[7]

So there you have it: hearing voices at sea is not a pathological condition. It's quite normal. Welcome to the world of sea-borne illusions. Of mirages, looming, towering, stooping and sinking. Of moons that change size, suns that change shape, horizons that bend, lights that change colour, and sounds that play hide and seek. Of waves that speak, ships that effervesce and whales that turn into baby elephants. For the sea has a lobsterpot full of tricks and illusions to confuse and beguile even the most rational 21st-century sailor.

CHAPTER 2

THE CURSE OF THE *BEAGLE*

The Strait of Magellan in winter is a grim place to be. Violent westerly gales come pounding across the Southern Ocean, throwing up enormous seas that crash against the southern coast of Chile as they are funnelled through the gap between South America and Antarctica. Not for nothing do the ends of both those land masses look like they've been punched sideways by an enormous sledgehammer, leaving behind the shattered remains of the islands known as Tierra del Fuego. The rush of sea heading from west to east creates currents of up to 8 knots in the strait, and katabatic winds come shooting down the steep mountains without any warning. Even when it's not windy, it's usually overcast and rainy, with temperatures rarely rising over 0°C (32°F).

Pity Pringle Stokes then. At the age of 32, he was appointed captain of her majesty's ship *Beagle* and sent on a mission to chart the southern coast of South America, including the Strait of Magellan, an undertaking that could take up to four years. It was the dawn of the British Empire and the Admiralty wanted to

21

find a safe route around South America so ships could head home from Asia without having to negotiate the dreaded Cape Horn. Unfortunately, although the Strait of Magellan had been discovered by the eponymous explorer back in 1520 and other sailors had sailed through it since then, no reliable charts had been produced of the area. Indeed, when Captain Bligh sailed to Tahiti in 1788, rather than risk the dangerous strait, he spent more than a month trying to cross into the Pacific via Cape Horn, before giving up and sailing east via Australia.

The expedition charged with changing all of that was headed by Captain Phillip Parker King, on the 330-ton survey ship HMS *Adventure*. King was an obvious choice to lead such a venture. Born in Australia, his father was the third governor of New South Wales, and he had already made four voyages surveying the coast of Australia. What's more, he was said to be knowledgeable about geology, ornithology and 'natural history generally': just the man for such a dangerous and demanding undertaking.

But what of his second-in-command, Pringle Stokes? Aged 32, Stokes had already served more than 20 years in the navy – including some high jinx trying to suppress the slave trade on the west coast of Africa – but this would be his first official command of a ship. Unlike King, he didn't have any relevant scientific knowledge, but a contemporary account said: 'though he was not practised in professional science, he had been studying in Edinburgh to attain mathematics, and he was moreover an indomitable seaman'.[1] In truth, he was probably considered a safe pair of hands rather than a brilliant officer.

The ship allocated to Stokes for the voyage was also a strange choice, given the detailed surveying work he and his crew would be required to undertake and the extreme weather they were likely to encounter. The so-called Cherokee class were famously bad sea boats: they were difficult to manoeuvre and had a nasty habit of sinking – more than a quarter of the 100 or so ships built to the design were either wrecked or lost at sea, earning the class the nickname of the 'coffin brig'. Stokes improved the ship's seakeeping abilities somewhat by having both the forward and aft decks raised, and adding a forecastle and poop deck.

The ship was 90ft long and just 24ft wide, so conditions on board were cramped (even with Stokes's modifications), especially when it was packed with provisions and equipment for several years at sea. A typical officer's cabin was 6ft long by 5ft wide and 6ft high, while the rest of the crew slept side by side in hammocks spaced just a few inches apart – enough to test the patience of the most tolerant sailor. Yet, when she set sail from Plymouth, the *Beagle* had more than 60 men on board, including a surgeon, an assistant surgeon, a carpenter and 10 marines to impose discipline.

The two ships sailed from Plymouth on 22 May 1826, surveying several islands in the Atlantic before stocking up with provisions at Rio de Janeiro and heading south. The expedition's base for the first two years was a safe anchorage at the eastern end of the Strait of Magellan known as Port Famine, in memory of the 300 Spanish settlers who died while trying to set up a colony there in 1584. During the first season, from February to April 1827, Stokes surveyed the more windswept and dangerous western part of the strait, while King took on the relatively easy southern and eastern section. Stokes's primary task was to determine the exact position of the rocks that marked the western entrance to the channel – Cape Pillar (Cabo Pilar) on one side and Westminster Hall Island

(Isla Westminster Hall) on the other – and to record safe anchorages in the strait itself.

Using inaccurate charts to guide him and having to cope with constant gales and driving rain, Stokes was faced with the unenviable choice of either surveying the coast from the *Beagle* and risking shipwreck, or working in the ship's boats and being exposed to winds and rain for days on end. He chose the latter, writing in his journal:

'Throughout that interval – five days – we were all constantly wet to the skin; repeatedly in doubling the various lands, we were obliged – after hours of efforts to pull the boat ahead of the violent squalls and cross turbulent sea that opposed us – to desist for a time and seek rest and shelter in any little cove that chanced to be at hand.'[2]

Bearing in mind that the only way to pinpoint a place accurately at that time was to measure the angle of the sun, moon and stars using a sextant and then to make complex mathematical calculations, the state of the weather had a major impact on the men's professional work as well as on their bodily comfort. As for the latter, in an age before foul-weather gear had been invented, the best protection Stokes could offer his men was some canvas for frocks and trousers, 'to be painted at the first opportunity'.[3]

Stokes's description of the landscape even in that first season is indicative of his state of mind:

'The nature of the coast was not such as to invite us much to go on shore; for it is either high steep rocks; or a narrow beach composed of knobs of granite attrited to roundness and slipperiness by the action of the tides, and skirted, almost at high water mark, by a scarcely penetrable jungle – Every where an utter solitude.'[4]

It's a long way from the description of the strait by Antonio Pigafetta during Magellan's world tour: 'I think there is not in the world a more beautiful country, or a better strait than this one'.[5] But then Pigafetta and friends merely sailed through the Cape of the Eleven Thousand Virgins (as the strait was originally called) and didn't have to spend years recording its every contour.

Perhaps Stokes did his job too well, for in the second season he was given the task of surveying the rest of the west coast, from the entrance of the Strait of Magellan up to latitude 47°S, a distance of some 400 miles (650 kilometres). Only this time, the expedition missed the summer season and instead faced the full brunt of the southern hemisphere's autumn and winter. Even Captain King complained in a letter to the Admiralty that 'the season was either not an ordinary one, or [...] it is the most inclement climate that has yet been experienced, perhaps, in the world'.[6]

As Stokes and his crew worked their way up the west coast of South America, they encountered an endless series of storms, and Stokes's journal became increasingly melancholy and doom-laden. Repeatedly he wrote, 'Nothing could be worse than the weather we had [...] here'; 'Here we were detained .[...] by the worst weather I ever experienced,'; and 'Another day and night of incessant rain.' And yet still the terrible weather continued. All the while, the ship's tenders were being smashed to smithereens, including the beloved yawl, whose 'loss was second only to that of the ship',[7] so that the ship's carpenter was eventually forced to build a new one from timber brought all the way from England for that purpose.

The weather also took its toll on the health of the crew, with several dying through a variety of diseases, including the dreaded scurvy. By 15 June, so many men were ill that Stokes had to anchor the ship and stop work for two weeks to allow them to recover. He described his surroundings in typically mournful tones:

'Nothing could be more dreary than the scene around us. The lofty, bleak, and barren heights that surround the inhospitable shores of this inlet, were covered, even low down their sides, with dense clouds, upon which the fierce squalls that assailed us beat, without causing any change: they seemed as immovable as the mountains where they rested. Around us, and some of them distant no more than two-thirds of a cable's length, were rocky islets, lashed by a tremendous surf; and, as if to complete the dreariness and utter desolation of the scene, even birds seemed to shun its neighbourhood. The weather was that in which (as Thompson emphatically says) "the soul of man dies in him".[8]

Eventually, enough crew recovered to man the ship, and the *Beagle* set sail again for her scheduled rendezvous with Captain King and HMS *Adventure* at Port Famine. However, Stokes's mental state was deteriorating fast. For most of the journey south, he locked himself up in his cabin, and even though supplies were running low, he prevaricated and delayed progress, stopping needlessly, until the ship was almost out of food and he was forced to head in.

This caused a long and painful delay for Captain King and his crew as they waited for the *Beagle* to return before heading north to

Chiloé Island to restock the ships. As soon as the *Beagle* was anchored, King went on board and spoke to Stokes. In his official report, he wrote that Stokes 'expressed himself much distressed by the hardships the officers and crew under him had suffered; and I was alarmed at the desponding tone of his conversation'.[9] By the end of the visit, however, Stokes seemed to have cheered up and was already discussing the best way to continue the survey.

There were enough clues, however, for King to ask the ship's surgeon, when he returned from other duties two days later, to investigate Stokes's state of mind. On 1 August 1828, the surgeon reported back that the *Beagle*'s crew had been 'in daily expectation that [Stokes] would commit some serious deed, particularly as he had expressed himself to be weary of life and wished to meet his death',[10] but that he seemed in better health since arriving at Port Famine. This assessment proved to be wrong – just as they were discussing his case on board HMS *Adventure*, a message came that confirmed King's worst fears: Stokes had shot himself.

If Stokes had hoped for a swift end to his unhappiness then he was to be disappointed. Unlucky to the end, his shot entered his brain but wasn't sufficient to kill him outright. Instead, he lingered on in agony for 12 days, while gangrene spread through his wound. Four days of delirium were followed by three days during which he was surprisingly lucid and made a strange and pathetic confession to Captain King.

For months, Stokes had been deceiving his commander. Unable to cope with the exacting surveying work expected of him in such challenging conditions, Stokes had delegated most of the work to his second-in-command, Lieutenant Skyring. Rather than admit failure, however, he had presented the work to Captain King as his own.

'Every chart, plan and calculation which he from time to time supplied me with bore his signature,' King wrote in a confidential letter to the Admiralty, 'but [...] the two former were entirely the work of Lieutenant Skyring and the calculations mere copies of that officer's work.'[11]

Not only that, but Stokes's navigational judgement had been critically affected by his deteriorating mental state, and several times the *Beagle* had been put in dangerous situations 'into which her Commander had unwarily and rashly rushed without any regard to the lives of so many people under his protection'.[12] Only the timely intervention of the ship's master, Samuel Flinn, saved the ship from destruction, as King wrote:

> 'The state of Captain Stokes' mind drove him at times to such desperate acts, as regarded the conduct of the ship, in which he would be controlled by no one, but by the Master Mr Flinn, that the officers and I believe every person aboard consider their lives being saved only [due] to his praiseworthy and seaman-like conduct.'[13]

Stokes had sworn his officers to secrecy but must have known his duplicity would be discovered – which is why he had attempted to delay the inevitable meeting with King by lingering unnecessarily before the rendezvous at Port Famine. Locked in his cabin and knowing the likely outcome of his actions would be a court martial, followed almost certainly by professional and personal ruin, Stokes descended into a spiral of depression that was only momentarily relieved by the arrival of King. When the surgeon visited on 1 August, he must have known his time was up and shot himself rather than face the consequences.

After another four days of 'most intense pain',[14] the gangrene did what the bullet had failed to do, and Stokes died on 12 August. A post-mortem examination revealed the bullet lodged in his brain, as well as 'seven or eight'[15] barely healed knife wounds on the chest. Stokes, it seemed, had been trying to kill himself for weeks. His body was buried close to Port Famine with a simple cross bearing the inscription: 'In memory of Commander Pringle Stokes RN, HMS *Beagle*, who died from the effects of the anxieties and hardships incurred while surveying the western shores of Tierra del Fuego [cross] 12-8-1828'.

In his official report on the expedition (as opposed to his confidential letter to the Admiralty), King glossed over Stokes's deception and his previous attempts to commit suicide. Instead, he wrote a generous tribute:

'Thus shockingly and prematurely perished an active, intelligent, and most energetic officer, in the prime of life. The severe hardships of the cruize, the dreadful weather experienced, and the dangerous situations in which they were so constantly exposed — caused, as I was afterwards informed, such intense anxiety in his excitable mind, that it became at times so disordered, as to cause the greatest apprehension for the consequences.'[16]

The ship's log was more perfunctory. The first entry for 12 August 1828 reads: 'Light breezes and cloudy. Departed this life Pringle Stokes, Esq, Commander.'[17]

History has been harsh on Pringle Stokes, and he is usually dismissed as an incompetent captain who even botched his own suicide. It is more likely, however, that he was just an ordinary man asked to perform an extraordinary task and found wanting; an ordinary man driven to madness. Even the most skilled sailor would balk at spending months on end navigating around treacherous rocks in a remote part of the world, with minimal support and in often terrifying weather conditions. Stokes's task demanded he make precise astronomical measurements and calculations and then extrapolate them into accurate representations of shorelines and seabeds. Failure meant not only court martial and personal disgrace but also being held responsible for future shipwrecks if his charts were proven to be inaccurate. The stakes could hardly have been higher.

Some, such as Stokes's commander King and his successor Robert FitzRoy, were truly exceptional men and rose to the challenge of such a task. Others, such as Stokes, were lesser men and were not successful – and who, really, can blame them? Knowing the circumstances he was facing, Stokes's failure and subsequent breakdown should incite pity rather than scorn.

In the usual run of things, Stokes's suicide would have been washed under the unstoppable tide of history; another life lost to Patagonia's inhospitable shores. Instead, his death set in motion a chain of events that not only would affect those immediately around him but would ultimately impact on our whole understanding of the world. For, much as Stokes might have liked his final months to be forgotten, the events that followed his death would ensure that the first captain of the *Beagle* would be immortalised for ever, if only by association. And, strangely, they would involve another tale of madness at sea – and another suicide.

Before Pringle Stokes had even been buried and his epitaph carved, King had appointed Lieutenant Skyring to succeed him. It was a logical decision, given that Skyring knew the boat inside out and had been carrying out most of Stokes's work for the past few months anyway. The two ships duly sailed north, *Beagle* to Montevideo and *Adventure* to Rio de Janeiro, where King had a meeting with his commander-in-chief Sir Robert Otway on HMS *Ganges*. Far from endorsing King's appointment, however, Otway had already chosen another man for the job: his own lieutenant on the *Ganges*, Robert FitzRoy, then just 23 years old.

FitzRoy had everything to recommend him. His family was descended from King Charles II, albeit through an illegitimate offspring, and at least three of his ancestors had been admirals. Like Stokes, he had joined the navy when he was 12 years old, and had passed his exams at Portsmouth Naval College with 'full numbers' (ie full marks), the first pupil to do so.

But FitzRoy had a skeleton in his cupboard that would haunt him throughout his life. His uncle Robert Stewart, the Second Marquess of Londonderry, had served in the British government as Secretary of State for Foreign Affairs in the crucial years following Napoleon's defeat. After 10 bruising years, during which he became increasingly unpopular with the public and the press alike, he became ill from overwork and gradually tipped into mental illness. Although guns and razors were removed from his reach, he managed to commit suicide, using a small penknife to slash his throat. The coroner's verdict was suicide due to temporary insanity – which saved the family from the ignominy (and difficult legal ramifications) of a 'deliberate' suicide, but left them with the stigma of madness. FitzRoy was just 17 when this family tragedy happened, and it made a lasting impression on him.

The young lieutenant's first command got off to a rocky start when, just a few weeks after he took charge, the *Beagle* was knocked down by a sudden gust off Uruguay and two men were lost overboard. Despite this unfortunate beginning, he seemed to have initially made light work of the task that ultimately drove his predecessor mad. Unlike Stokes, who usually moored the *Beagle* close to the survey area, FitzRoy preferred to moor her in a safe anchorage and then set off with the small boats, sometimes for weeks at a time. He loved these camping trips, sleeping out of doors in this spectacular and barely inhabited landscape.

However, FitzRoy's heavy reliance on these small boats was to have unexpected consequences. Three months into his first season, in February 1830, one of the *Beagle*'s whaleboats was stolen by Fuegian natives. Already infuriated by the locals' tendency to help themselves to anything they could lay their hands on, FitzRoy and his men set off on a wild goose chase, finding bits of their boat in settlements up and down the coast, taking hostages and then losing them repeatedly, and even shooting an indigenous man dead. After nearly three weeks' chase they finally gave up and sent two of the three children they had managed to hang on to back to their families. The third, a nine-year-old girl they named Fuegia Basket, they kept, more or less as a ship's pet.

'She seemed to be so happy and healthy,' FitzRoy wrote in his journal, 'that I determined to detain her as hostage for the stolen boat, and to try to teach her English.'[18]

Over the following few weeks, FitzRoy acquired three more Fuegian captives: a teenage boy he bought in exchange for a few buttons (and duly named Jemmy Button), and two young men in their twenties (York Minster and Boat Memory). His avowed plan was to take them back to England, educate them, and then return them to Patagonia to spread the word of God. But there's little doubt he also regarded them as interesting biological specimens; also in the ship's hold were the body of the Fuegian shot dead during the boat hunt, body parts of two others, and 'the prepared skin of the head'[19] of a fourth unfortunate soul.

Back in England, Boat Memory soon died of smallpox, but the other three Fuegians became a talking point among the upper echelons of society, as FitzRoy introduced them to his influential entourage. They even had an audience with the new King William IV and his wife Queen Adelaide. What happened next is not entirely clear, but the evidence suggests that York Minster started to show undue interest in the young girl, Fuegia Basket. Rather than face a scandal, FitzRoy decided to return the three of them home as quickly as possible. With the help of influential friends – including the celebrated Admiral Beaufort, inventor of the Beaufort wind scale – he persuaded the Admiralty to fund a second mission to Tierra del Fuego and onward around the world, collecting navigational data.

However, FitzRoy had already spent a year on the *Beagle* and had seen what had happened to Stokes. Moreover, he was keenly aware of his uncle's suicide and realised he might be susceptible to depression too. So, rather than risk years of loneliness, he suggested taking a 'well-educated and scientific person' on the voyage 'in order to profit by the opportunity of visiting distant countries yet little known'.[20] Captain Beaufort wrote to several people, including the Professor of Botany at Cambridge University, who in turn passed on the message to his favourite pupil, saying: 'He [FitzRoy] wants a man (I understand) more as a companion than a mere collector & would not take anyone however good a Naturalist who was not recommended to him likewise as a gentleman.'[21] The pupil's name was Charles Darwin.

And so the man who was to transform our understanding of the world hitched a ride on a ship towards his meeting with destiny, having been invited on board in effect to prevent the captain from going mad. Whether he succeeded in that mission is open to discussion.

After a thorough refit, the *Beagle* left Plymouth once again on 27 December 1831. For the next four years, FitzRoy and Darwin shared a cabin, and the young botanist was able to observe his 'beau ideal of a Captain'[22] at close quarters. Years later he would write:

'Fitz-Roy's temper was a most unfortunate one, and was shown not only by passion, but by fits of long-continued moroseness against those who had offended him. It was usually worst in the early morning, and with his eagle eye he could generally detect something amiss about the ship, and was then unsparing in his blame.'[23]

Among the crew, FitzRoy was known as 'hot coffee'[24] for his sudden flashes of temper, and many would feel the effects of his mood swings in the stripes on their backs, as they were flogged for often trivial offences.

After surveying the coast of Argentina, the *Beagle* arrived in Tierra del Fuego in January 1833. There, FitzRoy dropped off the three Fuegians, along with Richard Matthews, the missionary charged with setting up a Christian mission. They were also supplied with an improbable array of equipment, courtesy of the Church Missionary Society, including wine glasses, soup tureens, fine white linen, top hats and a mahogany dressing case. Within days, the whole lot would be plundered by the indigenous people and Matthews would give up his attempt to set up a mission and scuttle back to the safety of the *Beagle*. FitzRoy's attempt to 'civilise' the Fuegians had utterly failed.

By the winter of 1834, the incessant work combined with financial worries was taking its toll on FitzRoy, and he sank into depression. 'I am in the dumps,' he wrote to his friend Admiral Beaufort. 'It is heavy work – all work and no play [...] Troubles and difficulties harass and oppress me so much that I find it impossible to say or do what I wish. [...] Continual work – and heavy expense – These and many other things have made me ill and very unhappy.'[25] Darwin described FitzRoy's mood as 'bordering on insanity'[26] and wrote to his sister, 'The Captain was afraid that his mind was becoming deranged (being aware of his hereditary predisposition).'[27]

Overwhelmed by his task, FitzRoy resigned his post and appointed his second-in-command, Lieutenant Wickham, to take over and return the ship to England. FitzRoy had reached the same point as Stokes six years earlier and must have seen where he was heading. Only some sweet talk by Wickham persuaded him that he didn't have to go back to Tierra del Fuego, but could continue northwards to the Galapagos and ultimately complete the voyage around the world. Once again, chance intervened to ensure Darwin kept his appointment with history.

Two years later, FitzRoy sank into another depression when the *Beagle* pulled into Sydney, and Darwin was again prompted to write to his sister:

'He is an extra ordinary, but noble character, unfortunately however affected with strong peculiarities of temper. Of this, no man is more aware than himself, as he shows by his attempts to conquer them. I often doubt what will be his end, under many circumstances I am sure, it would be a brilliant one, under others I fear a very unhappy one.'[28]

Prescient words indeed.

FitzRoy and Darwin both made it home in the end, and each would go on to play major roles in their respective fields: Darwin by creating the concept of evolution and FitzRoy by creating the concept of weather forecasting (a phrase he himself coined). FitzRoy would also eventually found the Meteorological Office and, for a time, his daily weather forecasts were printed in *The Times*, the first such forecasts to ever be published.

But his past would come back to haunt him. When Darwin published his *On the Origin of Species* in 1860, FitzRoy was devastated. He had by then adopted a more literal reading of the Bible, and was tormented by the idea that he had inadvertently helped Darwin formulate theories that directly challenged the concept of Creation. At the now-famous debate between Thomas Huxley and Bishop Wilberforce in Oxford later that year, FitzRoy stood up with an enormous Bible and implored the crowd to 'believe in God rather than man',[29] but was laughed down and humiliated. His personal capital fell further when, after three years, *The Times* axed his weather forecast and poked fun at the 'First Admiral of the Blew'.[30]

Finally, he could bear no more and, on the morning of 30 April 1865, he went into his dressing room and, with hideous inevitability, slit his throat with a razor blade.

CHAPTER 3

PLAGUES OF THE SEA

Madness at sea has been around for a long time. You could argue that the first people to attempt to navigate the ocean must have been mad – in the same way that Michelangelo was mad when he tried to design a machine to make man fly. Certainly, from the moment man created boats that could sail away from land and therefore be swept off course and out to sea, a stand-off was created between sailors and nature. By trying to harness the wind and waves, man was pitting himself against a merciless force, and there could only ever be one winner. It's this elemental battle that Hemingway depicts in his novel *The Old Man and the Sea*, in which an elderly fisherman crosses the border into obsessive madness in his attempt to catch a prize marlin, in spite of everything the sea throws at him. Such battles have doubtless been played out on the ocean for thousands of years.

The condition became a global phenomenon when sailors began to venture further afield, exploring unknown lands and facing unpredictable weather and inhospitable climates. Packed together in the confines of a small ship, these men had to work together, whether they liked each other or not, to survive terrible storms, maddening calms and the hidden dangers of uncharted waters. They had to sustain themselves on the most basic food and drink and live cheek by jowl in often grossly unhygienic surroundings. Once they reached land, they had to negotiate with various different races of people with alien cultures, customs and habits – not to mention strange foods. Some were friendly, many were not. Far from home, they only had their fellow crewmates for support, in a social system that was deeply hierarchical and unapologetically macho, and where discipline was paramount. In these circumstances, madness was practically an occupational hazard.

One of the major problems encountered by these early explorers was the climate. Sailors from the relatively mild northern countries simply could not cope with the tropical heat. This was a general issue with all migrants, whether on board ship or on land, but it seems to have taken a particularly nasty form among sailors. The problem was especially pronounced on windless days and at night, when the build-up of heat below decks could make the men delirious. Their mad frenzy was accompanied by an irresistible desire to throw themselves into the sea. The condition was known as calenture (from the Spanish *calentura*, or fever) and was first observed by Spanish sailors in the 17th century.

Calenture was described by the French physician François Boissier de Sauvages de Lacroix in his *Dictionnaire des Sciences Médicales* in 1771:

'This disorder comes on during the night, while the patient is asleep: he awakes quite delirious, his looks animated, and his gestures express fury; he speaks long and incoherently; quits his bed to run on the deck or forecastle, where he imagines seeing trees and enamelled meadows in the water; this illusion so delights him, that he expresses his joy with a thousand exclamations. He then endeavours to throw himself into the sea, and, at last effecting his purpose, he is infallibly lost, in case his companions be not either quick or many enough to prevent him putting his mad project into execution. His strength is so extraordinary during this crisis, that four strong men are scarcely able to stop him.'[1]

The French psychiatrist Jean-Pierre Falret (who made the first diagnosis of bipolar disorder) returned to the topic of calenture in his 1839 treatise *Du Délire*. He made the point that the sailors wanted to jump into the sea not because they wanted to commit suicide but because, in their fevered state, they imagined the sea as something else. 'The sea appears to them as a field sown with grass and enamelled with flowers; they are desperate to exercise themselves in fertile fields, fresh and moist, which they imagine shaded and scented like the most idyllic grove.'[2]

Falret identified the illness as inflammation of the brain and described it as 'the sailor's arachnitis' or 'the navigator's encephalitis'[3] (both conditions resulting from inflammation of the brain). Another symptom was extreme nostalgia, a longing for home that is not hard to imagine among sailors trapped in an overcrowded wooden ship in stifling heat.

Several dramatic cases of calenture were reported during the 18th and 19th centuries, usually involving young men on their first voyages. One such was recorded by the naturalist Hugues Gaultier (sometimes referred to as Gautier), who was about to embark on an exploration of the Senegal River in 1795 when the crew of his ship became overwhelmed by the oppressive heat. All 30 of the men, including the ship's doctor, threw themselves overboard and were drowned. Another incident occurred when the temperature soared to 37°C (99°F) on board the French brig *Le Lynx* while she was sailing off Cádiz in 1823. With frequent calms and no awnings to shelter the crew while they were on deck, 18 of the 75 crew, all aged 18 to 30 years old and sailing for the first time, succumbed to calenture. The most dramatic case of all, however, was on board the *Dunesque*, stationed in Rio de Janeiro in January 1829. Here, lack of wind pushed temperatures up to an unbearable 39°C (102°F), and 100 of the 600 crew on board died.

This was the age of the four humors (black bile, yellow bile, phlegm and blood), and the treatment – as for most conditions, it seems – was bloodletting. This approach was described in one of the earliest accounts of calenture, which took place in August 1693 while the *Albemarie* was crossing the Bay of Biscay, when one of the sailors was seized by violent fits and was only just prevented from throwing himself overboard. Four of his crewmates subsequently had to hold him down while he was cut, first in the jugular, which didn't yield much blood, and then in two other veins. In the end, about 1.5 litres (2¾ pints) of blood was collected, after which the sailor calmed down and fell asleep. He woke up the next day apparently none the worse for his experience, apart from feeling rather tired and sore from his exertions.

Calenture dropped out of sight after the 19th century, presumably because sailors' habits changed and they were better able to cope with extremes of temperature. Better supplies of fresh water and a reduction in the amount of alcohol routinely issued aboard ships might both have contributed to this situation. The term is still sometimes used, but in a more metaphorical way – to describe the state of hypnosis that sailors fall into while staring at the sea, which is often accompanied by a strong urge to throw themselves over the side. This ocean trance is thought to be responsible for some of the many cases of sailors inexplicably 'lost at sea'. Some believe it might even explain the disappearance of media tycoon Robert Maxwell, who fell from his yacht off the Canary Islands in November 1991.

Despite the undoubted impact of calenture, the great killer of the Age of Discovery, and one of the major causes of mental disorder, was scurvy. It's been estimated that more than 2 million sailors died of this preventable disease between 1500 and 1800 – far more than were killed in battle or by any other illness. Most of the great voyages of exploration were affected. More than 100 of the 170 crew on Vasco da Gama's voyage to the East Indies in 1497 died of scurvy, while half the 250 crew on Magellan's attempted circumnavigation of 1520 lost their lives to it. One of the worst outbreaks was on an expedition led by Sir George Anson to attack Spanish galleons in South America. Of the 2,000 men who set off from Britain in 1740, only 600 came back. Four died in battle, a few died of injuries sustained while carrying out their duties, but the vast majority – nearly 1,400 men – died of scurvy.

The symptoms of the disease were not pretty. The English surgeon William Clowes, who served in the Royal Navy, described the condition in 1596:

'Their gums were rotten even to the very roots of their teeth, and their cheeks hard and swollen, the teeth were loose neere ready to fall out [...] their breath a filthy savour. The legs were feeble and so weak, that they were not scarce able to carry their bodies. Moreover they were full of aches and paines, with many blewish and reddish staines or spots, some broad and some small like flea-biting.'[4]

Scurvy also had a devastating effect on the sailor's mental state. In his account of Anson's round-the-world voyage, the Rev Richard Walter reported how the disease was characterised by 'a strange dejection of the spirits, and with shiverings, tremblings, and a disposition to be seized with the most dreadful terrors on the slightest accident.'[5] Elsewhere, he added 'idiotism' and 'lunacy'[6] to the list of symptoms.

The Scottish physician Thomas Trotter gave a more detailed account of the mental deterioration of its victims:

'The mind in the beginning and throughout the disease, is timid, anxious, and desponding; but towards the fatal period, there is generally a total indifference and seeming torpor of every faculty. [...] But in the advanced state of the disease, the disposition to sleep seemed to be one of the most unfavourable symptoms; it was constantly changed to a coma and delirium; and none but one with this symptom ever recovered.'[7]

More recent studies of scurvy and vitamin deprivation have confirmed that patients suffered from depression, hypochondria and hysteria.

Perhaps the strangest impact of the disease was on the sailors' nervous systems. Their senses became so heightened that a sudden noise, such as a gunshot, could kill a person in the later stages of the disease. Grown men would be reduced to tears by the slightest disappointment, such as a change in the weather. Even positive experiences, such as the scent of flowers or the taste of fruit, could prove fatal. In his autobiographical novel *Omoo*, Melville described the effects of smell on an affected whaleman:

> 'The Trades scarce filled our swooning sails; the air was languid with the aroma of a thousand strange, flowering shrubs. Upon inhaling it, one of the sick who had recently shown symptoms of scurvy, cried out in pain, and was carried below. This is no unusual effect in such cases.'[8]

We now know scurvy is caused by a lack of vitamin C in the victim's diet – something that was always a danger on ships that were at sea and away from sources of fresh fruit and vegetables for weeks or months at a time. The tragedy was that the cure, a plentiful supply of citrus fruit, was repeatedly discovered and ignored. The British explorer Sir Richard Hawkins reported the positive effects of oranges and lemons as long ago as 1593. A few years later, in 1601, the privateer Sir James Lancaster reported to the Admiralty on the benefits of a daily dose of lemon juice, but his report was ignored. Even a controlled experiment by the Scottish surgeon James Lind in 1753 failed to change their Lordships' minds, and it wasn't until 1795 that a daily dose of lemon juice was finally made compulsory on all Royal Navy vessels. By then, 2 million sailors had died in terrible physical and mental distress – all for the want of a few lemons.

The so-called plague of the sea wasn't vanquished yet, however, since the cure only worked so long as a supply of fruit and vegetables was readily available. Where this wasn't possible – such as following a shipwreck – the disease re-emerged, in all its horrific manifestations. This became all too evident to the crew of the Arctic exploration ship HMS *Investigator*, sent to search for the Northwest Passage in 1850, who started showing symptoms of scurvy when their supply of limes ran out after two years at sea. These were described by the interpreter (and missionary) John Miertsching, who reported on the state of the crew as they readied themselves for their third winter in the ice, with the ship by now trapped where they would eventually have to abandon it:

'October 14. For a short time now we have noticed in one of our officers, Lieutenant Wyniatt [*sic*, correct spelling Wynniatt], strange actions that have puzzled everyone. Yesterday they took shape in complete madness, and he, like Bradbury, must now be watched day and night lest he do violence to himself or his shipmate. He passes the night with frightful shouting and raving. Today he slept a few hours and then began again to jest, laugh, weep, sing, and whistle; neither threats nor kindly admonition have the least effect on them. [...]

'October 16. Our two distracted comrades are no better yet; they sleep by day; by night they weep and rave. Today I again visited Mr Wyniatt; he kissed my hand and wept without speaking. [...]

'October 31. The deranged seaman, Bradbury, has grown quite peaceful; he speaks little and sleeps much; Mr Wyniatt, on the other hand, raves and jests frantically as ever.

'November 5. The poor sick Wyniatt is causing much trouble with his raving and babbling. I am the only one beside his servant whom he allows to approach him, but his mind seems utterly unsettled.'[9]

By January, Wynniatt had to be tied up because he was threatening to kill the captain and set fire to the ship, and both he and Bradbury spent most of their time howling and raving. Surgeon Armstrong was apt to blame 'lunar changes', but also thought Wynniatt might have a 'hereditary predisposition' to the disease as he had been previously guilty of 'slight eccentricities'.[10] Despite this, both men recovered from their illnesses and were eventually rescued – although only after they had endured a fourth winter in the Arctic. Remarkably, out of a crew of 66, only three died of scurvy during the entire five-year ordeal – a result that would have been virtually impossible only 55 years before.

CHAPTER 4

INTO THE VOID

Despite the relative improvements to life on board and the reduction in the incidence of scurvy, the question still remains: who in their right mind would organise such a venture in the first place? What type of person would devise a scheme to explore the blank areas of terra incognita and then pursue that vision through thick and thin? Who would have the conviction and self-belief to sail out across an empty sea with no guarantee of finding anything on the other side, apart from yet more sea, and risk the lives of dozens of other sailors on the basis of a mere idea?

The answer is someone like Christopher Columbus. The world's most famous explorer and 'discoverer' of the New World (even though we know native Americans already lived there and some Vikings probably visited it long before he did) was a driven man with an almost abnormal desire to succeed. He was the ultimate entrepreneur, if you like, which is appropriate given that he was the supposed founder of the land of entrepreneurs. But Columbus also had his dark side, and his strengths would also prove to be his weaknesses. His genius, ultimately, came at the price of his sanity, and even that genius was seriously flawed.

From the outset, Columbus believed he was on a divine mission from God.

'With a hand that could be felt,' he wrote, 'the Lord opened my mind to the fact that it would be possible to sail from here to the Indies, and he opened my will to desire to accomplish the project. This was the fire that burned within me.'[1] Later, he claimed the Holy Spirit had told him: 'God will cause your name to be wonderfully proclaimed throughout the world [...] and give you the keys of the gates to open the ocean, which are closed with strong chain.'[2]

The crux of his vision was that his discovery of a westward route to the East would bring untold riches that would fund an army to rout the heathen Muslim from the Holy Lands and spread the influence of Christianity. However, his religious fervour was mixed with so much self-interest and self-aggrandisement – he insisted on being given the hereditary title of Admiral of the Ocean Sea, being made viceroy and perpetual governor of whatever lands he discovered, and getting a 10 per cent cut of all future commerce from these lands – that it's hard to believe he was not delusional. His behaviour bears all the hallmarks of someone with a Messiah complex.

Columbus's maniacal obsession with this plan and its God-given importance meant he refused to listen to the best scientific advice of the day. It was by then generally accepted that the world was round, and astrological calculations suggested the distance from Portugal to Asia must be around 17,700 kilometres (11,000 miles). Yet despite this, Columbus not only miscalculated the size of the earth, making it much smaller than it really is, but also exaggerated the size of Asia, and concluded that the distance he had to travel was only 4,000

47

kilometres (2,500 miles). It was a gross miscalculation that led to him being branded a 'madman' and meant his proposed expedition was rejected by a succession of experts for seven years, before it finally found favour in 1492 with Queen Isabella of Spain.

So convinced was Columbus of his own righteousness that, when he finally set sail across the Atlantic later in 1492, he only took supplies for 21 days – leaving the crew to go very hungry indeed for 10 days before they finally made a lucky landfall in the Bahamas. Their landfall was 'lucky' because of course this wasn't the east coast of Asia, as Columbus believed, but some unknown islands next to a completely different continent.

By the time he set off on his second voyage in 1493, Columbus (born Cristóbal Colón) had reverted to the Greco-Latin version of his name, Christoferens, meaning literally 'Christ-bearer'. He also insisted on signing all his documents with this cryptic symbol:

.S.
.S.A.S.
X M Y
Xpo FERENS

More than 500 years on, no one has conclusively worked out what it means, apart from the last line, which is Xpo, from the Greek for 'Christo', and Ferens, Latin for 'carry'.

During his third voyage, Columbus claimed to have discovered the entrance to the Garden of Eden off the coast of Venezuela, and during his fourth and last voyage he announced he had discovered King Solomon's mines. The gold from these mines, he assured Ferdinand and Isabella, would allow them to mount a crusade for the Holy Lands. Despite this professed piety, however, Columbus was merciless to the indigenous people of the islands he ruled, effectively pursuing a policy of genocide against them. When he didn't uncover the gold he expected to find, he sent Isabella slaves instead, even though she had asked him not to.

Columbus had some wacky ideas about geography too. In 1498 he wrote to Isabella:

'I have always read that the world comprising the land and water was spherical [...] But [...] I have now seen so much irregularity that I have come to another conclusion respecting the Earth, namely, that it is not round, as they describe, but of the form of a pear, which is very round except where the stalk grows, at which part it is most prominent; or like a round ball, upon part of which is a prominence like a woman's nipple, this protrusion being the highest and nearest the sky, situated under the equinoctial line, and at the eastern extremity of this sea [Gulf of Paria].'[3]

In 1502 he published *The Book of Prophecies*, a collection of passages from the Bible that supported his belief that his mission was preordained by God and that he personally was destined to free the Holy Lands. It was at this stage, according to the biographer Gianni Granzotto, that Columbus began to move 'farther and farther away from reality' and his imagination 'turned more and more into a vehicle for mad ravings'.[4]

So wrapped up was Columbus in his mystical visions that to his dying day he insisted he had discovered the eastern edge of Asia and not a new continent, despite all the evidence to the contrary. It would take another explorer, Amerigo Vespucci, to prove that the land was indeed a separate entity and thereby give his name to the new continent.

Columbus was thus widely regarded as 'mad' in his own time and has retrospectively been diagnosed as suffering from bipolar disorder (aka manic depression). American 'bipolar' expert Karen R Brock wrote:

> 'Columbus was hypomanic, driven, and grandiose in the beginning, but he became increasingly delusional, probably manic, and possibly psychotic as time progressed. [...] Big ideas, big egos, and big goals – all hypomanic traits – sometimes make for big discoveries, big business ventures, and world-changing events. Columbus achieved all three.'[5]

The list of bipolar sufferers is instructive: Winston Churchill, Michelangelo, Mozart, Picasso, Isaac Newton and Albert Einstein. Not such bad company after all.

Of course, Columbus wasn't the only highly driven and socially inept ocean sailor roving the High Seas. A strong sense of purpose and a willingness to think outside the box were prerequisite characteristics for a successful expedition leader during the Age of Discovery, or at any other time. The trouble was, it was sometimes a thin line between discipline and authoritarianism; between running a 'tight ship' and working your crew to death.

The most famous despot of them all, Captain Bligh, is also often described as 'bipolar'– though it seems likely he was just a little deaf. Hence his propensity to shout.

Bligh was on a mission to transport breadfruit trees from the Pacific to the Caribbean when in April 1789, a few weeks after leaving

Tahiti, a group of sailors led by Fletcher Christian mutinied and cast the captain and 18 crew adrift in a 23ft open boat. The trigger for the mutiny was a trivial argument about some missing coconuts, but the roots of discontent went much further back and centred on Bligh's domineering attitude and his apparent humiliation of Christian over the preceding weeks.

Historians are divided as to whether or not the captain of the *Bounty* really was a ruthless tyrant – it's been convincingly argued he was no stricter than most naval officers of that era. However, either way, there's long been a fascination with the mental state of his chief adversary, Fletcher Christian, with much of the intrigue stemming from a conversation between Christian and Bligh just before the captain was cast off. According to Bligh, it went something like this:

'When they were forcing me out of the ship, I asked him if this treatment was a proper return for the many instances he had received of my friendship? He appeared disturbed at my question, and answered, with much emotion, "That, captain Bligh, that is the thing; I am in hell, I am in hell." '[6]

According to Christian's brother, who collected survivors' accounts of the incident, the interchange had been more along these lines:

'Captain Bligh, addressing himself to Christian, said, "Consider Mr. Christian, I have a wife and four children in England, and you have danced my children upon your knee." Christian replied, "You should have thought of them sooner yourself, Captain Bligh, it is too late to consider now, I have been in hell for weeks past with you." '[7]

51

Either way, the whiff of mental torment has led generations of historians to speculate about Christian's state of mind. Was he drunk, as some claim? Was the mutiny merely a 'moment of madness' that he later regretted? Was he enacting some rebellion against a father figure (Bligh and Christian had sailed together several times before and Bligh appeared to have taken the younger man under his wing)? Or had he simply been mentally befuddled by the sensual delights of Tahiti? After all, a mutiny on a naval ship in those days was no small matter and could result in only one thing: death.

More recently, the arguments have become a bit more sophisticated. When Glynn Christian, a direct descendant of the *Bounty*'s first mate, updated his biography *Fragile Paradise*, he asked a group of psychiatrists to give an assessment of Christian's mental health. He reported:

'For the first time I have had a genuine diagnosis of his physical state at the time he rebelled, and the experts concluded that he was experiencing a form of mental breakdown on the day of the mutiny. It is a state called brief psychotic disorder, which can last from a day to a week, but then you go back to normal. He was described as wild-eyed and dishevelled, which also points to temporary madness. Bligh also said Christian was insane.'[8]

Elsewhere, commentators have pointed to Christian's sweaty hands (according to Bligh, Christian was 'subject to violent perspirations & particularly in his hands so that he soils any thing he handles')[9] to suggest he suffered from generalised anxiety disorder – that is, he was a worrier. Others have said he suffered from psychoneurosis, another stress-related condition.

As if that weren't enough, Christian's descendants in both Cumbria and the Pacific island of Pitcairn (where 50 per cent of the inhabitants can trace their ancestry back to Fletcher and his fellow mutineers) have been the subject of several studies that show strange genetic mutations. One such study traced the development of a rare hereditary brain disease, similar to Parkinson's, that occurred among Christian's family in England and his progeny on the islands. Another report suggests that the descendants of the *Bounty* mutineers suffer from unusually high rates of migraines, while yet another shows they have better-than-average eyesight.

One of Bligh's problems was that he didn't have a strong chain of command. Because of her size, the *Bounty* didn't carry the usual tier of commissioned officers – Bligh was the only commissioned officer on board, and even he was a mere lieutenant rather than a fully fledged captain. Neither did the ship have a regiment of marines to enforce discipline, as most bigger craft had. Instead, Bligh was surrounded by a bevy of 'young gentlemen', mostly there thanks to their family connections, who served as part of the ship's crew but were outside its strict disciplinary code due to their social status.

This mutiny was not an isolated incident. Just two years after Bligh met his nemesis in the Pacific an almost identical situation resulted in the downfall of another British naval officer, George Vancouver. He was leading an expedition of two ships charged with surveying the west coast of America, which had recently been handed over to England in the Nootka Conventions of 1790, and for four years he was host to a particularly well-connected bunch of 'young gentlemen' who tested his authority at every turn.

The story goes that as the ships crawled their way along the mist-shrouded coast, meticulously taking soundings of every inlet and creek, tension on board the overcrowded vessels increased by the day. Vancouver, gradually enfeebled by a mystery illness, swung between extremes of geniality and violent rages, so that his crew feared he might be going mad. The degree of his unhappiness could be measured by the severity of his punishments. According to Greg Dening, author of *Mr Bligh's Bad Language*,[10] only 19 per cent of Bligh's crew were flogged, receiving an average of one-and-a-half lashes per flogging, compared with 45 per cent of Vancouver's crew, with an average of 21 lashes – an astonishingly high average even by the standards of the day. Indeed, while Admiralty regulations recommended a dozen lashes for most serious crimes, Vancouver was known to administer up to five dozen lashes at a time. One wretched marine received a total of 148 lashes during the course of four floggings.

Some historians have suggested that Vancouver displayed many of the symptoms of an untreated hyperthyroid condition – including premature ageing, deafness and mood swings – which must have tormented him throughout the voyage, making him more than usually grumpy. Others speculate that he might have suffered from tuberculosis, the repercussions of malaria, or even shellfish poisoning. His own journals show he was frequently hit by severe headaches and exhaustion, and by the end of the voyage was unable to go out in the ship's boats to do the surveying work himself.

Vancouver's big mistake in all this was to pick a fight with a particularly influential 'young gentleman': Thomas Pitt, cousin of the then Prime Minister and also cousin of the First Lord of the Admiralty. Given his social status, Pitt should have been immune to serious punishment but, perhaps to make a point or simply because he was enraged by the man's arrogance, Vancouver ordered him to be flogged several times for minor offences. Pitt never forgave him and, on their return to England, pursued a vendetta against Vancouver that ensured he was never given credit for his considerable achievements.

Vancouver died a broken man three years later, aged 40. It was left to his brother to publish the edited journals of his voyage a few months after his death, to almost no acclaim.

Severe as Bligh and Vancouver had been in meting out their punishments, they were mere chickens compared with Howes Norris, captain of the whaleship *Sharon*. Norris was a misanthropic whalehunter with a looming presence who had already had to quell one mutiny on his previous ship. Little wonder, then, that when the *Sharon* set off from Newhaven, Massachusetts on 25 May 1841 on what should have been a four-year voyage to the Pacific, Norris was in no mood for playing games. From the outset, he bullied and beat the ship's steward George Babcock – probably a fugitive slave – and as the hoped-for catch of whales failed to materialise, so the beatings got worse. Finally, on 1 September 1842, Norris beat the wretched Babcock to death.

'So ends as cold-blooded a murder as was ever recorded, being about eight months taking his life,'[11] wrote the third mate, Benjamin Clough.

Norris's account in his journal was somewhat different: 'Wind from NNE Middle and Latter parts calm. At 9am George Babcock died very suddenly – he complained of having the cramp.'[12]

With Babcock gone, Norris turned his attention to the Pacific islanders (known as Kanakas by the whalers) he had enlisted to replace some of the two dozen crew who had deserted ship since the start of the voyage. The Kanakas weren't the only ones to feel the sharp edge of his frustration, though – one man who attempted to desert was tied up hand and foot, brutally beaten and then cast off in a canoe, never to be seen again.

By November 1842, the *Sharon* was sailing with a depleted crew of 17 men, including four Kanakas, when some whales were spotted 1,125 kilometres (700 miles) north of Papua New Guinea. Two boats were lowered with six men on each, leaving Norris, a young Portuguese steward and three Kanakas on board. The steward was sent up the rigging to signal the location of the whales to the men in the boats, leaving the captain and the three Kanakas on deck. One whale was soon killed and the *Sharon* went to retrieve it, while the whaleboats carried on with the hunt. Instead of cutting up the carcass with their cutting spades, however, the Kanakas used this opportunity to exact revenge on their brutal boss. One slice of the cutting spades cut him almost in half at the waist, while another slice nearly took his head right off. The captain collapsed on deck in a pool of blood.

Seeing the gruesome events taking place below him, the steward, safely out of reach in the rigging, started signalling to the whaleboats to come back. When that didn't work, he cut the lines for the sails to prevent the Kanakas from escaping. When the whaleboats eventually caught up with the *Sharon*, they found the Kanakas standing on the ship's bulwarks, stark naked, covered in sweat and blood, wielding cutting spades and shouting at them. It turned out they were trying to persuade one of their fellow Kanakas in the boats to jump in the water and join the mutiny. When the man refused, he had to quickly duck as a well-aimed axe flew through the air where his head had been. An array of missiles followed: axes, hammers, belaying pins, lumps of wood, and anything else the Kanakas could get their hands on.

In the face of this onslaught, the men on the whaleboats decided to hang back until nightfall. As darkness fell, one of the Kanakas started beating a tin pan, while the other two drummed the deck planks around the captain's body. They were obviously traumatised by the day's events, and their ritual banging seemed to be some attempt to exorcise the dead man's ghost. Under cover of this noise, the third mate, Benjamin Clough, climbed through a window in the back of the ship. As two of the Kanakas came to find him, he mortally wounded one by pulling out his eye and almost cutting off his head (the sabre was apparently too blunt to do the job properly), and shot the second dead. Only then could the rest of the ship's crew be persuaded to join him on board the ship.

A horrific scene greeted them on deck, as the ship's pigs (kept to provide the crew with a fresh supply of meat) had made the most of the mayhem to feed off Captain Norris's part-severed head. They now scuttled about the deck with pieces of his skull in their mouths – a fitting enough end to one of the sea's most sadistic men. His body parts were collected by the crew and given a sea burial after breakfast the next day. According to Clough's account of the voyage, the seven pigs were then knocked on the head and thrown overboard too, presumably because no one fancied ingesting anything containing parts of Norris's brain.

The third Kanaka, the cook George Black, was eventually found hiding in the ship's hold. He was taken to Sydney, where he was promptly locked up in jail while the authorities decided what to do with him. Since the murder had taken place on an American ship, and as neither the victim nor the accused was a British subject, the courts decided there were no grounds to prosecute him in the Australian courts. However, when the *Sharon* sailed off without him, a writ of habeas corpus was issued, because Black had still not been charged with any crime, and he was promptly released without charge.

The *Sharon* story can be interpreted in two ways. Most of the newspapers of the time gave a one-sided account of an American skipper murdered by natives from the 'cannibal islands'[12] – as if their race was explanation enough for their terrible deeds. The madness of their actions was judged to be a kind of cultural insanity – the inexplicable behaviour of a primitive people that it was pointless to try to understand. It took a group of Sydney philanthropists to read between the lines and realise that Black's explanation of his actions – because 'the captain was cross'[14] – held the clue to a whole host of horrors that had taken place *before* the murder. The Kanakas had been driven to commit the mad acts because of the appalling and racist abuse by the captain. Unusually, in this case, history has come down on the side of the underdogs, and Captain Norris can be dismissed as part of the greater evil of colonialism and racist outrages that started with the Age of Discovery.

CHAPTER 5

RUM, LUNACY AND THE LASH

HMS *Victory* in Portsmouth is an icon of British maritime history. It's the ship from which Nelson commanded the Battle of Trafalgar, effectively ending Napoleon's plans to invade Britain, and on which he died during the closing stages of the battle. However, despite its historical significance, most 21st-century visitors to the ship will remember only one thing: its low deckheads (ie ceilings). With less than 5ft (1.5m) headroom in places, anyone of average height or more will find it almost impossible not to bump their heads on the deck beams at some point during their visit. This might sound trivial, but it's an issue that goes to the heart of the matter, for what's annoying to 21st-century visitors was potentially fatal to many 18th- and 19th-century sailors. According to the former Physician to the Fleet Sir Gilbert Blane – responsible for, among other innovations, the use of lime juice to get rid of scurvy – seamen in 1815 were seven times more likely to go mad than the general, shore-based population. Seven times. It's an extraordinary statistic that would result in any company or institution being closed down nowadays. And the reasons Blane gave were: 'intemperance, and blows to the head',[1] the first often leading to the second.

Social historian Michael Lewis confirmed this thesis, suggesting that low deck beams on ships were to blame because sailors forgot to duck while under the influence ('for then habit and discretion alike are apt to desert a man')[2] and hit their heads on the unyielding timbers. Certainly, the navy's habit of issuing seamen with daily rations of alcohol – 4.5 litres (1 gallon) a day of beer or, when that wasn't available, 285ml (½ pint) of rum, to be mixed with water – can't have helped with their short-term memory, or with their long-term mental health, for that matter.

'The Navy had a much higher rate of head injuries than the army,' says Andrew Baines, curator of HMS *Victory*, 'partly because of the cramped conditions on board ships. The crew were literally knocking themselves senseless.'[3]

Low deck beams and free booze weren't the only reasons Britain's sailors were going mad. The spreader bars attached to HMS *Victory*'s deck beams provide one clue, for it was from these that the men's hammocks were hung, just 40cm (16in) apart – and that was considered luxurious compared with most other ships, where they were only 35cm (14in) apart. Up to 460 men slept here, swinging in unison, endlessly, as the ship carried them over the waves.

And it's not as if they all wanted to be there. At least half of the men serving in the Royal Navy at the time of the Battle of Trafalgar were press-ganged into service. Most were pilfered from merchant ships, but many were petty criminals who chose to serve in the navy instead of going to prison. Others were mere children (13 was the official minimum age for ships' boys, though many started much younger) who were 'sent off to sea' because they were causing trouble back home. Some of them didn't know how to sail; most couldn't swim. For these new recruits it must have been a shock indeed to suddenly find themselves in this strange environment, where the slightest misdemeanour was likely to result in public flogging and the smallest slip of the foot could send them overboard.

Then there were the battles. The horror of naval warfare at this time was a brutal combination of heavy gunfire and hand-to-hand combat. During the Battle of Trafalgar in 1805, HMS *Victory* carried 104 guns, the most efficient of which were fired every 90 seconds. Each round sent a cannonball weighing up to 1.25 tons straight into the bowels of the enemy ships. The noise alone would have terrified most people.

As the *Victory*'s own Lieutenant Lewis Rotely put it:

'A man should witness a battle in a three-decker from the middle deck, for it beggars all description: it bewilders the senses of sight and hearing. There was the fire from above, the fire from below, besides the fire from the deck I was upon, the guns recoiling with violence ... reports louder than thunder, the deck heaving and side straining. I fancied myself in the infernal regions, where every man appeared a devil. Lips might move, but orders and hearing were out of the question: everything was done by signs.'[4]

He wasn't exaggerating. By the time the Battle of Trafalgar ended, HMS *Victory*'s foretopsail was pockmarked with the holes of 90 cannonballs, gunshots and other missiles that had passed through it in the space of five hours. And she was on the winning side. The sail still survives and is on display at the Royal Navy Museum in

Portsmouth, an apt metaphor for the damage inflicted on countless sailors' brains by centuries of naval warfare.

Whatever the reasons for the high rates of mental illness in the navy, the Admiralty did at least try to tackle the problem. From August 1755, and possibly earlier, mentally ill seamen were sent to Hoxton House, a privately run mental asylum in north-east London. As the wars between Britain and France dragged on, the number of seamen needing treatment steadily increased, and from 1794 to 1818, an astonishing 1,289 seamen were sent to Hoxton – an average of 53 per year. Not that it did them much good. Of the 1,289 admitted, only 364 were discharged as cured (and 102 of those were later readmitted), while 494 were sent to Bethlem Royal Hospital (popularly known as 'Bedlam') – presumably because they were considered incurable. Of the remainder, 52 escaped and 272 died.

The figures were shocking enough to warrant an investigation by the Admiralty, and in 1812 the first Inspector of Naval Hospitals, John Weir, paid several visits to the 'Lunatick Asylum' run by 'Mssrs Miles & Co'. On 13 November he filed his report, and it was every bit as grim as suggested by the modern cliché of an 18th-century mental asylum. Weir described how 20 officers were kept in a space the size of a living room – measuring a mere 5.8 x 4.3m (19 x 14ft) – and were looked after by a single keeper. The officers were 'mixed indiscriminately with other Maniaks', so that 'some are chained down to their seats, some are handcuffed, and some are raging with inconceivable fury, whilst others are calm and tranquil'. He went on to report how the chained patients frequently 'answer the calls of nature' where they are sitting, so that 'the air becomes so vitiated from this circumstance, and from so many persons being crowded together in so small a space, as to render it unfit for respiration'.[5]

The men's quarters were even worse. There, 106 seamen and 20 prisoners of war were kept in two rooms that were 7.9m (26ft) long by 4.9m (16ft) wide – a space smaller than a London Tube carriage – under the care of two keepers. Again, they were mixed together 'without the least regard being paid to the mild or violent forms of their disease'. Basic equipment, such as tables, plates, knives and forks, was not allowed, with the result that 'it is impossible to conceive a more uncivilized appearance than they exhibit at their meals'. The air was 'unfit for respiration' due to the 'insufferable effluvia' (excrement) emitting from the 'furious patients', and the only other place to go was a small dank yard, with no shelter or benches, of which Weir said, 'it is hardly possible to convey an adequate idea of the miserableness of this situation in the rainy season'.[6]

The sleeping quarters were 1.8m (6ft) long by 1.1m (3ft 8in) wide, shared between three men who slept one above the other in narrow 'cots' – and even then they weren't guaranteed their own bed. As Weir noted: 'At Bethlem each Patient is allowed a Bedroom to himself, in order to prevent any unnatural propensities, but at Hoxton they not only sleep three in a room, but, in six cases, two in abed – an impropriety so glaring as to need no comment.'[7]

In many ways a man ahead of his times, Weir was concerned about the men's diet, which typically consisted of: 450g (16oz) red meat, 450g (16oz) vegetables, 55g (2oz) cheese, 570ml (1 pint) broth, 1 litre (2 pints) tea, and 2 litres (4 pints) 'small beer' per day. Far from being under-nourishing, he concluded, it was 'too stimulating and nutritious a nature, and more calculated to increase than to retard the progress of Insanity'.[8] He was particularly critical of the amount of cheese given to the men, and recommended the 'Half and Low'[9] diet given in naval hospitals – whereby the amount of meat and vegetables eaten by patients was reduced, while their milk intake was increased. Given that the diet of a sailor in Nelson's navy amounted to about 5,000 calories a day (the equivalent of eating 20 Big Macs), he probably had a point.

However, what Weir was most furious about was the lack of medical treatment at Hoxton. Many men, he reported, had never received 'a single grain of Medicine' in 12 years at the asylum, even though some might clearly have benefited from it. He could not explain this omission, he said, 'unless it be from the mistaken supposition that Insanity is not to be cured or abated by medical aid, or unless it be imagined that Maniacks are not entitled to the same assistance as Patients labouring under other complaints'.[10]

Far from attempting to cure the patients, Weir suggested the regime at Hoxton House was designed to detain them as long as possible in order to maximise the company's profits. Moreover, he noted: 'I conceive, from having observed Patients lying perfectly naked, and covered up in straw, and others unnecessarily loaded with chains, that uncalled for severity is practised towards them.'[11]

Weir concluded that the care offered at Hoxton was 'radically defective'[12] and appealed to His Lordships' compassion, writing:

'It will readily be acknowledged that Maniacks are of all pitiable objects, the most entitled to protection and commiseration – as such we would imagine that it should be the boast of a generous Nation to provide Asylum, where those who may have been deprived of their intellects whilst employed in the service of their country, should be rendered as comfortable as the nature of their situations would possibly admit. We see ample accommodations in all our Naval Hospitals and Marine Infirmaries for the recovery of the Sick and Wounded of the Navy, whilst the wretched Maniacks are placed in a situation where the object appears to be more to get them out of the way, than assist in their recovery.'[13]

His position was supported by Rear Admiral Garrett, who was reported as saying: 'A seaman who has lost his reason in the service of the Crown should receive the love and attention on a scale not less than a seaman who has lost a limb in the same cause.'[14]

Weir suggested building a dedicated hospital for the care of mentally ill sailors, and couched the idea in terms he knew would appeal to his masters:

'On the principle, therefore, of humanity as well as of Necessity, I would humbly suggest that some other Building be appropriated exclusively to their accommodation. I am of the opinion that it should be conducted on such a widely different plan, as not only to strike the eye of the observer with admiration and afford the greatest possible comfort to the Maniaks themselves, but be a lasting memorial of the humanity and wise policy of the present Naval Administration.'[15]

Not only that, but it would cost the Admiralty half as much if they looked after the patients themselves.

Six years after Weir's report, Block F at Royal Hospital Haslar in Gosport was converted into a mental asylum, and in August 1818 the 126 patients remaining at Hoxton House were transferred to the new facilities.

✳　　✳　　✳

The records of many of the sailors treated at Haslar, along with the hospital's journal, still survive and are contained in a pair of boxes at the National Archives in Kew. Together, they form an extraordinary paper trail of the most important turning point in the history of mental health in the navy. There's Weir's landmark report, with its small, painfully neat handwriting; another report from Lord Somesuch complaining about the cost of building new facilities; and then the case studies themselves: dozens upon dozens of reports of mentally ill seamen sent to Haslar for treatment.

Written on thick parchment paper in often unintelligible longhand, they are tied in neat bundles by year – just one for 1822, a few more for 1823, and then dozens more every year from 1824 onwards. The reports are mesmerising, partly because of the stories they tell, of lives gone awry and unfortunate souls who stood little chance of recovery – but also because of the language, with its beautiful rhythms and unusual choice of words, at once just the same as modern English and yet intriguingly different.

And then there's the journal itself, which follows the lives of all the patients at Haslar from 1830 to 1838, recording any incidents of note from their arrival at Haslar through to either their release or (more often) their ongoing incarceration or death. Also written in longhand, the journal jumps crazily, as one page was filled and the entry continued in the next available space, weaving in and out of the journal. Despite its broken narrative, however, it too makes compelling reading.

Both sets of reports contained tales of derring-do on the High Seas, of injuries received in combat, of concussions caused by errant bits of rigging or by falling down from aloft. There was Lieutenant Thomas Mackeson of His Majesty's Schooner *Cornelia*, struck down by fever off the coast of Africa and relieved of his command after becoming violent and suicidal. Or take Edward Barrett, a cook on HMS *Royal Fredrick*, who was 'deprived of his arms and right eye in naval engagements' and behaved in 'a violent, inconsistent and highly irrational manner'[16] (and who can blame him?). And how about George Lloyd, also a cook, this time from HMS *Argonaut*, who 'has lost the left leg but how cannot be learned',[17] as well as Captain Winne, hit by a block (ie pulley) when he was a midshipman in 1787 and thirty years later confined to an asylum.

These were the brave, heroic sailors of popular imagination, struck down in the course of their duties in faraway lands, the victims of the harshness of life at sea in the 18th and 19th centuries. But, in truth, they were the exceptions. Closer scrutiny of the case studies reveals how tragically mundane most of the patients' stories were. The reasons sailors went mad at sea, it seemed, were very similar to the reasons non-sailors went mad on land.

These included sailors being victims of 'private misfortunes',[18] such as John McKinzay from HMS *Spartiate*, who was apparently overwhelmed by the death of his father and the 'ill behaviour' of his brother, both of which 'preyed upon his spirits'.[19] There was the painful jealousy of husbands leaving their wives at home to fend for themselves, such as James Purches, who was 'extremely jealous of his wife and thinks that Dr Wilson and many others have taken improper liberties with her'.[20] Causes also included the paranoia of men stuck on a ship at close quarters for months on end, believing their crewmates were trying to kill them, and the delusions of patients who believed they were the King of Denmark or had some special connection with God. And, again and again, there was the curse of drunkenness, usually described as 'intemperance' or, as one doctor put it, 'the free use of spirituous liquor'.[21]

Others had more puzzling symptoms, such as purser Edward Griffin, who 'fancies that he has bats [and] mice in his belly, and they repeat every word he utters',[22] and 66-year-old James Holloway, who 'never enters a gate or a doorway without running in and out'.[23] Or take John Parker, who was frequently found with 'twenty or thirty wooden spoons secreted about his person'[24] and who fashioned knives out of the handles of beer mugs, or the ship's barber, Edward Craig, taken in because he was 'flighty and extravagant in his manner and conversation and [had] occasional fits of laughter without any apparent cause'.[25] According to his notes, the latter was bled and 'purged' (ie made to vomit) before being discharged a few months later as 'unserviceable'.

Some patients were harmless enough, and even at times amusing, such as Lieutenant James Bowdick, wounded in action off Copenhagen, and whose doctor wrote:

'It is supposed when he was in Ireland, the free use of spirituous liquor had been the cause of his imbecile state of mind. During the period of my observation, his delusions have consisted in an idea of possessing great wealth, constantly speaking about his large estates, and immense capital in the funds. When he leaves his present situation, he fancies he is to marry a rich Irish widow, who resides in an elegant cottage in Blackheath. He is so much pleased with his present keeper [ie Lt Bowdick himself] that he has engaged him as his steward, at two hundred per annum.'[26]

Not surprisingly, given the central role religion played in everyday life at this time, religious delusions occurred frequently and were often the source of some barely concealed humour in the doctors'

reports. For instance, William Duke, a 21-year-old seaman on HMS
Heron,

> 'was found walking about in the night in a state of apparent insanity,
> which was characterised by the constant repetition of the Church
> Prayers, and quotations from the Scriptures, in a loud voice, and
> which continued night and day in spite of every persuasion. He
> conceived he had had some communication from Heaven, which
> while it promised its own Redemption, told him to warn others of
> their hopeless state.'[27]

Others were clearly dangerous, such as Patrick Walsh, a seaman
suspected of killing several men. His doctor wrote that he:

> 'fancies that there is no crime, but rather a meritorious act, in killing
> a Frenchman, Spaniard, American or native of any other country
> with which England is at war, which he thinks is at present the case.
> And also any person who would blaspheme the Holy Ghost or Virgin
> Mary or speak disrespectfully of the Pope. Under these impressions
> it is believed he has destroyed two or three of his fellow creatures!!
> His health is generally good and for the most part his behaviour – but
> owing to the above statements it is considered prudent to keep him
> strictly confined.'[28]

However, while the reasons sailors became mentally ill might
have been depressingly similar to those of their counterparts on
land, there's no doubt that the sea magnified their problems. Living
in a rugged macho environment far away from their families and
any other kind of emotional support, it's easy to see how the sailors'

personal difficulties could become exaggerated in their own minds and get out of hand. Just as a hand appears larger when looked at underwater, so the sailors' mental problems loomed larger and more frightening under the ocean's uncompromising lens.

Whatever the symptoms, the cures on offer were hardly any better than the illness. Doctors in the 18th and 19th century tended to blame everything on the existence of 'bad humors' in the body, which could be cured by purging. At Haslar, there seems to have been an obsession with 'loosening the bowels' of patients, with a variety of laxatives being prescribed almost automatically, while other substances were given to make patients vomit. Another regular treatment was a blister or a 'seton' (a piece of thread passed through the skin), both of which were applied to the back of the neck to allow the bad humors to run out. Bloodletting was also commonplace to relieve a 'determination of blood to the head',[29] including placing leeches on the patient's temples to suck out the blood. And then there was that old favourite, mercury, once thought to cure syphilis (also a cause of madness), but that was more likely to lead to a slow death from liver and kidney poisoning.

These methods were inflicted upon William Kemp, who was taken to Haslar in 1830 for his violent and noisy behaviour and, when a course of mercury failed to cure him, was given the following treatment:

'Since the commencement of his present illness his bowels have been kept open by the compound Rhubarb Pill, the compound aloetic pill and small doses of the Sulphate of Magnesia, and Tartrate of Antimony. A Blister was applied to his head without benefit, but the cold affusion had the effect of composing him and rendering him less noisy.'[30]

And what of poor William Kiddall, a seaman admitted to Haslar in 1826 with Mania? Six years later, on 17 August 1832 at 11.30am, he was 'observed to yawn'. As he 'could give no account of his sensations' he was put to bed, and at 2pm, induced by his keepers, 'vomiting and purging commenced'.[31] The report goes on:

'He was then put into a warm bath and Brandy, Aromatic Spirit of Ammonia [ie smelling salts] & Tincture of Opium were given, with a view to arouse the powers of life, which were evidently very low; but no reaction took place. At 4pm he was again put into a bath and Venisection [blood letting] was performed on both arms & internal jugular, but scarcely any blood came away, and the little obtained was viscid and extremely dark coloured. A branch of the temporal artery was then opened and about a drop of blood of the same appearance could be procured.'[32]

By 9.30pm he was dead.

✳   ✳   ✳

This was a critical time for the treatment of mental health in the UK. Public attitudes were changing and there was growing outrage at the abysmal treatment of patients in the nation's mostly private and therefore run-for-profit mental asylums. It was the beginnings of 'moral management' – an approach that was far more progressive than it sounds and that essentially advocated the treatment of patients through therapy rather than restraint and medicine. One of the most notorious cases, which proved to be a turning point for mental health reform in the UK, was that of an American sailor incarcerated at Bethlem.

James Norris was in his early forties when he was admitted to Bethlem in 1800, and soon established a reputation as one of the most violent and dangerous patients in the hospital. In 1804, after stabbing a keeper with a knife and attacking two other men, he was put into solitary confinement. Various methods of restraint were tried, with little success. Thanks to his unusually slim hands and wrists, Norris seemed able to slip out of his manacles and used them as weapons to attack his keepers. The contraption that the resident apothecary John Haslam and his cohorts eventually devised to restrain him, and in which he was imprisoned for over 10 years, is the stuff of horror films:

'... a stout ring was riveted around his neck, from which a short chain passed to a ring made to slide upwards or downwards on an upright massive iron bar, more than six feet high, inserted into the wall. Round his body a strong iron bar about two inches wide was riveted; on each side of the bar was a vertical projection, which being fashioned to and enclosing each of his arms, pinioned them close to his sides. This waist bar was secured by two similar bars which, passing over his shoulders, were riveted to the waist bar both before and behind. The iron ring around his neck was connected to the bar on his shoulders, by a double link. From each of these bars another short chain passed to the ring on the upright iron bar...'[33]

It was in this hellish device that prison reformer Edward (Lord) Wakefield found Norris when he visited Bethlem in 1814. Appalled by this and the sight of other semi-naked men and women chained to the walls as if they were 'vermin', Wakefield commissioned an artist to make a drawing of Norris, which was turned into an engraving. It was an act of propaganda genius. The image of the unfortunate American sailor, 'confined in Irons in a manner repugnant to humanity',[34] was published in several newspapers and widely distributed as a print. It led to a national outcry and prompted a Parliamentary Select Committee inquiry that ultimately ended the use of chains in the UK and elsewhere. The outrage Norris's case aroused is also credited with leading to the Madhouses Act of 1828, which attempted to regulate the treatment of mental patients in private hospitals.

The Admiralty must have been aware of this changing climate of opinion when it inspected its own facilities in 1812, and then transferred its mental patients to Haslar in 1818. No doubt spurred by the hammering the reputation of Bethlem was receiving at the hands of Wakefield and others, it ordered an inspection of its new premises in 1824, this time by one Dr Burnett. The report is a fascinating snapshot of a society in the process of change; of progressive Enlightenment thinking clashing with the outdated attitudes of the previous generation. It also explains the sudden increase in reports of mental cases to the Admiralty from 1824 onwards, which was unrelated to any increase in 'Naval Maniaks'.

For, while Dr Burnett admired the buildings and the grounds, he reprimanded its superintendent Dr Dods for not doing more for the patients. The doctor had, he said, a 'misunderstanding as to the difference between a place of confinement for Lunatics simply, and one in which measures were to be taken for their cure also'[35] – a comment that goes to the heart of the new versus old-guard approaches to mental health.

Dr Burnett castigated Dr Dods for relying on outmoded cures (namely setons and tonics), for not attending post-mortems, and for not keeping a journal with details of his patients' symptoms and medical treatment.

'The treatment of Lunatics is of a nature to require more attention and patient investigation, than any class of disease to which mankind are liable,' he wrote. 'Of equal variety are the hallucinations of the Maniac, and it is of great importance that the Medical Attendant should be well acquainted with them, for by this means only will he be enabled to direct with effect the moral management of his patient...'[36]

He recommended that 'a minute account of every symptom or hallucination' of new cases should be entered in the Medical Register, along with 'every circumstance which preceded or accompanied the disease previous to his admission',[37] and that a copy of these reports should be sent to the Victualling Board within a fortnight.

The sudden increase in reports from 1824 onwards suggests Dr Dods complied with the second request, although of his journal there is no sign. Instead, the first page of the journal at the National Archives contained this sombre note:

'Thursday, 11th November, 1830, Charles Dods, Esquire, Senior Surgeon of the Royal Naval Hospital, Haslar, and Superintendent of the Lunatic Asylum, died suddenly; in consequence of which the temporary Charge of that Institution devolved upon James Scott, MD, Lecturer, Curator of the Museum, and Librarian. A List of the Patients, then in the Asylum, is subjoined.'[38]

The doctor is dead, long live the doctor! No sooner had Dr Dods had died, in unexplained circumstances, than his successor Dr Scott took over, and his very first action was to start a journal. Significantly, he backdated each entry to 1818, with a pointed comment that previous volumes are 'nowhere to be found'.[39] His entries included detailed descriptions of each patient's symptoms and, where available, their past histories, and there were columns for both their 'medical treatment' and their 'moral treatment'. Not only that, but there were gruesome descriptions of post-mortems, or *sectio cadaveris*, including examinations of the patients' brains and innards. As an ardent phrenologist, Dr Scott was interested in how the different parts of the brain related to the patient's illness, and, while his conclusions might now be regarded as simplistic, this work did at least herald the start of a more scientific approach to mental illness. The modern age of rational neuroscience was on its way.

❊   ❊   ❊

Haslar was closed down in 2009 and the site offered for redevelopment as a retail, residential and business centre. Before that happened, however, a group of archaeologists was allowed in to excavate some of the graves in the Paddock. Some 8,000 or so bodies were buried here between 1753 and 1826, including many of the 1,690 British casualties from the Battle of Trafalgar, as well as those mentally ill patients transferred from Hoxton House who died while in Charles Dods's care. The bodies that were exhumed between 2009 and 2013 appeared to be mostly male, heavily built, with the strong upper bodies that would come from years of pulling ropes. Their injuries ranged from sword wounds to missing legs and teeth, and among them was someone with a crushed skull and broken jaw consistent with falling from a great height, such as ship's rigging, and landing face first on a hard object, such as a deck.

The findings confirmed what was already apparent: life in Nelson's navy was brutal and unforgiving. But they also suggested that it wasn't completely without heart. The archaeologists studying the remains of that unfortunate sailor who smashed his skull falling from the rigging concluded that he must have been kept alive for about three months, probably being fed through a straw, before dying from an infection. That such care was forthcoming at Haslar suggests a degree of compassion for one's fellow man that was clearly missing at Hoxton House. It would, however, take another 100 years for the mental health revolution to be fully sanctioned by the Royal Navy.

CHAPTER 6

THE REAL MOBY DICK

First Mate Owen Chase was repairing a boat on the deck of the 87ft whaleship *Essex* when he looked up and saw a sight that would haunt him for the rest of his life. About 25 metres (30 yards) away, on the windward side, a large sperm whale, about as long as the ship, had surfaced and was swimming straight towards them at considerable speed.

'Helm hard up!' he shouted to the helmsman, but it was too late. The whale struck the bow of the ship with such force that the men on deck were knocked off their feet. The vessel was brought to an immediate halt, 'as if she had struck a rock,' Chase later wrote, after which she 'trembled for a few seconds like a leaf'.[1]

Moments passed as the ship's crew looked at each other in disbelief, and the whale passed under the ship, came up on the other side and lay on the surface of the sea, apparently dazed, too. Then the bow of the *Essex* started to sink down into the sea. Coming back to his senses, Chase ordered the crew to man the pumps and signalled to the other whaleboats to return to the mother ship.

Meanwhile, 450 metres (500 yards) to leeward, the whale thrashed around in the sea, opening and closing its jaws 'as if distracted with rage and fury'. As he prepared the ship's boats to abandon ship, Chase heard someone shout, 'Here he is – he is making for us again.' Chase looked up and saw the whale bearing down on them once more, this time going twice as fast as before. Its head was half out of the water and its tail thrashed the sea as it propelled its 70-ton weight forwards 'with tenfold fury and vengeance'.[2]

'Helm hard up!' he shouted again, but again it was too late. The whale struck the bow of the ship, this time at a combined speed of 9 knots, completely smashing the planking. It then passed under the ship again, reappearing to leeward, before it dipped underwater and vanished from sight.

The whole incident lasted less than 10 minutes, Chase later wrote, but it would have a profound impact not only on the lives of the vessel's crew but on how mankind viewed its relationship with the world's biggest mammal, for this was the first recorded incident of a whale attacking a ship in a premeditated manner, as if in revenge rather than simply in self-defence. Moreover, it was this aspect of the story that so fascinated Herman Melville when he read Chase's account and that prompted him to write his seminal novel *Moby Dick*. However, while Melville chose to focus his attention on Captain Ahab's mad obsession with the whale before the sinking of his ship, in the real-life story the sinking marked just the beginning of the crew's drift towards insanity.

In fact, the *Essex* took a remarkably long time to sink, and for the next two days the ship's captain, George Pollard, and his crew scavenged food and equipment as best they could for the difficult voyage ahead. The ship had been wrecked in the middle of the Pacific, 2,250 miles west of South America and just south of the

Equator. The nearest land was the Marquesas Islands, 1,200 miles to the west, but, in a supreme piece of irony, Chase and others believed the islands were inhabited by cannibals and should be avoided at all costs. They thus persuaded Pollard to sail the much longer route east, towards South America. The only means of transport for the 20 men were the three lightweight whaleboats – little more than overgrown dinghies – that they had saved.

They estimated that they had enough provisions to last them 60 days – assuming they ate half their usual rations. However, as their bread became contaminated by salt water and lack of wind slowed their progress, they soon had to go on quarter rations. Already, their thirst and hunger were almost unbearable, yet, no matter how desperate the men became, they never questioned the need to ration the food and only once did someone steal any for themselves. After a month at sea, they stumbled across an island, but there was little there to sustain them so most of them set off again; three decided to stay on the island, and were eventually rescued by a passing ship three months later.

The rest carried on sailing eastwards and, after two weeks at sea, had their first death. Matthew P Joy, the second mate, who had been in charge of the third boat, had a 'weak and sickly constitution'[3] and died on 10 January. He was sewn into his clothes, weighed down with a heavy stone, and lowered into the sea.

Two days later, the boats were separated, and Chase and his crew had to carry on alone. A week later, another man died, this time as a direct result of starvation, and was also buried at sea. Despite their worsening state, Chase decided he had no choice but to halve the men's food rations yet again, leaving them with just 35g (1½oz) of bread per day to live on. The reduced rations began to affect their minds as well as their bodies, as Chase wrote; 'our speech and reason were both considerably impaired'. Worst affected was Isaac Cole, who became delirious and turned into 'a most miserable spectacle of madness'. 'He spoke incoherently about everything, calling loudly for a napkin and water, and then – lying stupidly and senselessly down in the boat again – closed his hollow eyes, as if in death.'[4] After several hours writhing around in agony, he died later that afternoon.

This time, rather than launch Cole's body into the deep, Chase made a shocking suggestion. With only three days' rations left and hundreds of miles still to go, he said, their only option was to use the dead man's body to prolong their own lives. In other words, to eat him. The alternative was to die themselves. The rest of the crew agreed, and they set about their gruesome task without further ado.

'We separated the limbs from the body and cut all the flesh from the bones,' wrote Chase, 'after which we opened the body, took out the heart, closed it again – sewing it up as decently as we could – and then committed it to the sea. We now first commenced to satisfy the immediate cravings of nature from the heart, which we eagerly devoured...'[5]

Appalling as it was, their deed was by no means unprecedented in maritime history. Examples of cannibalism among sailors date back to at least 1710, when the crew of the *Nottingham Galley*, shipwrecked on a tiny island off the coast of Maine, ate the body of the ship's carpenter to stay alive. The practice was usually justified as a 'custom of the sea' and accepted as a legitimate means of survival – though its status in law would later be challenged. On some ships, the dead bodies were chopped up and used as bait to catch fish, which at least avoided the charge of cannibalism.

For Chase and his crew, eating their comrade probably saved their lives. The meat, once cooked, kept them going for several more days – long enough for them to be picked up by a passing ship. By that time, 89 days had passed since their ship was sunk and they had sailed for 3,500 miles – an astonishing feat of endurance.

Over on the other two boats, things were following a similar, but even more dramatic, course. Both boats ran out of food soon after they parted from Chase's company, and within the space of just a few days, from 23 to 28 January, two men died on each boat and were consumed by the rest of the crew. As Captain Pollard later recounted, 'We roasted [their remains] to dryness by means of fires kindled on the ballast-sand at the bottom of the boats.'[6] At this point, Captain Pollard's boat lost sight of the second mate's boat and they carried on separately. Three days later, with no food left at all, the four remaining men decided to cast lots to see who would go next. The lot fell to the cabin boy, Owen Coffin, the captain's cousin. Pollard had promised Coffin's mother he would look after the boy, and was deeply upset by this turn of events.

'My lad, my lad,' he shouted, 'if you don't like your lot, I'll shoot the first man that touches you.' But the boy was resigned to his fate, and quietly laid his head on the gunwale, saying, 'I like it as well as any other.'[7] The executioner's lot fell to Charles Ramsdell, himself just a teenager, who shot the boy with a gun.

'He was soon dispatched,' said Pollard, 'and nothing of him left.'[8]

Ten days later, another man died, and the two remaining men, Captain Pollock and Charles Ramsdell, ate him too. By the time the last two men were picked up by a ship, on 23 February, they were completely delirious. Barely more than living skeletons themselves, they sat among the remains of their former comrades, smashing the bigger bones of the arms and legs – the femur, the fibula and the humerus – with a hatchet to suck the last bits of goodness out of the marrows. Even when rescuers appeared, they barely noticed them, and, too weak to move, sat in the bottom of the boat, stuffing their pockets with the smaller bones of fingers and feet – the distal, middle and proximal phalanges, the metatarsals and the tarsals. As they were lifted aboard the rescue ship, the two men were more spirit than body, their bodies wasted away and their minds in free fall.

The fate of the men on the third boat is not known for certain. A whaleboat with four skeletons on board was later found washed up on a nearby island, but the remains were never positively identified as being those of the missing men.

Most of the survivors of the *Essex* tragedy went straight back to sea – after all, there weren't that many other options available to them in 19th-century Nantucket. Fourteen months after taking up his next command, however, Pollard was shipwrecked again and thereafter renounced the sea and became a nightwatchman. He never set sail again. Owen Chase carried on whaling for another 20 years, and was married four times – his first two wives died soon after childbirth and the third he divorced after discovering she had been unfaithful to him while he was at sea. Towards the end of his career Chase complained of pains in his head, which related to his ordeal on the *Essex* and which plagued him for the rest of his life. His torment resurfaced in other ways as, when an old man, he became anxious about starving and hoarded food in the attic of his house. By 1868 his headaches had become unbearable and he was described as 'insane'.[9] He died the following year. The book he wrote about his experiences, composed with the help of a ghostwriter as soon as he returned to Nantucket, has never been out of print and has been translated into more than 200 languages.

CHAPTER 7

ADRIFT

Shipwreck was a sailor's worst nightmare. It was what every major decision made aboard ship was designed to avoid: from recaulking the ship's planking, to watching the weather, planning the ship's passage, navigating correctly, manoeuvring the ship... When a ship was wrecked, its crew had to cope not only with terrible physical demands but also with profound mental anxiety. For a ship's captain, it was the ultimate failure and could cast a shadow on the rest of his career. Perhaps it's therefore not so surprising that many captains chose to 'go down with the ship' rather than live with the consequences of their mistakes. For those sailors who survived the immediate disaster, their apparent good fortune often turned out to be the start of another, far worse mental journey.

In some ways the crew of the *Essex* were lucky: at least they had the ship's boats to escape on – even if in the end they must have wished they had perished with the ship. For many, or most, passengers and crews wrecked on ships in the 18th and early 19th centuries, there was no means of escape and hundreds died due to a lack of lifeboats. During

83

most of the Age of Sail, there were no rules governing the number of lifeboats (which included ship's boats) ships should carry, and most vessels went to sea with far fewer than were needed to carry everyone on board.

Even when the Passengers Act was introduced in 1849 specifying a minimum number of lifeboats, the quota was based on a ship's tonnage rather than on the number of passengers it carried. That meant a 1,000-ton ship carrying 300 passengers only had to have six lifeboats – the same number as a 2,000-ton cargo ship with a crew of 30. The prevailing view was that too many lifeboats would clutter up the ship's deck and be more of a hindrance than a help, and that losing half the people on board was simply 'a price worth paying' – an acceptable risk that passengers implicitly accepted the moment they set foot on board a ship.

It was only after the sinking of RMS *Titanic* in 1912, with the loss of 1,500 lives (ie nearly 70 per cent of the people on board), that pressure grew for ships to carry sufficient lifeboats for everyone on board. The principle was finally enshrined in the International Convention for the Safety of Life at Sea (SOLAS), adopted by the UK in 1914.

One of the most gruesome shipwrecks of this era was that of the French frigate *Medusa*, immortalised in Géricault's painting *The Raft of the Medusa*. The 1,080-ton ship was on her way to Senegal in July 1816 to take over command of the colony from the British. Nearly 400 people were on board, including would-be settlers, an army regiment, and the new governor of Senegal and his wife. The captain of the ship was a minor aristocrat, Hugues Duroy de Chaumareys, who hadn't been to sea for 20 years but was given the job as a reward for his support of the French monarchy. As they approached the north-west tip of Africa, de Chaumareys insisted on taking the shorter route close to land, despite advice to keep well offshore, and the *Medusa* went aground on the notorious Arguin Bank.

This in itself wasn't an insurmountable problem, and the ship could have been saved had de Chaumareys immediately jettisoned some cargo and lightened the *Medusa* so she could float on the next high tide. However, he was reluctant to lose any of his precious cannons and instead ordered a raft to be built, so the cargo could be unloaded onto it and then loaded back onto the ship once she refloated. After four days, though, a gale sprang up and the *Medusa* started showing signs of breaking up, forcing de Chaumareys to give the order to abandon ship. This was long before the era of lifeboats, and the only means of reaching the land, just 30 miles way, was on board the six ship's boats – and the raft.

The ship's evacuation followed a strict hierarchical order, with the captain, the ship's officers, and the governor and his entourage nabbing the best boats, while the settlers, soldiers and a few remaining sailors were dumped on the raft. Seventeen men decided not to risk it, and stayed on board the ship (only three survived). The original idea was that the ship's boats would tow the raft to land, but when it became clear that this might prove hazardous, the lines were cut and the raft was left to fend for itself.

It was a devastating moment for the 146 men and one woman on the raft, as they watched the ship's boats row away to safety and abandon them to their fate. The gale was raging and the raft, already semi-submerged by the weight of people on it, was continually bombarded by 'mountains of water'.[1] The front and back of the structure flexed alarmingly as it was driven up and down the waves, so the only relatively safe place to stand was in the middle – and there was such a crowd there that several people were trampled to death. The rest had to hang on to the raft as best they could. The only food on board was a sack of soggy biscuits, and the only drink a barrel of water and several barrels of wine.

Twenty men died on the first night, either swept off by waves or deliberately jumping into the sea. By the end of the second day, as it became clear that no one was coming to rescue them, a group of soldiers seized a barrel of wine and, in a drunken frenzy, started trying to destroy the raft, hacking at anything and anyone who got in their way. The mutiny turned into an orgy of violence as the soldiers beat, bit and stabbed the officers and others trying to maintain calm.

By now, even those who hadn't drunk wine were feeling the effects of being lashed by wind and submerged in sea for hours on end. 'The manner in which we were affected had something very extraordinary about it,'[2] wrote two of the survivors, Jean Baptiste Henri Savigny and Alexandre Corréeard.

> 'Some threw themselves at once into the sea. Mr Savigny had the most delightful visions; he fancied he was in a beautiful country, amid objects which delighted all his senses; some rushed on their companions with drawn swords, asking for the wing of a chicken or some bread; some asked for hammocks, "to go repose between the decks of the frigate"; several thought that they were still on board the Medusa; some fancied they saw ships or a harbour, before a fine city. We were less affected during the day-light, but the return of night increased our disorder.'[3]

When the sun rose on the morning of the third day, it revealed a terrible sight. The raft of the *Medusa* was littered with bodies and splattered with blood as if it were a human abattoir. In one night, more than 60 people had been killed in a crazed bout of violence. And the horror didn't stop there. Out of their minds with hunger and thirst, some of the survivors started eating the bodies of the dead. Using knives and swords, they hacked off limbs and peeled the skin off torsos, eating the raw flesh and drinking the blood to sate their thirst. To make it more palatable, they hung strips of flesh from the rigging to cook in the sun. It was a scene of utter debasement.

The following day, 10 more men died and were all buried at sea, except for one who would, as Savigny and Corréeard put it, 'nourish those who, only a short while before, had clasped his hands in friendship'.[4] By the eighth day, only 27 people were left alive, and they were down to their last barrel of wine – all the other barrels having been thrown overboard by the rampaging soldiers. Twelve of the survivors (including the only woman on board) were terribly ill and 'no longer in full possession of their senses'. Rather than waste their limited resources on them, the strongest group decided to improve their own chances of survival by pushing the weakest ones over the side, 'thus at once terminating their suffering',[5] according to Savigny and Corréeard.

By the time the raft was discovered by another French ship, only 15 of the 147 people who had boarded the raft 13 days before were left alive. The rest had all been murdered or washed overboard, or had committed suicide, lost their minds – or been eaten. There was uproar in France when news of the disaster leaked out, and the story soon became a symbol of the corruption of the Bourbon regime, as the authorities first attempted to cover it up and then gave de Chaumareys a lenient three-year prison sentence, despite his incompetent and immoral actions. It was, however, the making of the young painter Théodore Géricault, who interviewed survivors and studied body parts to paint

87

his first major work, *The Raft of the Medusa*. But, while the painting was read as a damning indictment of the royalist regime, it also captured another major concern of the age: man's relationship with nature. *The Raft of the Medusa* showed how impotent man is when pitted against the might of the sea, and the extremes of physical and mental anguish endured by its victims; no other painting captures more dramatically the aftermath of madness at sea.

Getting on board a ship's boat or a lifeboat was no guarantee of survival either – as the privileged majority who made it onto the *Medusa*'s boats discovered. The annals of maritime literature are chock-a-block with stories of shipwrecked sailors going through unspeakable suffering as they drift about the ocean on inadequately provisioned liferafts – so much so that they are sometimes referred to as a separate literary genre. In most cases, the only food and drink on board was whatever the crews could grab as the ship was going down, which was almost always inadequate. And with lack of food and water (water especially) usually comes madness.

Such an occurrence was recorded by the master of the *Maria Hay*, sailing from Peru to London laden with guano, who gave a detailed account of the gradual deterioration of the crew after their ship sank in a storm in March 1872. When the 18 men took to the ship's pinnace (an open boat measuring 27ft long and 6ft wide), their total stock of food consisted of a small cask of water, two bags of bread, five pieces of salted meat and some tins of preserved meat. The crew managed to survive another four days of gales in their small open boat, with freezing temperatures and sudden onslaughts of the dreaded pampero, the katabatic wind that shoots down the mountains of South America and turns the sea into 'a cauldron of boiling water'.[6]

After 12 days, they ran out of water, and the very next day the first signs of madness began to appear. Captain John Jones wrote:

'Friday, 5th [...] "Water", "water", is the unceasing cry, and there is none to give them; there remains now but a mite of rotten bread. On this day commenced the most distressing and appalling of our troubles, as one of our seamen, Charles Miller, showed evident signs of insanity from want of water. We have not moistened our lips today. Oh, what horror; how long is this to last! God have mercy upon us.

'Saturday 6th [...] How fearsome this is. Some have started drinking salt water in spite of all remonstrance from the rest, as we know it must cause a thousand times more thirst and accelerate the period of madness. Poor Miller has become quite insane, and so restless we can scarcely keep him in the boat.

'Sunday 7th [...] At 2am Miller died, raving mad. God knows who will be the next. [...] We buried poor Miller at 10am. [...] At 4pm another of us, Robert Hughes, began to show symptoms of insanity. Rain at last! [...] New life and hope now seemed instilled into our hearts [...] all except poor Hughes, who is too far gone for this world.

'Monday 8th [...] Another of our crew, named Laughran, shows symptoms of insanity. The new water does not seem capable of saving either him or poor Hughes. At midnight Hughes departed this life in a state of insensibility. Thomas Laughran is now raving mad, and in a most uncontrollable condition; the water does not seem to allay his madness. Possibly insanity may be the fate of all of us, one after the other.

'Tuesday 9th [...] Our sufferings I cannot depict. Our legs and arms are swollen from the effects of hard boards and salt water, being literally one mass of corruption.

'Wednesday 10th [...] A midnight, poor Laughran died, and shortly after another companion, William Brown, suddenly became mad, and lingered but a few hours. We buried him with Laughran, 10am.'[7]

Finally, after 18 days at sea, the crew spotted a ship and, with night falling, managed to attract its attention by flashing a light. Unable to move, they were carried onto the ship and treated 'with the greatest kindness, liberality, and care by the captain, officers and crew'.[8] Four men had died in appalling states of insanity brought on by drinking salt water, and the rest would only have survived a few days more.

It was generally accepted at this time that drinking sea water led to madness and was to be avoided at all costs, even if the scientific explanation wasn't fully understood until a few decades later. The issue is the amount of salt the kidneys can cope with. The body needs a certain amount of salt to operate, but too much and the organs will fail. The kidneys' function is to get rid of excess salt and other pollutants by expelling them through urine. However, the kidneys can only produce urine that is less salty than sea water, which means the more undiluted salt water a person drinks, the more salt builds up in their kidneys. That in turn forces the kidneys to create more urine to flush out the excess, which dehydrates the body and makes the person even more thirsty. So, unless salt water is drunk with plenty of fresh water to flush out the excess salt, it really is counter-productive to consume it.

MacDonald Critchley, a British physician who studied the issues of survival at sea, described the physical and mental effects of drinking salt water. There is:

'... immediate slaking, followed quite soon by an exacerbation of the thirst, which will require still more copious draughts. The victim then becomes silent and apathetic, with a peculiar fixed and glassy expression in the eyes. The condition of the lips, mouth, and tongue worsens, and a peculiarly offensive odour has been described in the breath. Within an hour or two, delirium sets in, quiet at first but later violent and unrestrained; consciousness is gradually lost; the color of the face changes and froth appears at the corners of the lips. Death may take place quietly: more often it is a noisy termination, and not infrequently the victim goes over the side in his delirium and is lost.'[9]

In some cases, drinking salt water could mean the difference between survival and death. So it was for the crew of the steamship *Columbian*, which caught fire 300 miles south of Newfoundland in May 1914, while carrying a cargo of highly explosive barium peroxide. Most of the crew escaped on three lifeboats, two of which were picked up by passing ships within a couple of days. The third, however, was not so lucky and drifted about for 14 days, gradually running out of food and water. By the time it was spotted by a US coastguard ship, only four of the 15 men on board were left alive, the rest having died of starvation and thirst.

Under the headline 'Axe drama in the boat of death', the *Daily Mirror* reported in lurid terms the story of Lifeboat No 3, 'in which death, hunger, thirst and stark madness stalked', and in particular of the 'plucky young Englishman',[10] 22-year-old Chief Officer Robert

91

Tiere, who tried to lead them all to safety. Tiere described how the crew were reduced to trying to eat the leather from their shoes, how most of them died one after the other, and how one of the last to die, a Russian oiler called Jakob [*sic*], went mad after drinking salt water.

'I was sleeping when Belanger [a seaman] woke me, and said that Jakob had gone crazy. He was sitting in the bow with an axe in his hand and swearing that he would go ashore for a drink. I talked to him a bit, and coaxed the axe away from him. I got him to go and lie down, and took everything I thought he could use for a weapon away from him, but I had hardly fallen asleep when he got the boat stretcher and came aft threatening to kill us all. There was nothing left but to tie him up.

'Jakob was ordinarily a very powerful man of about forty years of age, and [we] had all we could do to handle him. He was screaming at the top of his voice that we were trying to keep his money from him so that he could not go on the spree. [...] We had a pretty hard fight to get him under control, but we finally tied him down to the bottom of the boat and lashed him to the thwart. He lingered five or six hours longer, screaming at the top of his voice. Then he became exhausted, and we forced a little water between his lips, but it was no use, for about one o'clock on Saturday morning he died.'[11]

Although Tiere himself survived the ordeal, he developed gangrene and had to have both of his feet amputated.

In such circumstances, it's perhaps not surprising that some desperate sailors broke the ultimate taboo and practised cannibalism. From a strictly practical point of view, it made sense to use the body of dead crew to help the others' survival rather than throw it away. No one suffered, lives could be saved and it was, in any case, a 'custom of the sea'. The real problems started when there were no dead bodies to be consumed and lots had to be drawn to see who would sacrifice themselves for the sake of the greater good. In these instances, it didn't pay to be an ethnic minority, or foreign, or young, as the lots invariably fell on the most socially isolated members of the group.

This macabre trend became a gruesome reality when the Irish migrant ship *Francis Spraight* capsized off Canada in December 1836. The crew managed to right the ship but were left clinging to the hulk, without food and almost no water, for 15 days. Eventually the captain decided one of four teenage sailors who had survived would have to be sacrificed to feed the rest, and ordered them to draw lots. He justified selecting the youngest sailors on the grounds that the older ones had families to support. One by one, four of the crew were killed and eaten, meeting their fate with varying degrees of 'insensibility', according to John Palmer, one of the survivors, who wrote:

'It was astonishing to witness how different were the effects produced by their sufferings. The ravings of O'Brien and Beham, in their last moments, were like those of madmen, and whose greatest efforts (with fists clenched, and with gnashing teeth) appeared to be to commit violence on those of their shipmates by whom they were approached [...]. Burns, although he talked incessantly and incoherently, manifested a more harmless disposition. At one moment he would be engaged in singing some favourite sea song, and at the next would appear to imagine himself the commander of the wreck, calling on his shipmates (by wrong names) to attend to their duty. [...]'[12]

93

Once they had been consumed, the lot fell on the first mate, but, according to Palmer, the captain persuaded the crew to postpone his execution for a day by sharing out the liver and brains of the first victim, which he had preserved by soaking them in water. The survivors were discovered by a passing ship the following day, apparently waving the hands and feet of their dead shipmates to demonstrate their predicament. The first mate was thus saved, but the anticipation of being killed for meat had so terrified him that he had first gone deaf and then become delirious. Even after they made it back to England, the captain reported that the poor man 'still continued out of his senses'.[13]

Similarly, when the British collier *Euxine* sank in the South Atlantic in 1874, seven of the crew, including the captain, ended up on a lifeboat sailing towards Brazil. All their supplies were lost when the boat capsized in a storm, and after two days without food or water they suggested taking lots. Curiously, they drew lots three times and, each time, it fell to the same person: the youngest and smallest member of the crew, an Italian sailor called Franco Gioffey (or Francis Shufus, as they named him). According to the captain, Gioffey agreed to his fate: 'Shufus bore it with great calmness and showed the utmost resignation [...] He did not struggle or scream.'[14]

This version of the story was, however, contradicted by a different report, apparently from another member of the crew, who insisted: 'He then jumped overboard and attempted to drown himself, but was seized by his shipmates, dragged into the boat, his throat was mercilessly cut, and portions of his body were devoured by his former shipmates.'[15]

Despite the horrific deeds they had committed, the shipwrecked sailors were rarely criticised, let alone prosecuted, for their actions when they got home. Moreover, since their behaviour was accepted as a 'custom of the sea', the surviving sailors were generally extremely candid about what had happened – even in cases when their victims were deliberately killed to feed the rest. Even the relatives of those who were cannibalised seemed to accept the fate of their loved ones – one notable exception being the mother of Patrick O'Brien, the first teenager killed on the *Francis Spraight*, who hounded the ship's captain about her son's death and had to be bound over 'to keep the Queen's peace'. With public opinion firmly behind the survivors, the authorities seemed loath to interfere in such a well-established maritime tradition, which in any case invariably took place in the no man's land of the high seas.

Despite this, the *Euxine* marked the beginning of a change. Perhaps because of the contradictory versions of the story and the likelihood of a cover-up – the crew suggesting the victim had been more willing than he really was – the British colonial authorities arrested the crew when they arrived in Singapore and shipped two of them back to London to be tried. Apart from anything, there were many, both in the legal fraternity and among the public at large, who wanted a prosecution to clarify where the law stood on murder perpetrated 'by necessity'. They would have to wait, however, as due to legal blunders the case against the *Euxine*'s crew had to be dropped.

Another opportunity wasn't long in coming. The 52ft yacht *Mignonette* was sailing from Britain to Australia in July 1884 when she was hit by a storm and sank in the Indian Ocean. The skipper and all three crew managed to clamber into the yacht's 13ft dinghy, but they were only able to salvage two cans of turnips and no water. After nearly three weeks at sea, during which time they were forced to drink their own urine, the 17-year-old deckhand collapsed and slipped into a coma. The idea of drawing lots had already been mooted, but the boy's deteriorating condition made this unnecessary. At a signal, the mate pinned down the boy while the skipper pushed a penknife into his jugular vein and killed him. The three men then cut up his body and ate it.

The skipper later said: 'I can assure you I shall never forget the sight of my two unfortunate companions over that ghastly meal. We all was like mad wolfs who should get the most, and for men fathers of children to commit such a deed we could not have our right reason.'[16]

A few days later, the three surviving men were picked up by the German barque *Montezuma* and taken to Falmouth, where they were arrested and two of them charged with murder. The third man, who had not actually killed the boy although he had eaten him once he was dead, became the witness. The court dismissed the defendants' plea of insanity, on the grounds that their statements showed they had fully understood the enormity of what they were doing. Crucially, the court also refused to accept the lesser charge of manslaughter on the grounds of necessity (ie that the men had had to kill the boy in order to stay alive), a ruling that would have far-reaching legal consequences. The men were found guilty of murder and sentenced to death, but, partly because of public opinion, this was eventually commuted to six months' imprisonment.

By then, the Age of Sail was giving way to the Age of Steam, which in turn would give way to the Age of Diesel. Shipwrecks would, for a while, become a little less commonplace, and when they did occur there was a better chance of rescue, thanks to modern telecommunication systems. The cannibal lottery was thus not only outlawed but, perhaps more importantly, not so necessary. When a new age of mass shipwrecks did return, in the form of two world wars, most sailors were spared the mental and physical ordeals of their predecessors – although, as we shall see, they had other traumas to contend with.

CHAPTER 8

SHIPS OF FOOLS

Between 1840 and 1939, some 60 million people emigrated from Europe to start new lives in other countries around the world. Most went to North and South America, some to South Africa, and others to Australia and New Zealand. Nearly all went by ship. Initially, they sailed aboard square-riggers, subject to the whims of currents and weather, until steamships began to take over from the 1870s onwards. For those sailing to North America, the 'easiest' of these routes, the passage took about four weeks; for those sailing to New Zealand, it could take up to four months.

Conditions on board varied depending on the class in which you travelled. A typical ship of 210–240ft (about the size of the *Cutty Sark*) carried on average 340 people. A few lucky ones might be housed in first-class cabins on the poop deck, but the rest would be packed into the ship's hold with precious little scope for privacy. One observer commented that the space given to steerage passengers was less than half the minimum required by a 'common lodging house' and that the married quarters were like the 'Black Hole of Calcutta'. There were strict rules of conduct and segregation between social groups in what was described as a 'miniature republic'[1] at sea.

As you might expect of a journey by sail halfway round the world, the passage was full of perils, quite aside from the overcrowding. First, there was seasickness to cope with, which might in turn lead to dehydration. Ventilation below decks was often poor or non-existent. Drains frequently became blocked, and the stench of effluvia commonly filled the ship. Vermin ran rampant, ranging from cockroaches to bed bugs, fleas and rats – passengers were often forced to block ventilation ports to try to keep the rats at bay. Hygiene was poor, and there was the ever-present danger of disease. Lighting was by candle or oil lamps, so fires were a constant and very real hazard. Some 470 people died on one ship alone when the 1,220-ton clipper *Cospatrick* caught fire south of the Cape of Good Hope in November 1874.

The catalogue of potential woes didn't stop there. No sooner had passengers sailing down the Atlantic got used to life at sea than they hit the Doldrums. With no wind, the ships would drift across a featureless expanse of ocean, temperatures soaring above anything these Northerners were used to. Sunstroke was a common problem, as well as just sheer boredom. Within a few weeks, they would catch the Trade winds, and as they headed south, temperatures would drop dramatically, until eventually they would be dodging icebergs. Then they had to contend with terrifying storms and the inevitable leaks, from both above and below, as the caulking in the deck and hull planking was loosened by the movement of the ship. It wasn't uncommon for passengers to have to bail for their lives, as the bilges flooded and filled the hold with water.

Not surprisingly, many of the passengers on these ships, most of them setting off to sea for the first time in their lives, suffered some kind of mental trauma. One study of passengers' accounts of migrant voyages to Australia suggests that 8.5 per cent of them showed signs of mental disorder. Extrapolating that to the 3.5 million people who emigrated to Australia and New Zealand from 1821 to 1932 points to nearly 300,000 people suffering from mental illness on that route alone.

The diary of Jane Findlayson, who sailed from Greenock to Otago on the spectacular 1,300-ton clipper *Oamaru* in 1876, gives a moving insight into the deteriorating state of a fellow passenger during a sea voyage:

'16 Oct: There is a young Irish girl went wrong in her mind beside us. We did not get any sleep for 4 nights she talked on, so we complained to the doctor and she has been taken to hospital.

'20 Oct: The girl who went wrong in her mind is getting worse. She is harmless as yet. She has spoken and sung continually for nearly a week. She does not know any of us now. Her eyes are quite vacant.

'23 Oct: We passed a restless night owing to Lizzie. She is getting fractious now and tries to belt anyone who goes near her. She is quite near us here and keeps pelting at the door with her hands and feet. She is worn to a shadow and eats nothing scarcely.

'28 Oct: Lizzie is no better in her mind. She tries all she can to commit suicide and many a fright she gives us.

'7 Nov: Lizzie has broken the door of the hospital twice. She is more sensible than she was and when we ask her at the outside of the door how she is she knows our word fine and answers sensible enough. She has torn up her bed cloths with her teeth and a dresser of her own she had beside her. They have taken everything away out of the room. She now lies on boards with a strong quilt over her. We don't know how she lives with so little sleep.'[2]

Oamaru arrived in Port Chalmers on 16 December, after 88 days at sea, which was regarded as a fast passage at the time. Strangely, Lizzie's case was not mentioned in the ship's official report, which confined itself to observing that, on arrival at Port Chalmers, the *Oamaru* was placed in quarantine, with 31 cases of measles and two cases of enteric fever.

Lack of hygiene, overcrowding and poor ventilation meant that disease could and did spread rapidly on board migrant ships. Deaths were commonplace on these journeys, especially among very young children and babies born at sea. Grieving on a crowded ship floating in the middle of nowhere was a distressing experience, especially since the bodies had to be buried at sea within 24 hours, and there are many instances of parents and spouses slipping into depression, or worse, following the death of a loved one.

These include one Alfred Button, who was sailing to New Zealand on the full-rigged ship *Conflict* in 1875 when, seven weeks into the voyage, his wife and children became ill. Button became so depressed at the prospect of losing his family that he threw himself off the ship and died. The epidemic eventually killed 24 people, including his youngest child Harriet, although ironically his wife and his other two children survived. Another was Jane from Lanarkshire, who lost a child while on passage but told doctors it was leaving home that 'Crabbet her brain'.[3] Likewise, Bartholemew H, father of five, whose wife died while sailing to New Zealand, and who subsequently became so disturbed he had to be committed to Seacliff mental asylum when the ship arrived in Dunedin.

Another patient at the same hospital told doctors, 'I did not enjoy the Voyage out very much and have been rather queer since I have been here.'[4]

All sorts of people emigrated from Europe for different reasons, and once they arrived at their destination they were free to go their various ways. However, while they were on board ship, they were forced to live in close quarters for up to four months with whatever neighbours chance had brought them. This was particularly the case for single women, who were not allowed on deck as frequently or as easily as the men and had to stay in the ship's airless, claustrophobic hold for weeks on end. The all-too predictable bullying, petty rivalry and teasing – often featuring religion – proved too much for some.

One such female was a 20-year-old Catholic called Eliza, who 'became insane'[5] on the voyage from Ireland to New Zealand in 1876, and told doctors 'she was very badly treated by the other girls on board'.[6] Then there was Jane C, committed to an asylum in Auckland in 1874, who had complained the people on the ship 'spoke evil of her' and who was 'labouring under the delusion that people are trying to injure her'.[7] The doctor's notes mentioned that she had headaches and that 'her constitutional powers have ceased to act periodically as on land'[8] – ie her periods had stopped.

It wasn't just the female passengers. There was Charles McG, a Catholic farm labourer sailing from Ireland to Australia on the *Oruba* in 1893, whose mind was apparently troubled by 'his protestant fellows jeering him about religion'.[9] His wife told the doctor: 'He was not strange or essentric only he began talking about religion and as pious as the people were at home compared to the people in the ship he commenced talking about piety ten days before he got insane.'[10] He was committed to an asylum on arrival in Australia.

The big question in all of these cases was whether the patients were mentally ill before they boarded the ship, or whether their illness was brought on by their experiences at sea. It was a pertinent question at a time when counties in Britain were for the first time having to bear the expense of caring for their 'pauper lunatics',[11] thanks to various acts of Parliament. Already, local authorities were being accused of trying to palm their mentally ill constituents off on other parts of the country, and the new colonies provided another opportunity for offloading their responsibilities.

Rules passed in 1854 stipulated that immigrants to New Zealand should be 'of sound mind and body, healthy, skilful in their calling, of industrious habits, and good moral character',[12] and most other countries had similar requirements, or soon would. In practice, however, medical checks were cursory and inadequate. All but the most obviously sick got through, prompting one ship's surgeon to describe the examinations as a 'perfect farce'.[13]

A disproportionate number of mentally ill immigrants, especially women, came from Ireland. Some 25 per cent of inmates in mental asylums in New South Wales in the 1880s were Irish born, while in Nova Scotia 19 per cent of the mental patients came from Ireland, even though the Irish only accounted for 3 per cent of its population as a whole. There has been much speculation about why this should have been the case. Some have suggested the Irish potato famine of 1845–1850 may have caused an 'epigenic change'[14] in the country's population that made subsequent generations more susceptible to mental illness. Others blame prejudice against the Irish for making them more likely to be diagnosed as lunatic. Still others suggest there was a deliberate policy of 'shipping out' Ireland's mental patients to other countries, including Britain and its colonies, to avoid paying for their care.

There is ample evidence from surgeons' and passengers' journals on migrant ships to suggest that even people with a long history of mental illness were getting through the vetting system. There's the case of Jane T, for instance, who suffered from 'furious outbursts of maniacal excitement, shouting and whimpering almost in the same breath'[15] while sailing on the *Merope* in 1875, and had to be placed under 24-hour surveillance in the ship's hospital to stop her injuring herself. When she eventually calmed down, the surgeon noted her mental condition had regained 'its normal standard, which I am inclined to think was never very high'. A week later her condition was much improved, he reported, though 'a peculiar and characteristic look about her reveals a condition of intellect not altogether compatible with sanity'. It transpired she had been an inmate at Bodmin Asylum in Cornwall before emigrating, leading the surgeon to surmise: 'It is perhaps another of those cases where the Parochial authorities have tried to rid their Parish and the rate-payers of the charge of a Pauper or Lunatic by persuading her to emigrate – a practice which cannot be too strongly condemned.'[16]

It wasn't just the 'Parochial authorities' who were at it. There are plenty of examples of families shipping off troublesome relatives to save themselves the trouble and expense of caring for them. When Bridget O'K sailed to New Zealand on the *British Empire* in 1875, her screams were so 'dreadful' and 'frightening' she had to be locked up in the hospital room. When she broke down that door, she was locked up in the bathroom, where she proceeded to rip up the plumbing. Her brother confessed 'she was bad in this way before' and that he intended to put her in an asylum when they got to New Zealand. 'He evidently wants to get her off his hands,' concluded the ship's surgeon. 'The mystery is why he should have brought her here.'[17]

In some cases, the export of mentally ill relatives overseas was done out of good intentions, as there was a widespread, and not unfounded, belief that a trip at sea and a change of scene could provide a cure for mental illness. 'We did not know when we left England that she was insane,' wrote the nephew of Elizabeth, who sailed from England to New Zealand in 1894. 'The doctor thought it was obstinate hysteria, which a sea voyage might cure.'[18] Which seems fair enough, bearing in mind Thomas Cook would soon be advertising trips to New Zealand as an antidote for 'most minor or nervous ailments'.[19]

The reality for mentally distressed immigrants was of course very different, and if the challenges of the sea journey didn't get them, then the isolation and loneliness once they reached their destination would. Scottish physician William Lauder Lindsay had this warning for anyone who deluded themselves into thinking that the life of a shepherd might suit their mentally ill offspring: 'In Otago, shepherds are notoriously liable to insanity, this being ascribed by the colonists themselves to the solitary somber life among the hills.'[20]

Lindsay had his own explanation for the high rate of mental illness in the colonies. In his 1869 study of 'Insanity in British Emigrants of the Middle and Upper Ranks', he quoted one of his interviewees as saying:

'The predominance of this fearful malady (insanity) in New Zealand is, perhaps, partly ascribable to the fact, that many of those who emigrate to this country are of a romantic and unsettled disposition, and this leads to excesses of various kinds, which, I have no doubt, very frequently result in mental disorder.'[21]

That's just another way of saying that anyone who was willing to contemplate spending up to four months at sea in search of a new life must have had a certain spirit of adventure and non-conformity that might have put them on the margins of society back in the Old Country. It's a view supported by the psychiatrist Ørnulv Ødegård, who made a study of Norwegian immigrants in the USA. He found they were twice as likely to suffer from schizophrenia as their counterparts back home in Norway and concluded that this was due to a process of 'negative selection'.[22] People who were prone to schizophrenia were less likely to integrate successfully in their native countries and therefore more likely to emigrate.

Whatever the cause, the countries at the receiving end were keen to put a stop to this influx of undesirable immigrants and started to legislate against it. The Imbecile Passenger Act was thus introduced in New Zealand in 1873. This stipulated that any immigrant found to be of 'unsound mind' on arrival would be shipped back to their country of origin at the shipping company's expense. If the shipping company refused, they would have to pay a bond of £100, refundable after five years unless the person was committed to a mental hospital, in which case the money would be used to pay for their care. The rules didn't apply to those who were part of the government's assisted migration schemes as they had, in theory, been examined prior to departure – although, as we have seen, those examinations were far from thorough.

Despite these measures, in 1879 the New Zealand Minister of Immigration, James Macandrew, complained that 'cases of lunacy are alarmingly on the increase amongst immigrants to this country'.[23] That year, nine newly arrived immigrants were admitted to mental hospitals within a month of arriving in New Zealand, three of them straight from their ships.

Similar laws were passed in the USA, where the 1882 Immigration Act required the return to their homelands of 'any convict, lunatic, idiot, or any person unable to take care of himself or herself without becoming a public charge'.[24] In 1893, this was expanded to include anyone found to be mentally ill within a year of arrival – which was in turn extended to two years in 1903, three years in 1907 and five years in 1917.

The 1907 US Immigration Act widened the terms even further to include:

'All idiots, imbeciles, feebleminded persons, epileptics, insane persons, and persons who have been insane within five years previous; persons who have had two or more attacks of insanity at any time previously; paupers; persons likely to become a public charge; professional beggars; persons afflicted with tuberculosis or with a loathsome or dangerous contagious disease...'[25]

Great efforts were made to repatriate mentally ill immigrants to their country of origin, supposedly in the belief that they stood a better chance of recovery back home with their families, although in reality the financial burden of looking after them provided the real motivating factor.

There was outrage in Britain in 1858 when 'certain insane persons'[26] were shipped back from New York to Liverpool, at the shipping company's expense. The uproar prompted an American official to write to the *Evening Standard*, pointing out that two-thirds of the inmates in America's asylums were of European birth. While the authorities didn't object to looking after patients who 'became deranged' after their arrival, he wrote, they did have the right to 'prevent a systematic deportation of the deranged subjects or citizens of all other countries'.[27]

It turns out it was two-way traffic. The following year, in September 1859, the *Roscommon Messenger* reported the case of 'the lunatic woman' who was shipped back from Ireland to New York on board the steamship *Circassian*. Bridget McGilroy had apparently been brought to Ireland 'without either a letter or a friend, and destitute of the guidance of her own reason, lodged in a poorhouse'. The paper blamed the ship's 'heartless' captain who transported the woman to Ireland, presumably in return for payment, only for her to be shipped back again. 'It was pitiful to see this unfortunate woman as she proceeded to the vessel,' the paper reported, 'her wild and wretched appearance truely [*sic*] indicative of her mental infirmity.'[28]

Another poor soul shunted from one side of the Atlantic to the other was Margaret McPhillips of Newbliss in Co Monaghan, Ireland. In June 1889, she was charged with attempted suicide while travelling on the steamship *Devonia* from an unspecified port in America. According to the ship's agent, this 'respectable-looking woman' was smuggled on board the ship 'by some parties who wished to get rid of her'. He pointed out that there were no inspectors to check passengers travelling from America to Europe, as there were going the other way, because 'America was a free country'.[29] McPhillips was pronounced insane by the medical officer and sent to the Derry Asylum.

Other passengers were clearly suffering from a temporary mental disturbance brought about by the stress of their voyage, as was the case in the tragic story of madness at sea that unfolded on the Royal Mail steamer *City of Brooklyn* soon after she set sail from Ireland headed to New York in March 1873. The *Belfast Telegraph* reported what happened under the headline 'Thrilling Scene at Sea':

'When the vessel was two days out of Queenstown, a woman rushed up from the other steerage passengers, bringing her two little boys with her. She then threw them overboard in a frenzy, and then leaped overboard also. An alarm was raised, the steamer stopped, and a boat sent back. The woman, then a mile distant, was seen floating on the waves, supported by her clothing. She was reached and taken into the boat alive; one of the boys was found dead, the other was not seen again. The children were bright and pretty little fellows, and they had been the pets of many of the passengers. The mother was suffering from sickness, and became temporarily insane, in which condition she committed the strange, unmotherly act. She was apparently an intelligent and refined person, in somewhat destitute circumstances. She lived in Liverpool, but her husband was in America, and with the children was on the way to find him. When the *City Of Brooklyn* reached New York the woman was just recovering, and she was beginning to inquire for her children. It is singular that quite frequently insanity breaks out at sea.'[30]

Some passengers on the Cunard liner *Campania* had their own way of dealing with the stress of an ocean voyage. According to a report in the *Driffield Times* in March 1909, 'three Italians' who were on board the ship during a particularly rough crossing to New York took 'overdoses' of drink 'in the hope of securing relief' – whether from seasickness or fear, it's not clear. 'One after another, they became frantic, broke away from confinement below decks, and made for the rail with the object of ending their troubles in the sea.'[31] The three men were eventually seized and put in straitjackets until the end of the voyage. A passenger on the French liner *Savoie* caught in the same storm was less lucky: he apparently 'became demented very suddenly'[32] and, before he could be restrained, slit his own throat.

Another case of 'temporary insanity' took place on board the P&O ship *Victoria*, while sailing home from Australia in March 1890. Halfway between Colombo and Aden, a male passenger became deranged and jumped over the side of the ship. A boat was immediately hoisted out to rescue him, but its forward tackle broke as it was being lowered, throwing its 13 crew into the sea. 'There was then painful excitement on board,' reported the *Aberdeen Evening Express*, 'as it was generally known there were numerous sharks in the water.' Another boat was quickly launched, and the passengers on the *Victoria* watched while the second crew tried to save the others before the sharks tore them to pieces. In the end, 11 of the crew were rescued, but the other two and the man who had jumped overboard were not so lucky. The *Express* report concludes: 'The water for a considerable distance around was reddened by the blood of the three unfortunate men who were devoured.'[33]

Despite repeated instances of insanity on immigrant ships, there were no rules about how patients should be treated. A booklet entitled 'General information for the guidance of surgeons' published in 1912 contained some advice, including how to prevent suicide, but otherwise the issue was left to the discretion of the ship's surgeon. Violent patients were usually locked up in the hospital room to prevent them injuring other passengers, but more extreme measures were sometimes taken. For instance, one insane passenger on the *Forfarshire* was chained to the ship's capstan while travelling to Auckland in 1873. Meanwhile, the surgeon on board the *City of Auckland* had a straitjacket made for one passenger who became a 'raging lunatic' while sailing to New Zealand in 1877.

Even by contemporary standards, the treatment of mentally ill patients aboard these ships was shocking, as Lindsay wrote back in 1869:

'I have been told of cases of mania in wealthy and educated men, fastened in irons to confined sections of the hold during long voyages, in order to the prevention of danger alike to the patient, his fellow-passengers and crew. I have heard of maniacal patients possessing themselves of firearms or other lethal weapons, such as crowbars, and requiring, for the safety of the ship on the one hand, and of the lunatic on the other, to be hunted down with similar weapons like wild beasts. The confinement of insane patients on shipboard too frequently resembles those cases, still occasionally occurring at home, in which maniacs are kept in cages for long series of years without ablution, clothing, fresh air, or exercise – in a much worse plight, in truth, than the more fortunate, though equally ferocious, inmates of a menagerie.'[34]

The movement of people wasn't just out of Europe, of course, and the mental and physical suffering on slave ships was on a whole other level. Some 12.4 million slaves were shipped out from Africa between the 15th and 19th centuries – two thirds of them in the period from 1700 to 1808. Packed into ships' holds like cattle, they experienced many of the same problems as the migrants – such as seasickness, homesickness, lack of sanitation, heatstroke, and diseases including fever, dysentery and smallpox – only many times worse, due to the inhumane conditions they were forced to endure. Rape and physical abuse were commonplace. Those that showed signs of mental illness immediately lost their value as a commodity – after all, who would want to buy a mad slave? – and were usually beaten to death and thrown over the side. Many others committed suicide, either by starving themselves to death or by other means. It's estimated that 1.8 million slaves died on the infamous Middle Passage – the slave route from Africa to the Americas – many of them out of their minds with misery.

With the abolition of slavery in 1833, indentured labour was used to provide a cheap workforce, and thousands of workers were transported on ships from countries such as India and China to work in the British colonies. For many Hindus, the journey had the added stigma of taking them across the *kala pani* ('black water') – ie it involved crossing the Indian Ocean and therefore severing ties with the Ganges. To overcome this problem, some ships carried vats of water taken from the holy river to maintain continuity, but this wasn't always enough to assuage the workers' nerves.

Ship's surgeon James Laing confirmed that there was a particular issue with Hindus when he wrote:

'I *know* that many people die from Nostalgia. Can it be wondered at with all their caste prejudices, their leaving their native land, perhaps never to see it again, and being among people strange in habits, language and even colour? The excitement of everything keeps them up for a time, but soon dies away, and is followed by depression when they realise what they have done; and to prevent this I would urge their being employed as much as possible while on board, and encouraged in every available means of entertainment.'[35]

There are many instances of people committing or attempting to commit suicide on these voyages. These included 22-year-old

Hubraji, who lost the plot while sailing from India to Fiji in 1899, in turn singing, crying, laughing, defecating in her clothes and abusing her fellow passengers. She had to be rescued after jumping off the ship and, after a brief spell in an asylum in Suva, was returned to Calcutta.

Cultural prejudice meant that the workers' symptoms often weren't recognised or taken seriously. Rajani was so violent she had to be placed in handcuffs during a passage to Fiji in 1892. When she was taken to the asylum there, however, the doctor concluded that she suffered from a 'violence of character, or rather deportment' but that she was 'disorderly and not insane'. He classified her behaviour on the ship as 'riotous conduct' but said it was 'insufficiently weighty proof of insanity to turn the scale'.[36] Rajani was nevertheless dismissed from her indenture and sent home to India.

The voyages to the new lands weren't hellish for everyone, and there is evidence that many passengers benefited mentally not just from their new environment but also from the passage itself. In June 1853, for example, the *Inverness Courier* published a series of letters from former residents from the Isle of Skye who had emigrated to Australia and who described their various experiences. These included Alex Cameron, who had a wonderful trip out on board the *Georgiana*, making it to Port Phillip, Melbourne, in 13 weeks and clocking speeds of up to 12 knots on the way. No one died on the voyage, he reported, 'but one child' – a remarkable record judging by other reports.

Cameron had bought a fiddle in Greenock before leaving and wrote that he played it 'every night that we could stand on deck dancing'. Far from being kept below decks, the passengers on the *Georgiana* were encouraged to stay on deck as much as possible 'to keep them in active' and the ship's captain and pastor 'would force them to dance every night, and they was very few the nights they would not try it'.[37]

This gaiety aside, Cameron seemed most moved by the sights and sounds of the voyage, writing:

'If I was near you I could tell you many thing I have seen coming [*sic*], but it was the flying fish the greatest wonder that I saw; they was so numerous about the ship, they would fly 200 or 300 yards before they would hold; they are about the size of a big herring, the smallest of them; 3 or 4 of them jump on board, although the ship was very high. I saw shirks [sharks?] near the Cape…'[38]

Clearly a man in good mental and physical health, Cameron got a job as a shepherd, looking after 3,000 sheep, and seemed not to be troubled by the solitary nature of his work. 'I am weel [well?] in health since you saw me, very busy with my flook [flock?]. I must rise as soon as the sun, and go home at sunset,' he wrote. 'I have nothing but following them; and when they reach the boundarys, they will turn there – they will not leave the station to go to any place. […] We have not but small houses, but we have plenty to eat and drink. […] I think this is the best place in the world – so bonny.'[39]

Donald Macdonald also sailed on the *Georgiana* and reported that, before leaving Greenock, the ship's crew took 'French leave' – ie without the captain's permission – and in the ensuing fracas the captain shot the cook 'through the head'. Despite this inauspicious start, though, he was also favourably impressed by life at sea and said that he and his family were 'well-used, and treated most kindly, by the captain, officers, and crew of the ship; indeed, in one word, we were dealt with far beyond our expectations'. Soon after arriving in

Australia, Macdonald's wife Isabella gave birth to a baby girl, who died after nine days. Yet despite even this setback, he wrote that 'this is the country for the poor working man'[40] and begged his brother and sister to follow him.

Others clearly suffered trauma on the voyage but were able to carry on with their lives regardless. John Mackinnon from Roag, for instance, made the passage to Melbourne in 68 days, 'which was the quickest ever was known'. The ship was, however, ravaged by illness, and 53 children, two women in childbirth and one sailor died on this one trip. 'As for myself I did not feel as much as a sore head since I left home,' Mackinnon wrote. 'But, oh, Sandy! throwing out my two boys into the deep sea; it will never go out of my heart. The youngest died with the measles at crossing the line [the Equator]; and the other 6 days after with a bowel complaint.'[41]

Despite his personal tragedy, Mackinnon raved about Melbourne, 'the richest town of its size in all the world', and the high standard of living compared with Skye – although he qualified his enthusiasm with the comment, 'I would not advise a man with a weak family to come – but it is all for fear of the passage'.[42]

Donald MacCaskill's ship took 15½ weeks, 'from anchor to anchor', to sail from Liverpool to Port Phillip, Melbourne, and 'had most of the time very coarse weather'.[43] During the voyage, 27 children and eight sailors were killed by measles and 'the bowel complaint', and eight babies were born. Yet, despite the trials of the passage, MacCaskill revelled in his new-found affluence, writing:

'Dear sister, you can easily understand by this account that I have left the starvation behind. I can give as much to my dogs now, as I was getting to my family at home [...] This is a very wholesome country. It is not too warm, nor too cold either. […] as far as I know, there is no other place under the stars like this place, for poor people to live in.'[44]

The increasing use of steam engines by the end of the 19th century, followed eventually by diesel engines, meant that the passages to the new lands took less time and became more comfortable. The number of deaths on immigrant ships declined, as did the cases of lunacy. By the 1930s, the exodus from Europe had petered out, and the great ocean voyages under sail that those early immigrants undertook – along with the associated toll on their physical and mental health – became a thing of the past. New waves of migration would follow, often by sea, but the direction this time would be turned the other way, towards Europe.

CHAPTER 9

THE LORETTES OF NEW YORK

There was quite a crowd on board the *Evening Star* as she sailed out of New York harbour on 29 September 1866, headed for New Orleans. The steamer had a reputation for being one of the most luxurious passenger ships in America and, despite charging up to 50 per cent more than her rivals, was usually booked up months in advance. Along with half-a-million dollars of merchandise, the 2,000-ton vessel carried 278 passengers and crew, including leading Louisiana socialites such as the architect James Gallier, the Confederate general Henry William Palfrey, and Samuel Hardinge, the husband of famed Confederate spy Belle Boyd. To add some extra colour, there was an American circus troupe and an entire 60-piece French opera company, newly arrived from Europe.

However, what attracted everyone's attention was a group of 'frail women' (aka prostitutes) headed south for the winter, like a flock of brightly clad flamingos seeking warmer climes. The women had been hand-picked by a cabal of New Orleans madams to freshen their 'stock' for their 'mansions of pollution'.[1] There were between 45 and 95 of these 'unscrupulous lorettes'[2] on board (numbers vary in different accounts), many of them sailing under assumed names. Their fellow passengers were unimpressed, and several apparently cancelled their voyages when they discovered who would be sitting next to them in the ship's opulent dining saloon.

'The lorettes of New York are the most abandoned of abandoned women,' reported one newspaper, 'their profligacy and recklessness surprise even those who are cognisant of the extravagancies of *ceux dames* abroad.'[3]

After three days at sea, the *Evening Star* ran into a hurricane off the coast of Georgia, halfway to its intended stopover at Havana. As the storm raged, the ship's wheelhouse and paddle boxes were swept away by the waves, and the rudder was lifted off its mountings. As water poured into the ship, the passengers and crew formed lines – regardless of class or status – and bailed for their lives using buckets and any other containers they could find. The most dedicated workers turned out to be the New York lorettes. One surviving member of the crew, who worked side by side with 'those women', described how they 'worked bravely, nobly', even as the ship lurched over and seemed about to sink. 'They had more pluck than many of the men had,'[4] he told the *New York Tribune*.

Eventually, the captain announced it was no good; the ship was lost and everyone would have to save themselves as best they could. That's when the madness began. One survivor described the scene:

'The women, shrieking frightfully, rushed on deck in the most frantic manner, tearing their hair and in many ways acting more like lunatics than beings endowed with reason. Reason at this moment had certainly abdicated its throne, and nothing but the wildest stage of madness had the poor things come to. The men were equally as violent, though for such a scene it may have been

117

worse. The women commenced to divest themselves of their clothing, and madly and wildly plunged into the foaming surf, never to rise to its surface more.'[5]

From the comfort of an office desk, a New York newspaper reporter elaborated:

'It needs no very vivid imagination to perceive the result of bringing a swarm of these selfish, abandoned, wretched women face to face with death. The fierce struggling for the boats; the oaths, and screams, and blasphemy, and wild jargon of well-nigh forgotten prayers; the tearing of hair and the frantic gestures; the vain frenzied appeals to a stolidly selfish crew; the insane leaps into the boiling sea, the last terrible cries rising above the howl of the storm – all these things and more must present themselves to any one who speculates upon the scene on that sinking ship.'[6]

In common with most ships of that era, the *Evening Star* carried insufficient lifeboats for the number of people on board. Most of the passengers – especially the members of the French opera company, most of whom didn't speak English – didn't make it into a lifeboat and were soon drowned. Moreover, only four of the six lifeboats on board were successfully launched, and they were repeatedly capsized in the churning sea, throwing off survivors attempting to cling on to them. In the days that followed, two lifeboats were picked up by passing ships, while the other two faced longer journeys as they sailed 180 miles to shore. With no fresh water, many of those on the lifeboats – particularly the passengers – drank salt water and became delirious and threw themselves over the side. Most of the crew survived by drinking their own urine.

The cruellest twist, however, took place on the lifeboat commanded by second mate William Goldie. After a gruelling five days at sea, seven of the nine of the passengers on board had died – mostly having been driven insane by thirst and hunger – by the time the boat made landfall on the coast of Florida. The only passengers to survive the ordeal were 16-year-old Rosa Howard (aka Rosa Burns) and 20-year-old Annie Norton, both of whom were probably prostitutes. But the sea hadn't finished with them yet. As the surf swept the boat onto the beach, it capsized and both girls were drowned. Norton's body was found by fishermen later that evening, but Howard was eaten by sharks and, according to one report, only her 'perfectly formed' foot was found. Goldie managed to clamber to shore and walked through 12 miles of swamp to find help.

Of the 278 passengers and crew who set off from New York on board the *Evening Star*, only 24 survived – the vast majority of them crew. It was one of the worst disasters at sea and was widely discussed, until the sinking of the *Titanic* threw it into insignificance. As for the New York lorettes, despite the noble attempts made by some of them to save the ship, they were not only scorned but were blamed for the accident, with many saying the ship was bound to sink as it was 'loaded down with iniquity'.[7] An official inquiry blamed the captain for not avoiding the storm and said the ship was inadequately manned. The presence of a carpenter to repair the damage caused by the storm, the report said, might have averted disaster.

CHAPTER 10

MURDER, MAYHEM AND MADNESS

It's easy to romanticise the Age of Sail, when elegant ships cantered across the oceans powered by nothing but huge clouds of canvas. When ships were handcrafted from organic materials such as wood, hemp and cotton. When anchors were raised and sails hoisted by gangs of men singing uplifting shanties in unison. When ships visited exotic places mostly still untouched by the march of western civilisation.

However, as we've seen in the preceding chapters, this was also a brutal and violent time and life at sea could be tough and unforgiving. The human cost of these long voyages was astonishingly high. You only have to look at a map of 19th-century shipwrecks around the British Isles to realise the level of destruction being meted out on ships and sailors during the period. According to the British Register of Births, Deaths and Marriages, in the year 1884–1885, some 1,490 passengers on British ships lost their lives. If you include the crew, that figure rises to 2,769, and if you include fishing boats, it goes

ABOVE: The legendary *Flying Dutchman*, condemned to sail around the world forever, was spotted by King George V. In reality, it was probably a Fata Morgana, an optical illusion in which an object below the horizon is refracted above it. © *Getty Images*

BELOW: The author's father was one of 100 men rescued when HMS *Galatea* sank off Alexandria in 1941. He had nightmares about it for the rest of his life. © *Family of Clifford Robert Calver*

HMS *Beagle*'s first captain, Pringle Stokes, committed suicide after spending two years surveying Tierra del Fuego. He was replaced by Robert FitzRoy, who took Charles Darwin with him on his second voyage. *© Dea Picture Library, Getty Images*

As Captain Bligh and 18 men were cast adrift in the middle of the Pacific, chief mutineer Fletcher Christian cried out, 'I am in hell, I am in hell.' History is divided about Christian's mental state, though experts now think he may have been suffering from a 'brief psychotic disorder'. *© Media/Print Collection, Getty Images*

The crew of HMS *Investigator* suffered from scurvy after being trapped in Arctic ice for three years from 1850. Two of the men went raving mad and had to be tied up after they threatened to kill the captain and set fire to the ship. © *Historical Picture Archive, Getty Images*

Christopher Columbus was described as 'mad' in his own lifetime and has been retrospectively diagnosed as bipolar and suffering from a Messiah complex. © *Getty Images*

HMS *Beagle*'s second captain and the founder of the Met Office, Robert FitzRoy, was a tormented soul who ended up slitting his own throat with a razor. © *Getty Images*

ABOVE: Block F at Haslar Royal Hospital in Gosport was converted into a mental asylum in 1818 after the Royal Navy's previous facilities were found to be 'radically defective'. © Wellcome Library, London

LEFT: The inhumane treatment of American sailor James Norris, manacled in Bethlem Hospital for ten years, caused a national outcry and led to changes in the law. © Wellcome Library, London

Only 15 of the 146 people on the raft of the *Medusa* survived after members of France's aristocracy left sailors and soldiers to fend for themselves in 1816. Most were killed in an orgy of violence or driven mad from exposure and drinking contaminated wine. *© Fine Art Images, Heritage Images, Getty Images*

Benjamin Clough single-handedly recaptured the whaleship *Sharon* after her abusive captain was murdered by its Pacific Island crew in 1842. The only surviving native was released after a group of Sydney philanthropists took up his cause.

The crew of the whaleship *Essex* drew lots to see who would be eaten next, after the ship sank in the Pacific in 1820. First Mate Owen Chase was haunted by their deeds for the rest of his life. *Courtesy of the Nantucket Historical Association*

HMS *Indomitable* taking part in the Battle of Jutland in May 1914. Nearly 7,000 British seamen died in the only major naval engagement of World War I. The Royal Navy claimed there was little evidence of 'nervous disorder', though anecdotal evidence suggests otherwise.
© *Robert Hunt Library, Windmill books, Getty images*

Brothers Robert (standing) and Andrew Buchanan both served at Jutland on different ships. Andrew was discharged a year later suffering from 'neurasthenia', and later killed himself. © *Dot Tose*

Best known for coining the word 'psychedelic', Humphry Osmond trained as a psychiatrist while serving in the Royal Navy and wrote about mentally ill sailors he treated in Malta during World War II.
© *Ed Maker, The Denver Post, Getty Images*

Although revered as the father of singlehanded sailing, Joshua Slocum had a troubled life, being convicted of cruelty to his crew and in later life sent to prison for indecent exposure. *Courtesy of the New Bedford Whaling Museum*

A flawed genius, Donald Crowhurst invested everything in the 1968 Golden Globe Race. When his boat started falling apart, he pretended to be sailing around the world while actually pottering around the Atlantic. *© Rolls Press, Popperfoto, Getty Images*

Crowhurst's boat *Teignmouth Electron* was picked up in the Atlantic with two logs on board: a real one and a fake one. There was no sign of the boat's skipper, who is presumed to have jumped overboard after suffering a mental breakdown. *© Paul Popper, Popperfoto, Getty Images*

ABOVE: Bernard Moitessier, another competitor in the 1968 Golden Globe Race, decided to keep going after he rounded Cape Horn, and sailed for another three months to reach Tahiti to 'save his soul'. Many, including his wife, thought he had gone mad, though his book about the voyage earned him a cult following.

BELOW: The sea can provide therapy for many war veterans suffering from post-traumatic stress disorder (PTSD). Turn to Starboard, a charity set up by former RAF medic Shaun Pascoe, has taken hundreds of ex-service personnel sailing on a 91ft schooner donated by the Prince's Trust.

up to 4,632. In another year, 1881–1882, an astonishing 838 British sailing ships were lost at sea, equating to a total of 204,239 tons of shipping.

Indeed, so commonplace were shipwrecks and deaths at sea, that they deserved only passing mention in the newspapers of the day, often under a generic heading of 'Shipwrecks' relegated to the back pages. This extract from the *Staffordshire Advertiser* of 19 January 1895, following a particularly violent gale, gives the general idea:

'Intelligence reached Grimsby on Sunday morning to the effect that two vessels – one a brig and the other an Italian barque – had foundered in the Humber during the morning. A Hull steam trawler noticed the masts of the barque above water, and that there were 10 or 12 men clinging to the spars. They shouted for help, and an attempt was made to launch a boat, but it was swamped alongside. The trawler then went close to the sunken vessel, but a heavy sea unfortunately pitched her on to the mast, which snapped off, and the entire crew were drowned, the men being too benumbed by exposure to save themselves. The tug Gipsy arrived later in the morning and reported observing the masts of a vessel above water a quarter of a mile above the Middle Lightship, this being believed to be the brig which the lifeboat went out to find in the first instance. The crew of this vessel have also been drowned. [...] The German schooner Kate (Captain Williams) arrived at Granton on Saturday from Oldenburg with a cargo of empty bottles after a terrible passage, which lasted for 32 days. Several high seas swept over the vessel, carrying away all movable articles, smashing the leeboard, and damaging the bulwarks from stem to stern. One tremendous wave carried a part of the railing about 20ft up the rigging, where it still remains fast. One of the sailors became insane from the effect of the terrible weather. The Italian barque Theresina, from Liverpool to Trieste, with coal and coke, drifted on the rocks near Quinton Castle and was totally wrecked...'[1]

And so it goes on, cataloguing the fates of 12 ships and at least 50 crew lost in a single storm in just a little over half a column of closely packed text – and that's just in Britain.

Despite this rather nonchalant acceptance of how commonplace it had become, shipwreck was always traumatic for the individuals involved. Take the crew of the Norwegian barque *Dagny*, for instance, which was wrecked off the east coast of America in September 1893. The ship's master Captain Eskeland described the scene:

'In all my experiences of the sea I never saw such a sea nor such a storm. From the terrific strain we were soon aleak, and the order was given, "All hands to the pumps." We worked hard all night, the seas making a clean breach over us. As the night waned the storm increased in fury and daylight found the *Dagny* a complete wreck. The mainmast had gone by the board, together with the fore and mizzen topmasts. The rudder had been wrenched from its hangings, the bow port was stove in and stern-post gone. The vessel was now at the mercy of the elements and all hands were huddled together in the after-part of the vessel, kept afloat by the nature of the cargo [pine logs]. All the men had been injured, most of them having deep cuts on their bodies, which being irritated by the salt water caused terrible swellings...'[2]

By the time the ship was spotted by a passing ship, the *Dagny* was a semi-submerged wreck, its crew clinging on to the aft house for dear life. So physically and mentally battered were the men that, when the crew from the other ship tried to save them, they refused to budge and had to be dragged off by force. 'Their sufferings had unhinged their minds,' as the *Shields Daily Gazette* put it. A sailor called Olsen was particularly badly injured, and had a deep cut above the right eye. 'He is insane from the effects of the wound,'[3] reported the paper.

And what do we make of the crew of the Norwegian steamer *Ausgarius* who, within sight of land, were reduced to a state of madness and death in the space of just a few hours? The ship was steaming out of the Pentland Firth at full speed when it hit rocks and sank immediately, according to a report in the *Lincolnshire Echo* of 5 September 1895. Six crew made it safely to land on one boat, but the seven crew in the other boat lost their oars and drifted about the firth helplessly. One man managed to swim to shore and raise the alarm, and the boat was eventually towed to land. By then, however, the boat's crew seem to have gone though their own version of shipwreck hell. 'During the eight hours they spent in the boat,' the paper reported, 'two of the crew became insane and died, one of the bodies being thrown overboard, as the boat was near sinking, being full of water.'[4]

For some shipwrecked sailors, arriving on land was just the beginning of their troubles, and the repurcussions were felt by more than just the crew themselves. For instance, the normally quiet South Devon countryside was turned into a battlefield after the Italian brig *Maria Theresa* was shipwrecked on Prawle Point on 5 December 1872, and one of the ship's crew, 'maddened, it is supposed, by his loss', went on a rampage, stabbing his crewmates and local villagers. He seems to have taken a particular dislike to a local woman, who was just going about her own everyday business, striking her 13 times. A coastguard officer eventually arrived on the scene with a cutlass and with 'one blow from the sword cut him down,' according to the *Shields Daily Gazette*, 'and he was picked up dead'.[5]

Neither was there any peace for the survivors of the *Neptune*, after their ship was wrecked on the coast of Natal, South Africa, in 1891. In the ensuing chaos, only five made it to shore, while the remaining 53 drowned. The survivors spent several days near the scene of the disaster burying the bodies of the dead, before they started to walk the 170 miles to Natal. On the way, they were captured by 'a band of Zulus' who, according to the *Western Gazette*, tied them to trees and beat them with 'clubs made of rhinoceros hide'. By the time a party of Boer hunters chased the Zulus away, three of the men had died, and the other two were too badly injured to travel any further than Cape Town. One was said to be 'insane from the torture inflicted upon him, and is unable to say anything'.[6]

And it wasn't just shipwrecks that pushed sailors over the edge. Contemporary newspapers are full of accounts of 'mad sailors' climbing up the rigging and having to be shot down, or running senselessly up and down the ship's deck, or jumping into the sea – often having attacked or even killed their crewmates beforehand. The afflicted sailors' weapons include guns, knives, axes, belaying pins and chisels. In fact, so prevalent was the problem that the image of the 'mad sailor' became almost a cliché and was used as an avatar by society gents.

Another report, published in the *Falkirk Herald* of 18 August 1853, related the case of a crew member on the steamer *Firefly*, a 'smart, active, well-dressed fellow', who jumped onto the paddlebox as the ship came into the Clyde and shouted, 'Once, twice, thrice, here goes the bold sailor!' before jumping into the sea. 'Strange to say,' the paper reported, 'he maintained a perpendicular position' in the water, until a boat reached him and he put up a 'deadly struggle'[7] before being dragged back on board.

Or take the American ship *Cultivator*, aboard which there was a spate of madness on a trip from San Francisco to Queenstown in Ireland in 1874. Within hours of leaving California, the chief mate caught the boatswain stealing some clothes and shot him, injuring him so badly that he later died. On the same voyage, the *Morpeth Herald* reported, 'the cook [...] became mad and jumped overboard, and another of the crew is insane and has to be kept under restraint'.[8]

A decade later, the case of a 'mad' Malay sailor shot on board the British ship *Lady Douglas* because of his threatening demeanour became something of a cause célèbre during the winter of 1887–1888. On the way back from Western Australia, the seaman called Hassin hid in the coal in the ship's forepeak and threatened to attack the rest of the crew with a knife if anyone approached him. He was eventually put in irons but managed to escape and went back to the forepeak armed with more weapons and a box of matches. Although he hadn't actually attacked anyone, his frightening expressions and threats of 'Suppose I kill one, I die' convinced the rest of the crew he was a deadly menace. By mutual agreement, they shot him in cold blood and threw his body over the side.

When the ship returned England, four men, including the captain, were arrested and tried for murder. Their excuse was that they had acted in self-defence and that Hassin was mad, though when cross-examined the worst they could say was that he 'looked something like a madman' and was 'inhuman in his behaviour'[9] because he never looked anybody in the eye. The jury found against the four men, and they were duly sentenced to death. In the weeks that followed, some 6,200 people signed three petitions asking for 'royal clemency' on the grounds that the men had feared for their lives and the safety of the ship. Their sentences were eventually commuted to life imprisonment.

The captains of these ships were under particular pressure. Not only did they have to ensure that their ships arrived at their destinations safely and on time, but they also had to maintain discipline among a crew made up of disparate characters, some of them escaping trouble back home. Running a 'tight ship' was a job that demanded a special combination of courage, seamanship and human managerial skills that not all men possessed. With more and more ships going on longer and longer voyages, it's not surprising that some of the skippers found their responsibilities too much to bear. There are all-too-frequent stories of captains abandoning their ships, locking themselves up in their cabins, setting fire to their ships, shooting at the crew and, in many instances, shooting themselves.

Take Captain Wilkinson, who was taken to Guernsey Lunatic Asylum after he abandoned his ship *Why Not* on the French coast in September 1895, leaving the passengers to find their own way home. Or Captain Illum from the Danish schooner *Lyo*, who smashed the ship's cabin lamp and skylights in June 1894, and, when the mate tried to get him to bed, climbed up the rigging and refused to come down for three hours. Another time he randomly raised the ship's anchor in the middle of the night while the crew was asleep, and only swift action by the mate stopped the ship being wrecked. Illum was subsequently taken to an asylum in Leith.

And pity Duncan McGregor, the 56-year-old captain driven 'mad through worry',[10] according to a report in the *Lancashire Evening Post* in June 1909. McGregor, the master of the Newcastle steamer *Loughbrow*, had apparently had trouble shipping cargo in Gibraltar and left port abruptly without getting proper clearance from the authorities. The stress of the voyage seems to have got the better of him and, 70 miles south-west of Ushant, he locked himself up in his cabin and started shooting through the door. He was eventually coaxed out by the steward and given a cup of coffee, only to become 'excited' again and start threatening the chief officer with a steel spike. As he rushed down from the bridge, the ship lurched and he was thrown overboard. He was picked up by one of the ship's boats soon after, but never recovered consciousness. The inquest into his death concluded that he had fallen overboard 'whilst temporarily insane' and that 'the derangement [had] been caused by worry'.[11]

Many of the contemporary reports only hint at the drama that must have come before the ships' masters lost the plot. We cannot know what nightmares the captain of the Italian barque *Innocenza Rosa* went through before the coastguard boarded her off Dungeness in October 1893. All the *Sheffield Evening Telegraph* could say was:

'The vessel was water-logged, having been seriously damaged during the recent storms. The mate is reported to have been washed overboard and drowned. [...] The seaman in charge reported that for some days past the captain had been confined to his cabin having lost his reason. Another of the crew had been injured the day previous.'[12]

A common theme among these incidents is paranoia: captains thinking, or imagining, their crews are conspiring to kill them. It's an understandable scenario on a ship where the skipper usually kept himself resolutely apart from the crew and other officers. There were certainly enough real-life examples of mutiny to justify some caution on the captain's part, and it's a thin line between self-preservation and paranoia, as can be seen in the case of the (unnamed) captain of the British ship the *Regent*, sailing from Calcutta to New York. Suspecting that his crew were trying to kill him, he took the drastic action of going to his cabin and pumping four bullets into his head, 'preferring death that way to being murdered,'[13] as he later told the authorities. Amazingly, he survived this suicide attempt and was put ashore at St Helena, where he was pronounced insane. A surgeon extracted the two remaining bullets from his head (the other two presumably having gone right through) and he was put on a ship back to London.

Similarly, on a routine passage carrying sugar from Mauritius to Adelaide in May 1873, the captain of the Australian barque *Hannah Nicholson* became convinced his crew 'had a design on his life'. When the first mate told him this wasn't the case, he retired to his cabin complaining of 'a pain in his head', returning soon after with a revolver and shooting at several of the crew, narrowly missing the helmsman, before going back to his cabin and locking himself in. He stayed there for nearly a week, shooting at anyone who came near, until the ship pulled in at Portland Bay and the police were called on board. They broke the captain's door open and found him 'in a sitting posture, dead but not cold',[14] with a note in his pocket blaming the crew for his murder.

Several weeks later, a message in a bottle was found on a beach at Kingston, just south of Adelaide, with a note saying: 'Barque *Hannah Nicholson* – This is to let you know the crew and second mate intentions is to shoot me and throw me overboard; they shot the mate and a boy yesterday; they have been trying to catch me this three days. I have been battered in my cabin. Wm Leask'. On the other side of the paper was written: 'Barque Hannah Nicholson. This is to let you know that the crew has shot me and [...]'.[15]

Not all ship's captains were the swashbuckling types depicted in the public imagination, a fact confirmed by the story of the brig *Earl Vane*, which had to turn from home after the master was caught trying to scuttle his own ship. According to a report in the *London Evening Standard* in August 1844, the (unnamed) captain was 'a timid, nervous man' and, not being a very competent navigator, devolved some of his duties to the mate. In return, the mate 'treated the master with great harshness, and applied him horrible names'.[16] While sailing from Sunderland to Archangel, the ship was delayed by contrary winds. One of the crew was sick, another had a scalded foot and, to make matters worse, they started running out of food. The mate suggested turning back, but the captain refused, saying he'd rather sink the ship than go back. Soon after, the *Earl Vane* started taking on water and two holes were found in the hold; the captain eventually confessed he had bored them. The ship headed back to Sunderland, where the captain was arrested and tried, during which case his defence was insanity. He told the court he 'was much agitated by the very harsh treatment of the mate'[17] and for several days ate very little.

Despite their reputation for having 'a girl in every port', heartbreak was another common cause of breakdown among captains and crew alike, who often fell victim to another cliché: 'out of sight, out of mind'. One such was a 24-year-old seaman called Harris who in January 1841 climbed over the railings of the Tower of London, took his clothes off and threw himself into the muddy moat – 'evincing every symptom of insanity', according to the *Morning Post*. When he was eventually saved and dressed, he told his rescuers he had been 'intimate' with a young woman he was planning to marry when he came back from a trip to the West Indies, but when he returned he found she had married someone else. 'This preyed upon his mind very much,' the paper reported, 'and he resorted to drinking to drown reflection, which, combined with the loss of his sweetheart, has, it is supposed, driven him into a state of frenzy.'[18]

An excess of religious zeal is another recurrent theme among mad sailors. There's the story of a captain who attacked and killed two of his crew while suffering from 'acute religious mania' while sailing off Ascension, a remote island in the southern Atlantic. Then there's the 'insane sailor' who stormed the pulpit of Waltham Street Chapel in Hull in March 1821. When he pulled a parcel out of his jacket, someone shouted, 'He has got a pistol,' and, according to the *Sheffield Independent*, 'this operated like an electrical shock on the audience, some fell down for security, and others turned ghastly pale'.[19] The offending item turned out to be a flag, which the man wanted to drape from the pulpit while he gave a sermon. He was promptly seized and escorted out of the chapel.

The strangest story of religious mania, however, took place on the Dutch lugger *Nordsee* in the North Sea in September 1915. Having spotted the fishing boat drifting about 130 miles off Scarborough, a Norwegian steamer sent a small boat to investigate. It found the *Nordsee* had been smashed up and the whole crew, including the captain, were behaving very strangely indeed. The crew and their boat were taken to Grimsby, where the authorities discovered, by checking the ship's papers, that three of the crew were missing. The surviving men were cross-examined and admitted they had killed the three men and thrown their bodies overboard.

'The feud was the outcome of a religious mania which commenced with one man and then developed amongst the crew,' reported the *Nottingham Evening Post*. The paper went on to explain that, perhaps not surprisingly, drink also had a part to play. 'The crew of the lugger [...] had become frenzied with drink, and proceeded to dismantle the ship. The rails were torn away and thrown overboard, hatchways wrenched away, and the decks were practically cleared. The captain was unable to navigate the vessel, which drifted about until observed by the Norwegian steamer.'[20]

Even when safely ashore, sailors often behaved in antisocial ways, which at best put them on the margins of society and at worst landed them in prison accused of murder. Post-traumatic stress disorder might not have been recognised as such during the 19th and early 20th centuries, but its evidence was around for all to see and contemporary newspapers are full of accounts of horrible acts committed by 'mad' and 'insane' sailors.

Among the many examples was the Spanish sailor, 'believed to be insane',[21] who stabbed three people on the streets of Liverpool in January 1877 before plunging the knife into his own stomach and dying soon afterwards. There was also the seaman Archibald McConnochie, who escaped from the Royal Naval Hospital in Plymouth, where he was 'under treatment for insanity',[22] and laid his head on the track in front of an oncoming train. 'The head [was] completely cut in two,' reported the *Grantham Journal* of 20 March 1875, 'and death [was] instantaneous.'[23] And who knows what was going through the mind of Dominion Line employee John Sergeant when he stood at Sandhills railway station in Liverpool in September 1890 and pulled out one of his eyes with his own hands, and then attempted to pull out the other one too?

'He appeared to be quite mad and suffering from delirium tremens [alcoholic withdrawal symptoms, also known as "the shakes"],' reported the *Nottingham Evening Post*, 'and it required several men to hold him.'[24]

Poor Charles Hodges suffered from his experiences at sea long after he disembarked from the *Lowther Castle* – a 1,500-ton East Indiaman that embodied the very essence of the Age of Sail. Hodges was taken to a Thames police station in October 1830 displaying symptoms of madness. He was accompanied by his sister, 'a decent girl', according to a contemporary report, who told police that she and her three brothers were orphans left destitute when their parents died. Her brothers had gone to sea, and she had had to go into service. 'Her present brother's aberration of mind was attributed to a flogging he had received on board the *Lowther Castle*,' reported *Bell's Life*, 'after which he had never been right in his mind.' Hodges was sent to a lunatic asylum, while his sister 'threaten[ed] ulterior proceedings against his Captain for cruelty on board the Lowther Castle'.[25]

In fact, Hodges was not the first seaman to be flogged on the *Lowther Castle*. The previous year, Captain Bathie had quelled a mutiny attempt by flogging the main culprit and other ringleaders. His decisive action was quoted as an example of correct behaviour in a contemporary book on naval discipline and supported by the following statement in 1828 by the Lord Chief Justice, Lord Tenterden:

'It was, undoubtedly, the duty of a commander of a ship, whenever he saw the least tendency to mutiny, instantly to take means to repress it; for that purpose he was justified in inflicting whatever punishment might be necessary upon the individual whose conduct was likely to create danger; and, unless he inflicted wanton and unnecessary punishment upon any of them, he was not amenable to the law.'[26]

With such a clear mandate for strict discipline and the whole modus operandi of the empire potentially at stake, it's doubtful whether the mental fall-out of individual sailors was a very high priority for the British courts. Hodges' case, if it were ever taken to court by his sister, would have cut little ice.

By the beginning of the 20th century, there was greater awareness of mental illness and its causes – although its treatment was still rather haphazard – and it could be used as mitigation in criminal cases. For instance, when 27-year-old German seaman Koppe was charged with fare dodging while travelling on the Great Western Railway from Falmouth to London, his experiences in a recent shipwreck were cited in his defence – Kopee was one of the crew on the four-masted barque *Queen Margaret* wrecked off the Lizard in May 1913. Although he had a ticket for part of his journey, as far as Exeter, he refused to pay the rest and told the ticket collector he already had a ticket to New Zealand. A doctor's report concluded that Koppe was insane and that 'this was probably the lamentable result of his terrible experiences when wrecked'.[27] He was taken to an 'infirmary' for treatment.

Even Queen Victoria had a close brush with her very own mad sailor: David Bowen, a seaman from Cardiff, who was found wandering around Windsor Castle in November 1900. When asked what he was doing, he said he had come to see his mother, the Queen. He was apparently upset she hadn't visited him when she passed by his workhouse the previous Sunday. He was duly arrested and committed to a mental asylum rather than prison.

The plight of poor and destitute sailors, often suffering from mental health issues, was clearly a major problem throughout the 18th century and led to the formation of several societies to help them. The first was the Marine Society, formed in 1756, whose main purpose was to help with the recruitment of sailors for the navy, particularly those from poorer backgrounds. The Sailors' Society was accordingly formed in 1818 to 'promote the moral and religious improvement of the sailors of the day',[28] and three years later the Seamen's Hospital Society was created specifically to care for injured and destitute seamen – including those suffering from mental health problems. That was followed by the Mission to Seamen in 1856 and the Fishermen's Mission in 1881, both concerned with the pastoral care and welfare of seamen, fishermen and their families.

CHAPTER 11

SHELTER FROM THE STORM

In the summer of 1835, the Rev John Ashley was out walking on the coast of Somerset, looking out over the Bristol Channel, when his small son asked him a question that would change his and many other people's lives. How, the boy asked, pointing to the nearby islands of Flat Holm and Steep Holm, do the people who live there go to church? Ashley looked into it and discovered that there was no church or chapel on the islands, and so volunteered to visit them himself. While he was there, he started thinking about the fleet of 400 fishing vessels that regularly anchored off the Welsh coast, and discovered that they had no form of pastoral care either. Far from it. While the boats waited for a fair wind, the crews were likely to be stuck in their cabins, bored and lonely.

With true evangelical zeal, Ashley gave up his job as parish vicar and started visiting the fishermen as they lay at anchor in the Bristol Channel. After a few years, he bought his own ship, the cutter *Eirene*, which he fitted with a chapel and sailed with a small crew – all paid for with money inherited, ironically enough, from the West Indian slave trade. To start with, he was often rebutted and turned away from the ships he approached, but eventually, as sailors realised he was there to offer friendship first and religion second, they warmed to him and allowed him on board – anything to break the monotony of their long days at anchor.

In his history *Flying Angel: The Story of the Missions to Seamen*, LAG Strong says it wasn't uncommon for seamen to be reduced to tears during Ashley's sermons, and 'emotional breakdowns' were apparently regularly reported in the journals of the early mission workers. 'The simple fact was that, behind their grim exterior, their beards, their tobacco chewing, and the menacing knife at their belts,' Strong wrote, 'these Victorian seamen were lonely.'[1]

Over the next 15 years, Ashley visited 5,000 ships and sold 5,000 Bibles and prayer books to fishermen in the Bristol Channel. His efforts led to the formation of the Bristol Channel Mission in 1837, which in turn led to the creation of the Mission to Seamen in 1856. Soon, the operation expanded overseas, as it became clear that sailors travelling far from home were even more prone to loneliness and depression than those working in British waters. The organisation's logo was a picture of a flying angel, designed by the wife of one of its founders, which would soon be flown in dozens of missions around the world.

Part of the missions' job in the early days was to protect sailors from predatory loan sharks, known as crimps, who preyed on them in every port. The problem was that seamen didn't usually get paid until a few days after getting into harbour, which meant they arrived on shore penniless and an easy target for so-called boarding masters, who gave them credit for whatever they wanted and then fleeced them of all their pay when it arrived. It was the ruin of hundreds of sailors – and the families who depended on them. The turning point came one day in 1876, when the mission's first superintendent, Rev Robert Boyer, arranged for the seamen to be taken straight to the station by taxi and bundled onto trains before the crimps could reach them. The incident was widely reported and raised awareness of the sailors' plight and led to a change in the law to protect the seamen's wages.

The Flying Angel missions also organised events such as picnics, outings and dances to entertain the seamen – anything to keep them away from the bars and 'insalubrious centres of interest'[2] (ie brothels) that the chaplains believed were the cause of the men's downfall. To encourage 'temperance', they even introduced a pledge card that committed seamen to avoiding alcohol.

The organised events provided occasions for the chaplains to mix with the seamen and help them with any problems they might have. Strong describes one exchange that took place during a dance at a mission in Australia in the 1950s, while a band was playing and a group of local girls mixed with seamen from the crews of several ships in the port. A burly seaman asked to speak to the chaplain and, after much prevarication, eventually broke down. Strong described movingly how 'a seaman with massive shoulders and two days' stubble on his chin shook with the misery of a child'.[3]

It turned out that the man felt partly responsible for an accident that had taken place a few months before in another port in which a colleague had been killed. Although there was no implication of wrongdoing, the man was overcome with guilt, which the chaplain, in his dual role as counsellor and priest, had to talk him through.

The work of the Mission to Seafarers (as it is now called) continues to this day, with centres in 121 ports around the world. As recently as 2007, it launched an 88ft ship to provide pastoral care for the crews of up to 150 ships moored off the east coast of the United Arab

137

Emirates. The visits of this ship, MV *Flying Angel,* provide welcome relief for the 2,000 crews stuck on these ships, many unable to contact their families and often with little or no shore leave. Not much has changed, it seems, since the days of John Ashley – although this time the facilities offered on board include an internet cafe, telephones, a DVD library and a small convenience store. No doubt Bibles are available too.

CHAPTER 12

IN WHICH WE SERVE

By the time World War I erupted in 1914, the mechanics of naval warfare had been transformed beyond recognition. Warships were now made of iron and steel instead of wood and were powered by reliable diesel engines, rather than depending on the whim of the wind. Gun technology had developed to such an extent that ships could fire at each other when they were several miles apart, compared with the close-quarters combat in Nelson's time. Hand-to-hand fighting on ships was virtually a thing of the past.

Despite these advances, battles at sea could and did create carnage and human suffering on a terrifying scale. War was war, and sailors died or were horribly injured whether the enemy ship was a mile or a few feet away. This fact was demonstrated at the Battle of Jutland in 1916, the only major naval battle of World War I, when nearly 10,000 men (6,784 British and 3,058 German) lost their lives in the space of a few hours – some blown to pieces by bombs, others burned to death by fires, and many more drowned below decks when their ships were sunk.

Captain Raymond Poland was close by when HMS *Defence*, one of the flagships of the British fleet, sank in a matter of seconds with the loss of 900 lives, and later wrote:

'I saw *Defence* coming down our starboard bow heading straight at the enemy. She was banging away, and going full speed, masthead colours and all the rest of it and made a very gallant show. I saw three salvoes fall across her in quick succession, beauties. A flicker of flame ran aft along her forecastle head and up her fore turret, which seemed to melt. Then – whoof, up she went, a single huge sheet of flame, 500 feet high, mixed up with smoke and fragments. As it died I saw her crumpled bow, red hot, sticking up, about 30 or 40 feet of it, at an angle of sixty degrees and then that sank. I nearly vomited. God it was an awful sight. I couldn't get to sleep that night for thinking of it.'[1]

Another witness, Petty Officer William Willis, was on board HMS *Calliope* when the gun turret he was commanding was hit by an enemy shell. 'Wigg Bennet, my sight setter, was decapitated, his head falling into my lap,' he wrote. 'I was wounded in the left side. I can remember moving Wiggy Bennett's head, turning round to the crew and ordering the continuance of the action.'[2]

There were scenes of death and violent injury everywhere. As the ships' hulls were torn open by incoming shells, burning oil slicks turned the sea into an inferno, swallowing up any sailors who had fallen or jumped over the side. Below decks, the stokers were killed by heavy calibre shells and compartments were filled with debris and body parts. It was the same on the other side, of course, and many British and German sailors alike would suffer lasting trauma, as Gunnery Officer Johannes Groth discovered when he went to the rescue of his shipmates on board the German flagship SMS *Lützow*:

'Everyone had suffered from minor or severe burns. The minds and spirit of every man had suffered a severe blow – in some cases it meant they had to be discharged later on. As far as I know, only one man was fit for service again. Rescuing these wounded men posed tremendous difficulties as they were all raging to a greater or lesser degree and the entrance to the compartment was very narrow. In several cases their feet and hands had to be bound to make transporting them possible. Every one of them yelled for water continuously.'[3]

Despite the evident distress such experiences caused to sailors on both sides of the conflict, official figures suggested that the Royal Navy suffered a remarkably low level of mental illness during World War I. This view was upheld by Surgeon Captain ET Meagher, who reported that there was little evidence of 'nervous disorder' among British sailors after the Battle of Jutland, and claimed that in the last year of the war only 16 cases of shell shock were reported by the navy. The official line was that 'anxiety neurosis was less common in the Navy than the other services'.[4]

The reasons given for the navy's apparently charmed life was the impersonal, long-distance nature of naval warfare (though, as we have seen, when it comes close, it comes very close), the close-knit life on board ship, and a more rigorous selection process. Because of the smaller numbers involved and the more specialised nature of their work, both the Royal Navy and the Royal Air Force could afford to be more selective, whereas almost anyone could join the army. Others speculated that the navy's good mental health record was due to low levels of alcoholism (the regulation 'grog' had by then been reduced to 'only' half a gill – ie 71ml or nearly three 25ml 'shots' – of rum per day), as well as regular exercise and fresh air, and the stamping out of venereal disease.

Meagher himself hypothesised:

'It is not improbable that the sailor had a psychological advantage compared with the soldier. The life of the sea habituates him to dangers. He fights on board ship, on his own ground as it were. He cannot fail to recognize that the promptings of the instinct to flee from danger are impossible of fulfilment, and is therefore freed from a mental conflict [...] and in addition, he probably has the advantage of having experienced many battle practices, and is not the least gun shy.'[5]

But the real reason the Royal Navy showed such low rates of mental illness was because it hid them behind a euphemism. Rather than apply the label of 'shell shock', with all its associated stigma, the navy preferred to use the more technical-sounding 'neurasthenia', a term that was originally coined in 1829 to describe an illness of the actual physical nerves. It was given a more metaphorical interpretation in 1869 by George Miller Beard, who used it to describe a psychological condition with symptoms of fatigue, anxiety, headaches and depression, which he attributed to the relentless pace of modern, urban life (in 1869!). Freud would later put his own spin on it, suggesting it was due to 'coitus interruptus' and an over-reliance on masturbation that resulted in 'insufficient libidinal discharge'.[6] It was the lack of a healthy sex life, he suggested, that led to neurasthenia.

Virginia Woolf, Marcel Proust and William James were all said to suffer from the condition, which was usually treated with rest cures or, in extreme cases, electrotherapy.

The military relevance of neurasthenia was suggested by Carl Weidner in 1905 when he described the illness in a paper published in an American medical journal:

'[M]ore than the physical injury in these cases, there seems to be psychical effect, either immediately accompanying the accident, such as the horrible sight of suffering, the cries of the injured, the agony of the mangled bodies, and all sorts of horrible scenes; in addition to that, even if not injured himself, come the terror of personal danger, the mental agony, the fright, etc, affecting the victim profoundly.'[7]

In fact, neurasthenia was just the latest in a long line of names given to what is generally called war syndrome – the currently accepted term in 2017 being Post-Traumatic Stress Disorder (PTSD). During the Napoleonic Wars, soldiers (and presumably sailors) who came extremely close to cannon shots, although not physically injured, often experienced what was known as 'wind contusions' (or *'vent du boulet'* in French), which included tingling, twitching and even partial paralysis. During the Boer War, the condition acquired a new name, disordered action of the heart (DAH) – also known as irritable heart, soldier's heart, cardiac neurosis, da Costa's syndrome, neurocirculatory asthenia, and effort syndrome. Among victims of railway crashes it was known as 'railway spine'. More recently, doctors have identified Gulf War Syndrome, which combines a unique cocktail of symptoms including loss of memory, diarrhoea and terminal tumours.

And it's not simply a matter of the same illness under another name. In most cases, the particular conditions of battle – from the kind of weapons used to the sort of fumes breathed in – gave rise to particular types of mental disorders associated with that era or even, in the case of Gulf War Syndrome, that battlefield. It's entirely possible that the Royal Navy chose the term 'neurasthenia' rather than 'shell shock' to distinguish the condition from its land-based equivalent and indicate that a special set of circumstances applied, though there's no clear evidence that this was the case.

Whatever the terminology, it was an important diagnosis. During World War I, a non-participating soldier or sailor diagnosed with shell shock or neurasthenia would be sent to hospital for treatment, whereas the same man diagnosed as 'sane' could be shot for treason.

By adding cases of neurasthenia into the equation, the true toll of mental illness on Britain's 'senior service' becomes clearer. Meagher himself estimated that 20,000 men were diagnosed with the condition – a shockingly high figure for a force that totalled just over 400,000, equating to 5 per cent. By contrast, the army had to deal with 80,000 cases of shell shock – less than 1 per cent of the 6–7 million who served with the force during the course of the war.

The situation got worse as the war went on, as shown by the admission figures for the Royal Naval Hospital in Chatham. Whereas just 140 patients with psychological disorders were admitted in 1914, the figure went up to 635 in 1915, then 888 in 1916, 1,143 in 1917 and 1,390 in 1918 – a total of 4,196 admissions over five years. This increase was partly explained by the increasing success of German U-boats: whereas at the beginning of the war, British supremacy at sea was undisputed, by war's end, the threat had moved under water and all Allied sailors lived in constant fear of being sunk by a single, well-aimed torpedo.

But the official figures could only ever tell part of the story, as the emotional repercussions of battle were often felt long after the last shot had been fired. A case in point was that of Andrew Buchanan, who joined the Royal Navy in June 1914 on a 12-year engagement. He was on HMS *Indomitable* when she was sent to reinforce the British fleet during the Battle of Jutland and probably witnessed the sight of HMS *Invincible* being blown up with the loss of all but six of her 1,032 crew. Although Buchanan survived the battle, he was discharged 16 months later suffering from neurasthenia. His war was over, but he continued to suffer from mental health issues back on 'civvy street' and in 1923 he shot himself. According to Peter Coppack's book on the Battle of Jutland, Buchanan's family have always been convinced it was his wartime experiences that caused him to commit suicide.[8]

The horrors of World War I and particularly the experiences of soldiers in the trenches cast a long shadow over Europe. In the years that followed, much was written about the lasting mental, as well as physical, damage inflicted on those lucky enough to have survived. The collective trauma of soldiers returning from the front coincided with an increasing awareness of psychological issues and an explosion of interest in Freud's theories. Suddenly, the taboo on mental illness was lifted just a little – which was just as well given the number of displaced servicemen begging on the streets before the creation of the welfare state. Never again would shell shock be dismissed as 'malingering' – or would it?

Despite the heightened awareness of these issues, the Royal Navy went into World War II remarkably unprepared and strangely in denial. To start with, cases of 'war neurosis' were treated either at the two established mental units at Haslar and Yarmouth, or in general naval hospitals. Once again, there were surprising claims by medical officers about the low number of serious psychiatric cases coming off naval ships, with the special circumstances of serving in the Royal Navy once more being quoted by way of explanation: selective recruitment, high morale and the team spirit aboard naval ships. The point was also made again that, while at sea, sailors could only abandon ship by jumping over the side, which would almost certainly result in death, and even 'throwing a sickie' wouldn't take them out of the line of fire. As Surgeon Captain CH Joynt put it, 'the safest activity is steady devotion to duty rather than flight'.[9]

Strict naval discipline was another factor often quoted as sustaining sailors' morale, with a former engineering officer remarking that the rear-admiral's 'resolute and uncompromising attitude to dress and behaviour was a tonic to us all'.[10]

Desmond Curran, who headed the navy's new department of neuropsychiatry, despite having no previous military experience, wrote: 'In wartime there is a very real danger of over-emphasising the dramatic, such as exposure to enemy action, when less dramatic events, such as the regimentation and frustration of service life, separation from home, and domestic difficulties, may really possess more significance.'[11]

His words echo the experiences of 18th- and 19th-century sailors (see Chapter 5), for whom day-to-day concerns seemed to affect their mental state more than the 'dramatic' incidents of naval warfare. But was that really the case in the era of modern, mechanised warfare?

Once again, the figures tell a different story. In the first year of the war alone an estimated 5,000 naval patients were admitted to naval psychiatric units in the UK, rising to 6,141 in 1943 and 3,516 in the first six months of 1944, giving a total of nearly 25,000 for the whole war. Many, if not most, of these patients were successfully treated and returned to active service, but a considerable number were not; some 1,297 officers and men were discharged from the navy with psychoneurosis during World War II, compared with 6,207 from the army and just 685 from the RAF.

Moreover, contrary to Curran's claim, a study of British psychiatric units in the Middle East showed that almost 90 per cent of the 1,300 naval admissions were directly related to 'battle conditions', compared with just 35 per cent of army admissions.

Despite its apparently laissez-faire attitude, the navy responded to this crisis by opening five new psychiatric units at naval bases around the country – from Aberdeenshire to Cheshire, and two in Somerset. By war's end, 35 psychiatrists had been appointed to deal with the rush of cases (an average of more than 100 men per week throughout the war). By comparison, there were 43 psychiatrists working with the slightly bigger RAF force and 227 psychiatrists working with the much bigger army force.

Unlike the army, which had learned to treat its mental patients as close as possible to the battlefield (the so-called forward psychiatry approach), the navy waited until a ship returned to port to deal with the problem. With several hundred ships at sea at any one time, it was impossible to have a psychiatrist on every one, even if that was desirable – and experiments by the German navy, which tried posting psychiatrists on board U-boats, suggested this approach was usually counter-productive anyway. Wherever possible, however, British naval patients were treated in navy bases since experience had shown that once a seaman had been admitted to a regular hospital, 'it becomes difficult to get him into a proper frame of mind for going to sea again'.[12]

With no doctor on board to talk to, however, there was clear evidence that sailors suffering from mental disorders at sea tended to internalise their problems, rather than discuss them with their colleagues. There was doubtless an element of old-fashioned machismo here – the same macho culture that made it impossible for seamen to talk about mental health issues in the 18th and 19th centuries. The famous 'stiff upper lip' was still the order of the day, and it was considered unpatriotic to complain about personal problems, however debilitating they were.

The result was the Royal Navy's very own, customised war syndrome: the peptic ulcer. Before the war in 1936, the typical ulcer patient was described as someone 'in the firing-line of life's struggle' – and none were more in the firing line during World War II than Britain's armed forces. By 1944, the definition of the typical patient had been refined to 'highly-strung, determined people, conscientious, ambitious and active, driving themselves in an effort to attain a perhaps unattainable standard'.[13] Research showed that, while diet may have been a contributing factor to the illness, 'psychic traumata'[14] and stress were the main causes – both of which were in ample supply in a navy fighting a prolonged war.

Sure enough, by 1942 it was estimated that 14 per cent of discharges from the Royal Navy were due to digestive disorders. A year later, in 1943, it was calculated that stomach disorders accounted for 10 per cent of admissions to UK naval hospitals, of which 40–60 per cent were found to be peptic ulcers.

So prevalent were stomach disorders during World War II that it was nicknamed 'the gut war', inspiring a German naval psychiatrist to comment that 'in this war it is the stomach that shakes not the hand',[15] a reference to the shaky hands that were one of the symptoms of shell shock during World War I. The condition even made an appearance in one of Nicholas Monsarrat's novels, *The Cruel Sea*, in which a character comments that the navy puts ashore anyone who is suspected of having an ulcer, 'in case something blows up while you're at sea'.[16]

Naval officers were particularly at risk of getting peptic ulcers, and indeed all forms of mental illness. Unlike the army, in which rank was said to be a protection against mental disorders as officers were usually held back from the front line, the navy put all its men equally in the line of fire. The psychological responsibility for the safety of the ship and its crew, however, rested with the officers and often preyed heavily on their minds. The men least susceptible to mental illness were the petty officers, the 'middle' rank of the navy with jobs such as mechanic, signalman and gunner's mate.

But World War II wasn't just about repressed anxiety and stomach disorders. There were plenty of cases of expressed anxiety and disruptive behaviour – though ship's doctors, who usually had little or no training in psychiatry, often struggled to identify them as mental health issues. Surgeon Lieutenant Humphry Osmond, a psychiatrist based at the British naval base in Malta, made a study of 50 cases treated at the hospital during the war. His research showed how often ship's doctors misunderstood and misdiagnosed mental illness due to their own inexperience. Not one of the 10 cases of 'organic' (ie physical) mental illnesses Osmond identified were correctly diagnosed by ship's doctors, and nearly all the cases of schizophrenia were misdiagnosed as either hysteria, anxiety, depression or even malingering (ie faking it). As Osmond put it, 'it seems the appearance of supposedly psychogenic symptoms tends to reduce the ardour of the examiner'.[17]

Sometimes this lack of diagnosis could be given a positive spin and described as tolerance. For instance, a 19-year-old midshipman heading home from a spell of active duty in the Far East was considered just eccentric when he began discussing 'the problems of life' with 'all and sundry'[18] on his ship. But then things took a turn for the worse. Twice he ordered 30-degree turns for no obvious reason while on watch. He also ripped the badges off his uniform, and the day before he was admitted to hospital, broke into the ship's safe and tore up some Maltese pound notes that he said were valueless. No one thought to have him examined, however, until a passing medical officer happened to spot his strange behaviour. When examined, the seaman was 'restless, aggressive, overactive, unco-operative, and showed press of words and flight of ideas'.[19] It turned out he had been hallucinating, visually and aurally. He was diagnosed as schizophrenic and kept ashore for treatment.

He was spotted in time; others weren't so lucky. One 19-year-old ordinary seaman with a brilliant school record had similarly been accepted as simply 'odd or queer' and nothing was done about his behaviour – until he tried to commit suicide by jumping down the ship's funnel. After having his injuries treated, he was examined by a psychiatrist and his true state of mind was revealed: 'He was negativistic and showed many other features of regression, nose picking, fidgeting and tongue sucking. He complained of lack of true feeling and had nihilistic delusions of spiritual death.'[20] He too was diagnosed as being schizophrenic.

Many seamen chose a more final route. Osmond described the case of a sailor on another ship who was said to be behaving 'queerly', and who said he saw angels at the masthead. Before he could be examined, however, the man 'disappeared over the side'[21] – one of hundreds of men 'lost at sea', either because of accidents or from having committed suicide.

Misdiagnosis could work the other way, though. One man who ran amuck aboard a ship was thought to be 'mental' but on closer examination it turned out he had overindulged in the pastor's communion wine and was just 'dull, unhappy and drunk'.[22]

One of the great concerns for the navy was that no one should shirk work by faking mental illness. This was to some extent an outdated notion, born of a lack of understanding of the issue, but still prevalent in some ranks. Take, for example, this treatise by Surgeon Commander EW Anderson, a psychiatrist from the famous Maudsley Hospital recruited to shake things up in the navy, though his attitudes seemed already outmoded. The main problems, he wrote, were the 'second-class citizen' and the 'high-grade mental defective'. The former, who apparently took up a third of the time of a Service psychiatrist, complained of a 'triad' of headaches, dizziness and blackouts, but was generally 'useless' with a 'lack of will' and often 'more than a dash of positive roguery added'. While he didn't deny that such men probably experienced the symptoms they described, he believed they used them 'for the evasion of duty'.[23]

According to Anderson, these 'second-class citizens' came mainly from Liverpool and Glasgow and were often Irish Roman Catholics, with 'a fair sprinkling of Welsh'. 'The psychology of the Celt notoriously baffles the Saxon,' he wrote, suggesting that 'the ancient antagonism' was at work – ie some Welsh soldiers didn't feel inclined to fight 'England's war'[24] and pretended to be sick instead.

Osmond, a young graduate from Guy's Hospital, London, disagreed. He quoted the case of a 20-year-old leading seaman who was brought to the psychiatric unit in Malta. There had been a minor disciplinary incident aboard the ship, apparently, after which he had become suspicious and aggressive and complained of strange pains in his eyes, spine and testicles. He was duly treated with painkillers and sedatives, though the ship's doctor suspected he was malingering.

When examined by Osmond, he was 'dirty, unshaven, tousled, distractable and overactive' and 'wandered about the consulting room talking incessantly', which led Osmond to conclude that, far from faking it, the man was suffering from hallucinations and he diagnosed him as schizophrenic. 'The schizophrenic nature of this episode was plain enough later on but might not have been easy to diagnose in the acute phase,' he wrote; 'however, there should never have been much doubt that he was suffering from a grave mental illness.'[25]

Osmond went on to say that in four years of working as a psychiatrist in the navy, he had only come across one certain case of malingering and that the diagnosis should only be made 'with great reserve'. 'It need be confused but seldom with acute mental illness,' he wrote, 'and it is undoubtedly better to miss the occasional malingerer than to be so preoccupied with the problem of detecting him that a sick man suffers.'[26]

It's a judgement that made a plain break with the punitive approach of old-school doctors such as Anderson and heralded a new approach to mental health in the forces. In Osmond's world, patients were listened to and given the benefit of the doubt, rather than assumed to be subverting the system. Welcome to the 20th century.

The new methodology yielded some success, as can be seen in the case of a 40-year-old petty officer who started to 'feel shaky' while doing welding work on his ship. He was later discovered in a washing area shouting, 'Give me back my boys'[27] and, after several such incidents, he was admitted to hospital and given a course of 'hypo-analysis'.[28] The treatment revealed that two of his children had been killed during the Glasgow blitz, 'while his wife was out with a Polish airman',[29] and that the man was struggling to keep his emotions under control. Thus, instead of being labelled a malingerer and punished accordingly, he was instead diagnosed with hysteria and treated at the naval hospital in Malta.

A doctor's diagnosis could have important consequences for patients in other ways, too, and work against them when it came to punishment. One particularly violent 23-year-old able seaman, for instance, was brought to the psychiatric unit on a Neil Robertson stretcher (a combination of a stretcher and a straitjacket) and manacled with handcuffs and footcuffs. He had been seized while rampaging around a group of moored-up minesweepers, brandishing a hammer and knife, and, as well as destroying a lot of furniture, he had struck an officer on the head, causing minor injury. His medical officer diagnosed him as a case of acute mania, which would have meant treatment in a psychiatric unit, but Osmond concluded that this was incorrect given the man's previous history and reclassified him as a 'psychopathic personality'.[30] The sailor was duly court-martialled for striking a superior officer and given a two-year prison sentence.

And then there was the dramatic-sounding general paresis of the insane (GPI), as exemplified by one 35-year-old petty officer who was examined at Osmond's psychiatric unit in Malta, and who displayed all the classic symptoms of the disease: 'he was aggressive, cheerful, friendly, and had ideas of grandeur when first seen, but when thwarted he became ill-tempered, sullen and even violent'. On board ship, he displayed 'boastful and aggressive behaviour'[31] and, after being arrested for smuggling, started throwing other people's kit over the side. His original diagnosis was schizophrenia, but after various tests were carried out, it became apparent that he was suffering from 'general paralysis of the insane' (GPI), a disease brought on by syphilis.

The symptoms of GPI – mood swings, delusions, visual impairment, loss of memory, seizures – were first spotted in the 19th century, but it took another hundred years before the link was made with the advanced stages of syphilis. Famous cases of GPI include Wolf Larsen in Jack London's novel *The Sea Wolf*, who suffers from intense headaches, blindness and paralysis, and Al Capone, who died of the disease. By World War II, two cures had been discovered: infection with malaria (discovered in 1917), and treatment with penicillin (1928). Osmond's patient was treated with penicillin – which would eventually all but rid the world of GPI – but failed to respond and was being considered for 'malaria therapy'. It's not known if he was cured.

Osmond went on to make a name for himself researching the constructive uses of LSD and other hallucinogenic drugs, and famously coined the term 'psychedelic'. One of his high-profile clients was Aldous Huxley, who persuaded him to prescribe a dose of mescaline as an experiment and subsequently wrote about the experience in his 1954 book *The Doors of Perception*. In later correspondence, Huxley wrote: 'To make this trivial world sublime, take half a gram of phanerothyme [a made-up word meaning "manifest spirit"].'[32] Osmond responded by writing: 'To fathom Hell or soar angelic, just take a pinch of psychedelic.'[33]

Back in World War II, the situation wasn't much better in the US Navy. There, psychoneurosis (ie a term for mental disorders) was the top cause of 'non-battle' illnesses, accounting for 4.9 per cent of days off sick, followed by 4.7 per cent for catarrhal fever (a defunct term for respiratory illness), fractures (4.2 per cent) and malaria (3.1 per cent). It was also the main reason for dismissal from the US Navy, accounting for 15.7 per cent of discharges, followed by personality disorder (11.5 per cent) and, in fifth place, our old friend, the duodenal ulcer (3.8 per cent). In all, then, mental illness and associated conditions accounted for nearly a third of discharges.

There was therefore plenty of work for psychiatrists, including one young man called Otto Allen Will Jr, who served in the US Navy before making a name for himself in the field of psychotherapy. After training at Stanford University, he studied the cases of 34 'psychotic' prisoners sent for treatment at a US naval hospital during World War II, all of whom had been court-martialled for a range of crimes, ranging from murder to homicidal assault, striking an officer and (the majority of them) going absent without authorised leave (AWOL).

He found that most of them were very young: apart from one 42-year-old, they were all under 30, and 12 of them were under 20 years of age. The youngest was 17. More than half were of average intelligence (as tested by contemporary IQ scales), but 11 were below 'normal', including one 'mental defective' with an IQ of 51 and two 'borderline defectives'. Only five were of 'superior' or 'very superior' intelligence.

Will also questioned the prisoners about their sexual preferences and found that most of them, 27 out of 34, experienced no 'gross sexual difficulties'. Two of the men, however, showed a 'marked conflict over masturbation' and one had 'engaged in both heterosexual and homosexual activities and often secretly dressed in women's clothing'. Another four had apparently 'never displayed any interest in sexual matters'.[34]

Another study of US naval offenders noted that separation anxiety was 'quite rife' before, during and after battle. Symptoms included headaches, dizziness, stomach ache and enuresis (bed wetting). 'One of the most important dynamics behind this entire condition is the inability of these young men to remain away from home,' the report said. 'He feels that he simply must return "home" but this usually means to his mother.'[35]

Some offenders justified their behaviour by saying their superior officers looked scared while in battle, a claim the author briskly rejected as 'projected anxiety' on the part of the prisoner. Others said the sea became monotonous and they were afraid of it, to which the author responded, 'This is definitely insecurity.'[36]

The report also listed the most common reasons given by sailors for going AWOL, and once again they were mostly concerned with personal domestic issues, rather than with battle trauma. The top 20 excuses were:

1. No reason at all.
2. My train, bus or plane was late.
3. I can't stand work on my ship.
4. I wanted to see my wife and baby.
5. My mother kept me at home.
6. I had to see my girlfriend who was in trouble.
7. I can't keep away from girls.
8. I wanted to have some fun.
9. I got drunk and woke up late.
10. I had difficulty at home.
11. I could not get medical care.
12. I became nervous at my post.
13. I thought I wouldn't get caught.
14. I could not get advance in rating [ie promotion].
15. I wanted to get married.
16. I was afraid of the sea.
17. I got sick while on leave.

18. I didn't like the ship I was on.
19. I couldn't get on with the BM [Boatswain's Mate].
20. I didn't like my duty.

[Source: Hospital Corps Quarterly, Vol 19, April 1946]

Like his British counterpart, the author concluded that 'malingering is less common than generally thought', though he suggested that 'simulated suicide is not uncommon'.[37]

CHAPTER 13

ADRIFT AGAIN

Those sailors whose ship was sunk but who managed to get on a lifeboat stood a fair chance of survival. One study of 448 ships sunk during World War II found that 26 per cent of crews were killed before they had got on the lifeboats. Once on board a lifeboat, however, the majority were rescued fairly quickly – 30 per cent on the first day and 50 per cent within three days (even quicker for those on liferafts). Overall, the study showed that 68 per cent of the 27,000 crews that were sunk survived the ordeal. Most of the rest – those who didn't die immediately but weren't rescued in time – died slow and often delirious deaths on board the lifeboats.

Following the sinking of the *Titanic*, the number of lifeboats carried by commercial and naval ships had increased dramatically, so capacity was not usually an issue. The lifeboats themselves had remained pretty much unchanged, however, and were usually built of wood to a design that had been around for several hundred years. Various improvements had been made, including fitting spray hoods and bilge pumps and ensuring an adequate supply of blankets, but the basic design remained unchanged for most of the war. As more ships were sunk and longer voyages were made in lifeboats, the supply of long-life food carried on the boats was increased. From 1941, each lifeboat was required to carry 400g (14oz) of biscuits, milk tablets, chocolate and pemmican (energy bars) per person. The amount of water carried was also tripled to 3.1 litres (5½ pints) per person.

Despite this, for the unfortunate sailors who had to make long voyages on lifeboats, it was usually the shortage of water that pushed them over the edge. Dying of thirst and surrounded by sea, the temptation to drink salt water proved irresistible to some – just as it had for their predecessors 100 years before (see Chapter 7). And, as before, the result was nearly always fatal. The point was made by ship's carpenter Kenneth Cooke, who survived 50 days at sea on a lifeboat after the cargo ship *Lulworth Hill* was sunk in the South Atlantic in March 1943:

'Our greatest problem was water, all of us suffered from intense thirst, and after a while I noticed some of the survivors drinking salt water. [...] As they drank more and more, they rapidly became delirious, imagining they could see rivers of water and snow. One man became very troublesome, and had to be forcibly held down until he became too exhausted to struggle any more. [...] Some died from drinking salt water, others from exhaustion, and I think many men gave up hope, and lost the urge to struggle on for their lives.'[1]

A contemporary study of voyages made on lifeboats during the war suggested that the minimum amount of fresh water needed to survive was 120ml (4fl oz, or 1/5 pint) per day. Survivors who consumed less than that were much less likely to survive, with 28 per cent dying within six days and 90 per cent dying after 32 days. At that rate of consumption, the Ministry of War Transport's allowance of 3.1 litres (5½ pints) per person was likely to run out after 28 days at sea – unless the crews managed to supplement their supplies with rainwater.

For those who clung to liferafts with only the supplies they managed to grab as they abandoned ship, the loss of reason came much sooner. This consequence of thirst was experienced first hand by one Australian survivor of a Japanese prison ship sunk in the Pacific in September 1944, who clung on to a raft for five days before being rescued by an American submarine. His description of his ordeal and subsequent rescue shows how far his mind had become detached from reality:

'I thought could see lovely long grass growing on the waves, and the big waves had nice trees sprouting out from them. I could hear little birds singing in the trees, and the voice of Mary, Mother of God, talking to me, telling me that I would be saved and to have faith.

'Presently I heard other funny voices and a man's voice called out to me: "Okay, buddy, we'll soon have you out of that." I looked about me and saw a submarine near, and men were moving on it. Then I felt a hand at the nape of my neck and was rising, rising, rising out of the water until it seemed that I was soaring through the sky, with oil dripping off my face and all over nice white uniforms.

'Then I smelt something. I began to get breathless and then I began to cry. It was chicken soup. Later I could hear some women talking near me – American women's voices. They were American nurses. They fed me from a baby's bottle with milk and soup. So I found I was still on earth.'[2]

Another survivor from the same ship described how they came across another shipwrecked sailor, who was clearly hallucinating:

'On the fourth day the sea was very choppy, making it extra hard to keep a grip on the oil-slippery raft. During the morning we saw in the distance what looked like a case, but it turned out to be our ship's ice box. There was a Tommy on top of it, but he was completely dingbats. We told him to jump off on to the raft, but he replied: "I can't leave this island, Betty. I love her and she loves me." We took firm measures and got him on to a raft, but some hours later the raft broke away and we never saw him again.'[3]

Others seemed strangely immune to the effects of drinking salt water. When the cargo ship *Athelknight* was sunk in the mid-Atlantic in May 1942, 18 of the survivors spent nearly a month at sea in a lifeboat and sailed 1,200 miles to reach the Leeward Islands. During the voyage, the second officer tried to stop the crew drinking salt water, but several men disobeyed him. Those who succumbed, he noted, 'suffered most'[4] – all except one man. The Russian carpenter claimed he drank salt water regularly and it had no effect on him, though the officer still tried to prevent him doing so, in case it had 'a bad effect' on the other men.

Despite the countless stories of shipwrecked sailors hallucinating and eventually dying of thirst, the Ministry of War Transport was slow to act on an apparently workable solution: supplying lifeboats with 'stills' to make their own fresh water while at sea. The idea was first mooted in January 1942, but it took months of discussion and experimentation before the kits were finally ordered in July 1943, and even by 1944 many lifeboats still weren't equipped with them. By the time they were widely available, the crisis was virtually over.

The dramatic increase in shipwrecks during World War II and subsequent tales of survival at sea – usually involving sailors becoming delirious from drinking salt water – reignited the debate about drinking from the sea. For centuries, it had been an absolute rule that you should under no circumstances drink salt water, no matter how desperate you were, and indeed the whole weight of maritime literature seemed to support that view. However, in 1952 a French doctor, Alain Bombard, decided to challenge this golden rule. Setting off from Las Palmas in a 15ft inflatable dinghy, he sailed across the Atlantic surviving only on what food he could catch along the way. For 65 days, he drank the juice of crushed fish and plankton (which he called 'lobster purée') and small amounts of salt water, supplemented by rain water when it was available. The secret, he concluded, was to start drinking salt water as soon as the fresh water ran out, before the mind started hallucinating.

Remarkably, although he went through periods of deep despair, he stayed rational throughout the voyage. His most noticeable mental 'tic' was that he became increasingly superstitious, at one point calculating when he would reach land by the number of matches it took to light his (increasingly damp) cigarettes. He also developed a 'persecution mania', believing everything was conspiring against him, including the clouds that sailed all over the sky but refused to shelter him from the unrelenting sunshine. And he started to talk to the toy doll that his friends had given him as a mascot before he left the Canaries.

It was a different story for Hannes Lindemann. Inspired by Bombard, the German doctor set off on two daring transatlantic voyages, first in 1955 in a dugout canoe and then in 1957 in a canvas kayak. Like Bombard, his aim was to research methods for survival at sea and, with little room for supplies on either boat, he too lived mainly on what he could harvest from the ocean. He was particularly interested in the psychology of the 'castaway', believing that the mind would give in before the body. 'It is the undisciplined mind that drives the castaway to panic and heedless action,' he wrote. 'Morale is the single most important factor in survival.'[5] To prepare himself before and during the voyage, he used a system of autogenic training to strengthen his mental resolve, repeating self-affirming phrases such as 'I will make it' and 'Never give up'. He also used prayer and meditation to maintain his morale.

Despite all his preparation, Lindemann suffered far more from altered mental states, including hallucinations and delusions, than Bombard. The worse moment came after 55 days at sea, when, after days steering the kayak through a force 8 gale, he started drifting in and out of consciousness. First, he thought he heard a journalist he knew talking to him from a passing ship (the ship was real enough, but the voice was entirely imaginary). Then he imagined he was sitting in a rickshaw, with a black servant running beside him.

'"Boy," I asked, "where are we going?" "It is all right. We have to go through the surf," he answered, and as he spoke we plunged through. The deck was under water and came up again. I looked at the boy to the left. He wore black and snorted like a whale or horse, but he worked without talking back. "Boy, where do you boys live?" "In the west." West! The word reminded me of something. I knew it, and then I remembered the compass. Again I was off course. I looked at the boy on the left, but he had gone. A black horse rode there now, pushing the boat. Horses know the way home. I could rely on a horse. [...] Then I clearly heard the voice of Mephisto: "I do not see your water lies." I looked for my black boy and black horse at port side. I saw only a black outrigger [ie the canoe's stabiliser].'[6]

Lindemann's hallucinations were more likely the result of too little sleep rather than too much salt, as he soon recovered and was able to complete his voyage – arriving at St Martin after 72 days at sea and having lost 25 per cent of his body weight. His conclusion? Bombard must have taken a supply of fresh water with him, or he couldn't have survived as long as he did.

The debate rages on, but the official line from the past 300 years remains unchanged: do not drink salt water (or urine) if you want to stay sane.

CHAPTER 14

THE PILOT OF THE *PINTA*

The sun hadn't yet risen when Joshua Slocum set sail from the Azores on 24 July 1895 on the second leg of his pioneering round-the-world voyage. He had spent a pleasant few days on the islands, being looked after by the locals and relishing the taste of fresh bread after a three-week ocean passage from Boston, Massachusetts. By the time he set out to sea again, his 36ft sloop *Spray* was laden with food donated by his generous hosts. As the breeze picked up, he was pleased not to have to cook, and snacked instead on some local delicacies: plums and Pico white cheese. It was a mistake, he soon realised, and a few hours later he was racked by stomach pains. Unable to steer, he lashed the helm and, after reefing down the boat as best he could, headed down below. There, he curled up on the cabin floor and, in between spasms, started having strange visions. He later wrote:

'How long I lay there I could not tell, for I became delirious. When I came to, as I thought, from my swoon, I realized that the sloop was plunging into a heavy sea, and looking out of the companionway, to my amazement I saw a tall man at the helm. His rigid hand, grasping the spokes of the wheel, held them like a vise [*sic*]. One may imagine my astonishment. His rig was that of a foreign sailor, and the large red cap he wore was cockbilled over his left ear, and all was set off with shaggy black whiskers. He could have been taken for a pirate in any part of the world. While I gazed upon his threatening aspect I forgot the storm and wondered if he had come to cut my throat. This he seemed to divine. "Señor," said he, doffing his cap. "I have come to do you no harm.[...] I am the pilot of the Pinta come to aid you. Lie quiet captain," he added, "and I will guide your ship to-night. You have *calentura*, but you will be all right to-morrow."[1]

After reprimanding Slocum for mixing cheese with plums, the apparition broke into song and made as if to catch up with the *Pinta*, Columbus's ship, which he claimed was not far ahead. When Slocum awoke the next morning, the pilot had gone but *Spray* was still perfectly on course and 'going like a race-horse'. As he put it: 'Columbus himself could not have held her more exactly on her course.'[2] His only complaint was that, to be on the safe side, the mystery helmsman should have taken down the jib.

Slocum survived this and many other incidents during his three-year adventure, eventually dropping anchor in Newport, Rhode Island, in June 1898 to become the first man to sail singlehanded around the world. The book he wrote about the voyage, *Sailing Alone Around the World*, became an international best-seller and effectively launched the sport of singlehanded sailing. More than 100 years later, it's still one of the best-selling nautical books ever written.

The appearance of the pilot of the *Pinta* is not only one of the most famous passages in Slocum's book, it's also the first recorded instance of hallucination by a singlehanded sailor – a mental affliction that would become all too common in the future as sailors were driven to the very limits of endurance competing in singlehanded races.

Although the apparition is described by many writers as a 'ghost', Slocum himself never used that word. Quite the opposite, in fact: he prefaced the passage by saying he was 'delirious' and in 'a swoon' and later referred to his 'fevered brain'.[3] He clearly believed his 'strange guest' appeared as a function of his brain – or, more specifically, from an over-indulgence in plums and white cheese – and not as some superstitious force. Neither was he surprised when he reappeared the following night, this time in a genuine 'sleeping' dream.

Even before this incident occurred, Slocum had described his heightened mental state during thick fog – a time when a sailor is on high alert and likely to suffer from strain and exhaustion. To the modern reader it sounds more like tripping than sailing:

'During these days a feeling of awe crept over me. My memory worked with startling power. The ominous, the insignificant, the great, the small, the wonderful, the commonplace – all appeared before my mental vision in magical succession. Pages of my history were recalled which had been so long forgotten that they seemed to belong to a previous existence. I heard all the voices of the past laughing, crying, telling what I had heard them tell in many corners of the earth.'[4]

The difference between how Slocum describes his experiences and how King George V's tutor described the *Flying Dutchman* less than two

167

decades earlier (see Chapter 1) marks a fundamental shift in how such phenomena are perceived and in our understanding of how the brain works. According to the new thinking, the brain was not to be trusted any more than the body's other senses, which all had a tendency to play tricks on the mind. If someone witnessed something unbelievable, such as a ghost ship or a ghost pilot, then most likely it was unbelievable and it was our brain or our senses that were to blame.

Coincidentally, one of the defining moments in the development of this new approach took place just a few hours before Slocum set sail from Horta. On the previous night, 3,540 kilometres (2,200 miles) away at the Bellevue-Höhe villa in the suburbs of Vienna, Sigmund Freud had a dream that would transform the face of psychology. The dream became known as 'Irma's injection' and concerned a patient of his who was resisting his proposed treatment. Freud's dream was convoluted and obscure, but through detailed self-analysis he realised it was enacting certain wishes he had about the patient's treatment – mainly exonerating him from her continuing illness. In other words, the dream was fulfilling his subconscious wishes.

It was the first dream Freud had successfully analysed, and he gave it a pivotal position in his *Interpretation of Dreams* – the book that in turn laid the foundations of psychotherapy – published in 1899, the same year as Slocum's *Sailing Alone Around the World*. Freud's description of his 'eureka moment' is suitably momentous – and unexpectedly elemental (it could equally describe a yacht emerging on the crest of a gigantic wave in the Southern Ocean – the sense of movement and pace is identical):

'When, after passing through a narrow defile, we suddenly emerge on a piece of high ground, where the path divides and the finest prospects open up on every side, we may pause for a moment and consider in which direction we shall first turn our steps. Such is the case with us, now that we have surmounted the first interpretation of a dream. We find ourselves in the full daylight of a sudden discovery.'[5]

In truth, it's hard to imagine the crusty old captain being a fan of psychotherapy. Born in Nova Scotia to a large, impoverished family, Slocum ran away from home at 14 and served on sailing ships for 20 years, winning his first command when he was 25. He married in 1871 and, after a stint in the South Seas, carried cargo on the Pacific coast, mostly from San Francisco to Hawaii. Though it might sound idyllic, it was a tough life and, as well as surviving one shipwreck, the couple had to endure three of their seven children dying in childhood. One baby girl died while Slocum was unloading timber in the Philippines in 1879, and he had to pickle the body in brandy in order to preserve it for a decent burial back home. His wife Virginia wrote movingly of the event to her mother:

'I have not been able to eat anything till lately. Dear Josh has got me everything he can think of, my hands shakes so now I can hardley write. Dear mother my Dear little baby died the other day & I expect that is partley the cause. Every time her teeth would start to come she would cry all night, if I cut them through the gum would grow together again. The night she died she had one convulsion after the other, I gave her a hot bath and some medicine and she was quite quiet, in fact I thought she was going to come around, when she gave a quiet sigh and was gone. Dear Josh embalmed her in brandy, for we would not leave her in this

169

horrid place. She did look so pretty after she died. Dearest Mother I cannot write any more.'[6]

It's hard to imagine the effect such an experience would have on even a hardy soul such as Slocum, but around about this time his luck seemed to change – and perhaps his personality too. In 1883, he bought a one-third share in a large clipper that he later described as his 'best command',[7] although subsequent events seem to suggest it was exactly the opposite. On the very first trip out of New York, there was a mutiny on board during which the first mate was killed, and Slocum was later convicted of 'false and cruel imprisonment'[8] for putting another man in chains for 53 days during the same incident.

Things didn't get better on his next ship. Soon after setting sail, Virginia died while the ship was moored off Buenos Aires, and Slocum was apparently driven crazy with sorrow. Undeterred, he married his much younger cousin Henrietta less than two years later and set off again to South America, only to be faced with another mutiny. This time, he shot two of his crew, although a court in Brazil acquitted him on the grounds of self-defence. Smallpox and shipwreck followed and, after living on a beach in Brazil while Slocum built a 35ft canoe and then sailed the family 5,500 miles back home, his young bride decided she had had enough and left him.

And so, by 1892, Slocum was out of work, out of money and out of love. Aged 48, with his sailing skills having been made redundant by the advent of steam, he was effectively unemployable. Thus when an acquaintance gave him a rotten old fishing boat to do up, he jumped at the opportunity. It's hard not to see his setting off three years later on a lone voyage around the world as an act of defiance from a disenchanted, misanthropic man, rejected by his family and society – turning his back on a long and painful past.

In fact, Slocum's voyage and the book he wrote about it proved the making of him, and he was soon travelling the country on lecture tours and visiting President Roosevelt at his private estate. *Sailing Alone Around the World* was a classic 'boy's own' adventure, with plenty of acts of derring-do and even some cunning survival tricks, such as sprinkling the decks with tacks at night to scare off marauding Indians. Coming at the end of the Age of Sail, it appealed to a nostalgia for the pre-industrial age, when men were in control of their own destinies and took matters into their own hands, rather than relying on machines and distant masters to sort things out. It even prompted *Swallows and Amazons'* author Arthur Ransome to say: 'Boys who do not like this book ought to be drowned at once.'[9]

But Slocum's ghosts hadn't left him. In 1906 he was convicted of the indecent assault of a 12-year-old girl and sentenced to 42 days in prison. The charge was refuted by his supporters, who suggested he may have inadvertently exposed himself. Friends had noticed he had become 'much run down physically, and perhaps mentally. He was exceedingly lazy and indifferent to his surroundings',[10] and often walked around with his flies undone. Either way, the incident adds to the picture of a dysfunctional character, out of step with society and its rules of behaviour.

On 14 November 1909, Slocum set off on his final voyage, headed for the West Indies. He was sailing alone, and had apparently told friends he might head to South America to explore the Orinoco, Rio Negro and Amazon rivers. He was never seen again, and in July 1910 his erstwhile wife reported him lost at sea. It was another 14 years before he was declared legally dead. The ocean had consumed another of its own, without leaving a trace.

CHAPTER 15

HEARING VOICES

A prisoner in Dartmoor doesn't get hard labour like this; the public wouldn't stand for it and he has company, however uncongenial. In addition he gets dry clothing and undisturbed sleep. I wonder how the crime rate would be affected if people were sentenced to sail around the world alone, instead of going to prison. It's ten months' solitary confinement with hard labour[1]
Robin Knox-Johnston

Singlehanded sailing is the ultimate endurance sport. Uniquely, it pits a lone person against the elements, usually hundreds if not thousands of miles away from land, with only minimal logistical support. And, as many singlehanders have discovered, if you have an accident in the middle of an ocean, your chances of survival are very slim. Tony Bullimore, the 'upside-down' sailor who was rescued 500 miles from Antarctica after surviving five days in freezing waters in his capsized boat, was one of the lucky ones. Most capsized singlehanders disappear without trace.

It takes a particular type of person to embark on what one solo sailor described as 'ten months' solitary confinement with hard labour'[2] *for fun* – or even as a professional occupation. Not everyone is capable of threading a needle and stitching up their own tongue while sailing across the Indian Ocean, as one luckless sailor had to do during the 1992 Vendée Globe race. Words used to describe these sailors include: 'loners', 'egomaniacs', 'misfits', 'mavericks' and 'oddballs'. Or, in the words of French sailing legend Alain Colas (who himself vanished at sea without trace): 'We are a special brand of maniacs.'[3]

However, the greatest threat to the sanity of the singlehanded sailor is not great storms or broken equipment but isolation and loneliness. Sailing week after week, month after month without contact with another human being takes its toll on even the most antisocial sailor. Combine that with a repetitive activity such as helming, not to mention the sheer boredom of being surrounded by nothing but sea, and it's not surprising if the mind starts to perform pirouettes. One solo sailor in a major race, for instance, found himself sobbing his eyes out when he heard on the radio that the Labour MP Nye Bevan had died – not because he was particularly fond of the man or even because he agreed with his policies, but because he had no one to share such a momentous piece of news with and therefore had no way of processing his emotions.

The desperate loneliness of the singlehanded sailor was captured on tape by one person after being hit by a storm halfway across the Atlantic:

'Oh it's been absolute hell and I just don't understand how I could be so stupid (sobbing). (Crash. The boat gets laid flat by a wave.)

173

Oh Christ... Oh God I deserve everything I get... and I thought, "Well, the other boats, they managed, they got through the Gulf Stream". But of course a big boat can get through the Gulf Stream. I can't even get through a four-foot wave and I knew that when I started. I knew it and I said it and I said it and I said it. Oh God, oh Sandy, Sandy... (sobbing)... how could you love somebody so stupid...'[4]

Not surprisingly, the sport has attracted the attention of psychiatrists, curious to see how people perform in such extreme conditions. The first study was set up by one of the competitors in the inaugural Observer Single-Handed TransAtlantic Race, or OSTAR, from Plymouth to New York in 1960. David Lewis was a New Zealand-born doctor based in London who said he came up with the idea as an excuse for taking time off work. In the end, only three of the five competitors (including Lewis) took part in the survey, which consisted of a daily 'medical log' that measured their eating and sleeping habits, as well as their mental and emotional state. Chichester apparently refused to join in because he (or possibly Mrs Chichester) objected to being asked about his sexual habits (the questionnaire contained a question about whether the skippers were feeling 'sexy', and another asking if they were 'happy without female company' or whether they 'would enjoy [the] company of [the] other sex'[5]).

Lewis wrote up the results of his study in a five-page article in the medical journal *The Lancet* in which he noted the differences in 'mood variability' among the three competitors who took part in the study, with Subject C (himself) showing the most variability. He noted that only one subject experienced hallucinations, Subject C (him again), who saw or heard things on seven of the 54 days he was at sea, and that these arose 'at times of acute fatigue and under conditions of decreased sensory variation'.[6]

Lewis concluded that his hallucinations were not brought about by solitude and fatigue alone but by the combination of these factors in conjunction with a monotonous occupation, such as steering the boat, or keeping watch in fog or in the dark. And, writing at a time when space travel was at the forefront of everyone's minds, he suggested his observations might have some application for astronauts, who were reported to have experienced hallucinations.

As for sexual habits, he suggested that the two bachelors, Subjects A and C (Lewis and Hasler), showed 'a much closer correlation between the physical and social aspects of sex wishes' than the married man, Subject B (Val Howells), who was more likely to express longing for his family than sexual frustration. Lewis concluded: 'In none of the records did sexual wishes arise during or after fear and stress – a form of displacement described in some of the reports on wartime stress.'[7]

Howells' own account of the voyage was rather different. Within days of leaving Plymouth, the larger-than-life Welshman was reduced to tears and suffered violent mood swings and 'emotional switchbacks'. He soon found himself talking to his self-steering gear (Iron Mike) and his own alter ego, who mocked him for 'prancing about' in a jock strap ('...that thing he's wearing is sparse enough to make me sick. / Nature boy indeed! / Only a few weeks ago he wouldn't have been seen dead in that sort of kit.'[8]). He compared the state of mind of the singlehanded sailor to an Indian mystic sitting on a bed of nails, who has to leave the body behind while the mind 'abdicates' for the duration of the ordeal.

And, contrary to Lewis's analysis of Subject B as being less prone to sexual longing than the bachelors, Howells made frequent references to erotic dreams, needing 'the attentions of a good woman', and to the drawbacks of 'discipline' (a euphemism for abstinence). His book includes possibly the first description of a sailor having sex with the sea, as he found himself being aroused by the spray on the foredeck and enjoying an 'ocean-going caress'.[9] Appropriately enough for a singlehander in this self-questioning age, his main reading matter was *Is Sex Necessary? Or, Why You Feel the Way You Do*, by EB White and James Thurber.[10]

For this was the era of the 'self', when self-realisation and self-improvement began to seem more important than worrying about what the neighbours were thinking. The self-help movement started here in the form of pop psychology books such as *Sex and the Single Girl* (1962),[11] *Games People Play: The Psychology of Human Relationships* (1964),[12] *I'm OK – You're OK* (1967)[13] and *Everything You Wanted to Know About Sex (But Were Afraid To Ask)* (1969).[14] And let's not forget *Jonathan Livingston Seagull* (1970),[15] in which a seaborne bird is urged to be his 'true self, here and now'.

Singlehanded sailing, with all that it implied about developing greater self-knowledge and self-reliance, fitted in well with this new awareness. Reading books about how your mind worked was one thing, but setting off to sea on your own really brought you face to face with who you were. It was the ultimate journey of self-discovery, and the sport grew in popularity throughout the 1960s and '70s. At its peak in 1976, the OSTAR boasted 125 competitors, after which the number of entries had to be limited to 110 boats for reasons of safety. Not everyone, of course, was there to save their souls – some were seeking fame and glory, while others were just enjoying the ride.

But the times certainly were a-changin', and when the next questionnaire was handed out at the start of the 1972 transatlantic race, 34 of the 55 competitors agreed to take part. The results, published by author Glin Bennet in *The Lancet* later that year, were spectacular, with 12 skippers claiming they'd experienced some kind of hallucination – be it visual, auditory (sound) or olfactory (smell). Bennet's descriptions of the strange things the competitors imagined seeing, hearing or smelling give an insight into the trippy world of singlehanded sailing.

One example occurred after 33 days at sea, when sailor 'T' was changing a sail and spotted an object in the water. 'A baby elephant,' he thought. 'A funny place to put a baby elephant.' Later, he saw the object again. 'A funny place to put a Ford Popular,'[16] he thought. On closer inspection, he realised the object was a whale – yet at no time did he question the probability of finding a baby elephant or a Ford car bobbing about in the middle of the Atlantic.

Another competitor was clearly extremely homesick. Sailor 'K' had been helming non-stop during a storm and hadn't eaten a proper meal for 56 hours when he saw his father-in-law at the top of the mast. Again, he was quite unfazed by this unexpected apparition and carried on steering the boat. Later the same day, he looked into the cabin and saw first his wife, then his mother, and then his daughter lying on a bunk. He was mortified when he eventually realised none of his family was really on board and he was just staring at an empty sleeping bag.

One competitor had his own version of Slocum's pilot of the *Pinta*. Sailor 'A' was heading back towards Brittany in a storm but didn't dare take shelter in any harbour because of the dangerous coastline. Exhausted and running out of food, he decided to get some rest. 'He was lying on his bunk when he heard a man putting the boat about on to the other tack,' Bennet wrote. 'When he went up on deck to investigate, the man passed him in the passageway coming down as he went up. The boat had indeed been put about and was on the correct course. The process was repeated several times. The man was not recognizable.'[17] Needless to say, the man didn't exist, though how the boat changed tack on its own remains a mystery.

Another competitor smelled coffee in the air, even though he was hundreds of miles away from land and wasn't drinking coffee. Others heard voices in the rigging and one repeatedly had spots in front of his eyes. Several had dreams and premonitions of danger, some of which turned out to be true and saved them from dangerous situations. Unlike the previous race, none of the skippers admitted to feeling sexually deprived this time, although one man was spotted with an 'evocative Scandinavian poster'[18] in his saloon.

Indeed, so extensive were the hallucinations that Bennet was moved to write in *The Lancet*:

'... what is striking is the frequency and range of the psychological phenomena reported. Taken out of context they might be said to provide evidence of severe mental disorder, but what is their significance in context? Is there something special about the business of single-handed sailing that makes such phenomena common, or are they due to some peculiarity in the sailors themselves?'[19]

He suggests that the phenomena are the result of 'impaired function'[20] due to a combination of sleep deprivation, malnourishment, seasickness and sensory deprivation. It's the white-noise phenomenon, whereby a subject subjected to continuous noise for a significant length of time starts 'hearing' other sounds. In the case of the solo sailor, the wind in the rigging and the sea rushing past the hull create the white noise. This, combined with the lack of features in the sea or sky, especially in foggy weather, causes sensory deprivation that, combined with the other physical ailments, leads to hallucinations.

However, Bennet points out that these experiences are not exclusive to sailors, and that similar hallucinations are experienced by people travelling through polar regions and in high altitudes. This suggests either that these sailors are not as peculiar as they might appear, or that they share their peculiarity with people who travel in polar regions and high altitudes.

These solo transatlantic sailors all suffered from temporary mental disorders, in the form of hallucinations and delusions, usually brought on by lack of sleep, exhaustion and not eating enough. They soon recovered and, once the race was over, returned to their normal lives. All that would change, however, with the creation of the ultimate yachting challenge: sailing singlehanded non-stop around the world. Faced with navigating 30,000 miles of empty ocean without seeing another human being for months on end, a sailor's ability to stay sane in the new era of singlehanded racing would mean the difference between winning and losing – and, in some cases, between life and death.

CHAPTER 16

THE MADDEST RACE

The Sargasso Sea is a large area of calm, windless ocean in the middle of the North Atlantic Gyre. Surrounded by water, it has no coastline and has developed a unique ecosystem that hosts the sargassum seaweed after which it is named, as well as turtles, eels, shrimps, crabs and several species of fish. Tales abound of sailing ships becoming becalmed here and drifting about for years, before eventually being discovered with a crew of skeletons on board. Even Jules Verne couldn't resist including the Sargasso Sea in his 1870 book *Twenty Thousand Leagues Under the Sea*, describing trunks of trees torn from the Andes and the remains of various shipwrecks floating above the *Nautilus* as it ploughed its way through this 'herbaceous mass'.[1]

Into this strange world, so dead above water and yet full of life below, sailed the *Teignmouth Electron* in June 1969. The trimaran was one of the competitors in the Golden Globe Race and was nearing the end of its strange voyage. After eight months at sea, the boat was weathered and broken and had barnacles on its bottom. The yacht's progress slowed as it entered the fecund mid-Atlantic pond, and gradually became more erratic as its skipper became entangled in a mental quagmire of his own. The events that followed constitute one of the clearest and saddest cases of madness at sea – one that would be described as 'perhaps the most completely documented account of a psychological breakdown', with symptoms 'typical of classical paranoia'.[2] And, while the Sargasso Sea wasn't exactly to blame, it's hard to imagine it happening anywhere else.

Donald Crowhurst was an instrument manufacturer from Devon who had had some success with his Navicator, a machine that allowed sailors to plot their position using radio signals. Blessed with a brilliant mind, he was very good at coming up with ideas and 'talking the talk', but hopeless at the practical aspects of running a business. By the late 1960s, the Navicator was going down the pan and he was having to borrow money to keep his head above water.

When he heard about the Golden Globe Race, he immediately saw a chance of redemption. The event came about after Francis Chichester sailed singlehanded around the world in 1966, stopping once on the way, in Sydney. Chichester received international acclaim for his achievement, but even before he had got home, several sailors were already preparing to go one better: to sail singlehanded around the world without stopping. The *Sunday Times* formalised the contest by offering two prizes: the Golden Globe trophy for the first person to complete a non-stop circumnavigation, and £5,000 for the person to do so in the fastest time. The only stipulation was that competitors had to leave a British port between 1 June and 31 October 1968.

For Crowhurst, the race offered a chance not only to become a national hero (he'd always felt he was destined for great things) but also to save his business. By sailing a yacht fitted with all his latest inventions around the world, he would gain valuable publicity as well as winning enough cash to pay off his debts. His business partner was persuaded, and duly agreed to fund the project, on condition that Crowhurst paid back the cost of the boat if he didn't complete the voyage.

In truth, Crowhurst's campaign was doomed from the start. The boat was built in a hurry and, following a disastrous maiden voyage down the English Channel, he didn't have time to make the modifications the boat so badly needed before the 31 October deadline. Within hours of leaving the UK, the trimaran began to fall apart and seemed barely in a fit state to sail across the Channel, never mind around the world. Not only that, but it soon became clear that his estimated speeds were wildly optimistic, and he had little or no chance of winning either prize.

But Crowhurst was in a double bind. He had by now mortgaged both his house and the boat against the success of the project. If he dropped out, he and his family risked financial ruin. If he kept going, though, he faced almost certain death. Instead, he embarked on one of the most daring deceptions in yachting history: he began to falsify his journey. Feeding false positions to the press, he pretended to be sailing around the world and even started writing a false logbook of his imaginary journey, when in reality he was simply pottering around the South Atlantic. To make his log convincing, he listened to weather forecasts for the areas he was supposed to be sailing in, and worked backwards from fictional 'fixes' to the precise sextant readings for those points at the appropriate times. It was an audacious plan that arguably required a much greater degree of mathematical skill than navigating the actual course.

His strategy was to come a respectable third, behind Robin Knox-Johnston, the first to complete his 'loop', and Nigel Tetley, the contender for the fastest circumnavigation. That would give him maximum publicity, while ensuring his logbooks weren't scrutinised too closely. Everything changed, however, when Tetley, believing Crowhurst was close behind, pushed his boat too hard and sank 1,100 miles from home. Suddenly, Crowhurst was back in the spotlight as the favourite to win the £5,000 prize for the fastest voyage. The BBC and the *Express* newspaper were preparing to meet him off the coast of Cornwall, and a welcoming committee had been set up in his home town of Teignmouth, with 100,000 people expected to cheer him in.

However, as he entered the Sargasso Sea, the wind died and his boat slowed down, allowing him to wallow in his own thoughts. Had he been anywhere else, he would have been too busy taking care of the boat to think about his own problems. Instead, the repetitive motion of the boat floundering about in the ocean invited morbid contemplation about his own bogged-down situation, frustrated ambitions and stalled career. As the boat slowly went around in spirals across an empty sea 2,000 miles from home, so Crowhurst's mind spun in ever-decreasing circles.

He had by then spent nearly eight months at sea and, apart from a brief (and rule-breaking) stopover in South America to repair his boat, had barely spoken to another human being. Alone on his boat in the middle of the Atlantic, he had no one to share his agony with. It was clear he couldn't abandon the race, and yet it was equally inconceivable to finish and be found out as a cheat. Trapped in his own tangled web of lies, Crowhurst's only escape was to give up 'sailorising'[3] (as he called the process of sailing his boat), and to disappear into his own imagination.

Over the next few days, he wrote a 25,000-word manifesto he called his 'Philosophy'. His insight was that, after millennia of development, human intelligence had attained such a state that advanced minds could now 'progress towards cosmic integration'. It required simply 'an effort of free will'[4] to release the mind from physical constraint and achieve an eternal God-like state. It was the perfect escape from his conundrum: he could just vanish and be swallowed up by the universe.

His diary ends with a confession:

'Now is revealed the true
nature and purpose and power
of the game offence I am
I am what I am and I
see the nature of my offence.'

Then an appeal:

'I will only resign this game
if you agree that
the next occasion that this
game is played it will be played
according to the
rules that are devised by
my great god who has
revealed at last to his son
not only the exact nature
of the reason for games but
has also revealed the truth of

the way of the ending of the

next game that

   It is finished

   It is finished

IT IS THE MERCY'[5]

And finally a countdown, ending at 11:20:40 precisely.

No one knows for sure what happened next, but it's generally assumed that Crowhurst jumped off his boat into the deep Sargasso Sea, and drowned. His empty yacht was discovered by a passing Post Office ship on a routine run from London to the Caribbean on 10 July 1969. On board, carefully laid out on the table as if ready for inspection, were his diary and his logbooks, the real and the fictional.

The *Sunday Times* journalists Nicholas Tomalin and Ron Hall made a study of Crowhurst's ramblings and concluded they were:

'typical of classical paranoia, a psychotic disorder in which deluded ideas are built into a complex, intricate structure. Though founded on mistaken beliefs, the structure of paranoid thought has a strong internal logic and consistency [...] Most often, the delusional system is one of persecution, but, as with Crowhurst, a paranoid can also have delusions of grandeur, thinking himself to be a great mathematician or philosopher, or a second Messiah.'[6]

Under the title 'Psychological hazards of single-handed ocean sailing', *The Lancet* devoted 11 pages to the case, which author Glin Bennet described as 'perhaps the most completely documented account of a psychological breakdown'. He concluded that, while Crowhurst was an 'unstable character' and 'erratic in his personal behaviour', there was not sufficient evidence of mental problems before the journey to warrant banning him from the race. He doesn't offer a diagnosis, but refers to Crowhurt's 'breakdown', which he says shows 'in a particularly vivid way'[7] how someone can be overwhelmed by events.

He concludes:

> 'One of the functions of tragedy in the theatre is to present an intensified view of ordinary life. With the story of Donald Crowhurst we have such a story but, alas, one that is true. The crisis and the breakdown occurred on the high seas, but the steps which led to it in the first place and the remorseless way in which he became more firmly caught in the trap are clearly discernible, and the parallels with ordinary life are not hard to find. Individuals will make their own interpretations, but one powerful message that comes through from this story is the need to provide those in distress with the opportunity to express their real feelings when all around them the barriers are going up and the avenues of escape are closing.'[8]

There is something Shakespearean in the way Crowhurst unwittingly orchestrated his own downfall, not due to any great act of evil but through a simple inability to admit he was not up to the task. The 'intensification' Bennet alludes to was created by the backdrop of the unrelenting and unforgiving sea, which magnified Crowhurst's every mistake and questioned his every move. Unlike Shakespeare's characters, however, Crowhurst never learned from his errors, and to the last was unable to swallow his pride and ask for help.

Crowhurst's exploits have touched people in a way few sailing stories have before or since – his life has inspired novels, poems, plays, art installations and even an opera. Films have been made about him, and the remains of the *Teignmouth Electron*, lying abandoned on a beach in Cayman Brac, is still a place of pilgrimage for many fascinated by the Crowhurst saga.

For, despite his brilliant brain, once at sea Crowhurst was an everyman. Unlike Slocum, he didn't have a lifetime's experience of sailing, and before setting off on the Golden Globe was little more than a 'weekend sailor'. Whereas Slocum knew the ways of the sea intimately and was able to use it to achieve some kind of redemption, Crowhurst pitted himself against it and was defeated by it. And it's this humbling of a vain but essentially good man by an all-powerful element that makes his story so poignant.

* * *

While Crowhurst was battling with his demons in the southern Atlantic, the three other remaining competitors in the race (five others having dropped out before even making it out of the Atlantic) were ploughing their lonely furrows through the Southern Ocean. The doughty former Merchant Navy officer Robin Knox-Johnston was an unlikely leader, sailing one of the slowest, simplest and most dependable boats in the race. Not far behind and sailing much faster than the Englishman was the highly experienced French sailor Bernard Moitessier on his steel ketch *Joshua*. Bringing up the rear on his plywood trimaran was Nigel Tetley, who, having made a late start, was unlikely to be the first man home but was still hoping to be the fastest.

187

Moitessier had already sailed these waters three years before with his wife, when they sailed 14,200 miles from Tahiti to Spain and set a record for the longest distance sailed non-stop by a yacht (only to be beaten the following year by Chichester). The voyage, and the book he wrote about it, had turned him into a celebrity in France. This time round, he had lightened the boat, and *Joshua* was sailing 20–40 miles a day faster than she had done three years earlier. Moitessier felt in deep harmony with his boat and the ocean. He was practising yoga on deck, talking to his 'eldest brother' (a spiritual presence he also referred to as 'something very imminent in the air') and reaching 'a kind of indefinable state of grace'.[9] Whereas most singlehanded sailors expect to lose weight during a long voyage, Moitessier actually put on a few pounds during his months in the dreaded Southern Ocean, a sure sign of a man content in his element.

In due course he rounded Cape Horn three weeks behind Knox-Johnston, but if he kept up his current average speed of 120 miles per day – 21 miles per day faster than his rival – he stood a good chance of overtaking him before they reached England. The French were already planning a massive welcome party, and he would almost certainly be awarded the Légion d'Honneur. His place in history, not to mention a healthy bank balance, was assured.

But then Moitessier had a moment of clarity – or a moment of madness, depending who you believe. Rather than going back to the 'snake pit' and facing the media frenzy with all its 'false gods', he would instead carry on sailing to the Pacific, crossing the tracks he had sailed five months earlier, effectively beginning a second circumnavigation. It sounded crazy, but as he wrote in his log: 'leaving Plymouth and returning to Plymouth now seems like leaving from nowhere to go nowhere'.[10] He explained his thinking in a letter to the *Sunday Times* (thrown in a film canister onto the deck of a passing ship using a sling shot, since he had refused to have a radio fitted):

> 'My intention is to continue the voyage, still nonstop, towards the Pacific Islands, where there is plenty of sun and more peace than in Europe. Please do not think I am trying to break a record. "Record" is a very stupid word at sea. I am continuing nonstop because I am happy at sea, and perhaps because I want to save my soul.'[11]

His decision astonished the media and even those closest to him. Under the headline 'Wife's plea to yachtsman', *The Times* carried an article in which his wife Françoise expressed her fears that all that time at sea 'may have temporarily unbalanced him'.[12] Others questioned whether he was of sound mind, and wondered if he had 'seen things' – he was after all sailing the same waters that Slocum had been in when he was visited by his pilot of the *Pinta*. And, as everyone knows, strange things happen to people when they have been at sea for too long.

Three months later, when he finally dropped anchor in Tahiti after 10 months at sea, sailing non-stop, Moitessier got to give his side of the story, telling a reporter:

> 'You have to understand that when [some]one is months and months alone, he evolves; some say people go nuts. I went crazy in my own fashion. For four months all I saw were the stars. I didn't hear an unnatural sound. A purity grows out of that kind of solitude. I said to myself: "What the hell am I going to do in Europe?" I told myself I'd be crazy to go on to France.'[13]

It was a classic 'Laingian' moment, and absolutely of its time. RD Laing was a controversial British psychiatrist who argued that mental illness (and specifically schizophrenia) was a relative term and that sanity was simply measured by how closely people conformed to a mutually agreed set of norms. In his book *The Divided Self* (1960), he wrote that sanity was tested by the 'degree of conjunction or disjunction' between two people, where it is assumed that one person is sane and the other not, eg in a patient and doctor scenario. There is no definitive measure of insanity, he suggested, only a 'lack of congruity' or a 'clash' between the 'sane' and the 'insane'[14]

By common consent, the yachting establishment waiting to celebrate Moitessier's return considered itself the 'sane' party in this particular scenario. But of course Moitessier didn't see it that way. The insight he had gained after sailing for months at sea – just him, his boat and the ocean – was akin to that experienced by the Indian mystics who disappear to the mountains to meditate for months on end. And indeed, Moitessier had spent most of his childhood in Asia and was familiar with eastern philosophy. He rejected the materialism of the 'snake pit' not merely on personal grounds but on profound philosophical and ideological ones. The disjunction between the two sides could hardly have been greater, though which was 'sane' and which was 'psychotic' was a matter of opinion.

With the benefit of hindsight, it's clear that Moitessier did the right thing. By sailing on to Tahiti, he kept his integrity intact and yet still carved himself a place in history – but on his own terms. The book he wrote about his voyage in 1973, *The Long Way*, became a best-seller and is now regarded as a classic of sailing literature.

The consequences of such an extended period of isolation had far-reaching effects on at least one other of the Golden Globe competitors, too. After his yacht broke up just 1,100 miles from home, Nigel Tetley was awarded a £1,000 consolation prize by the *Sunday Times*, which he put towards building a new 60ft trimaran. His plan was to sail around the world again and set a new record, but he was unable to find a sponsor to back him. Devastated, on 5 February 1971, less than two years after his yacht sank in the Golden Globe Race, Tetley took a rope and hanged himself from a tree in woods near Dover.

Derek Kelsall, the designer and builder of Tetley's new yacht, was the last person to see him alive. 'Apart from his wife Eve, I probably knew Nigel better than anyone else at the time of his suicide,' he said. 'That is not to say I knew him well. Perhaps no one did. I don't believe there ever was a reasonable explanation of the suicide. There were a few stories, as there is with most boat people.'[15]

Robin Knox-Johnston was thus the only one of the nine competitors to survive the rigours of the ocean and to complete the circumnavigation, arriving back in Falmouth 312 days after he set off. In an effort to understand what makes a singlehanded sailor tick, his sponsor, the *Sunday Mirror*, got a psychiatrist to examine the former Merchant Navy officer before and after the voyage. The diagnosis on both occasions was the same: 'distressingly normal'.[16]

Knox-Johnston 'heard voices' just once on his voyage. It happened while he was reconnecting the ship's battery and he heard the sound of people talking in the main cabin. Although he described himself as 'not a superstitious person', his first reaction was to wonder if it were a 'supernatural occurrence'.[17] In fact, it turned out to be a cassette player that had switched itself back on when he reconnected the battery. He wrote in his log:

'On thinking over the incident later, I felt that my reactions had been perfectly normal, in fact I drew quite a bit of comfort from the fact that the sound unnerved me, not because there were voices, but because there were voices when I knew there couldn't be any. […] I thus convinced myself of my own sanity, or, more correctly, I reassured myself that I am still as sane as I ever was. There is a subtle difference. So far, therefore, no visions or voices.'[18]

It's an important observation. Unlike those OSTAR skippers who saw elephants floating in the middle of an ocean and imagined their families visiting them, *and didn't think there was anything unusual about that*, Knox-Johnston had enough clarity to realise he *shouldn't* be hearing things when there actually were voices talking.

It was typical of the unflappable Brit that, while the other competitors were struggling to keep a grip on their sanity, his only pseudo-hallucination turned out to be a very real and very sane radio-cassette player.

CHAPTER 17

TAXI DRIVER

The success of the Golden Globe Race and the huge publicity given to its competitors led to an explosion of interest in singlehanded sailing. It didn't seem to matter that only one of the nine competitors actually managed to complete the course, or that two of the others died – both of suspected mental breakdowns – during the race or soon after. Singlehanded sailing was suddenly 'sexy', not least because of the extreme mental demands it placed on competitors. By 1982, the first regular round-the-world race for singlehanded sailors had been created. The BOC Challenge was to be raced every four years and was made up of four legs, with 'pit stops' in between each leg to allow competitors to make repairs to their boats, bodies and brains. Despite this more benign approach, not all the skippers proved up the challenge.

Yuko Tada was a taxi driver from Tokyo who delighted the participants in the first BOC Challenge of 1982–1983 with his good humour and generosity. He was always the life and soul of the party, and his saxophone playing was one of the highlights of the race. During the Rio de Janeiro stopover, he also held an impromptu exhibition of his paintings on the dock in an attempt to raise much-needed funds for his campaign. It was so impromptu, the paint on the pictures was still wet!

One seemingly minor incident in this race, however, gave a hint of the events that would follow. It happened after Tada was awoken from a deep sleep in a hotel in Cape Town, just before the fleet headed south to join the Southern Ocean 'sleigh ride'. According to journalists George Day and Herb McCormick, who wrote a book about the race:

'Tada, still unconscious, could feel the boat breaking up, the water seeping through the hull. He was sinking, and he was not singing a sutra. He awoke screaming in Japanese. He tore at the wall and at the baseboard radiator. He needed to get out of the boat and save himself. Then he realized he was not at sea at all, but in a small room in a high-rise building. Deflated, he slumped against the mauled wall with his face in his hands, weeping. Tada had taken his first look at the southern ocean.'[1]

You don't need to have read Freud to interpret the unconscious and conscious fears expressed in this dream – of confined spaces, of sinking, of being overwhelmed by the sea. Yet, despite this apparent warning, Tada carried on with the race and not only survived the Southern Ocean but finished first overall in his class by nearly two days.

Tada came back in 1990, this time with a lighter, more modern boat he had designed himself. However, *Koden VIII* was a failure and finished second to last in the first and second leg of the race. The second leg, from Cape Town to Sydney, was a particularly gruelling one, and the yacht was repeatedly knocked down. The journey took him 51 days, compared with 30 days for the class winner. Apparently devastated by this loss of face, Tada withdrew from the race and, a few days later, committed suicide. This time, the Southern Ocean had proved too much.

CHAPTER 18

MIND GAMES

Modern telecommunication systems have transformed the life of the singlehanded sailor. Whereas the Golden Globe skippers were out of contact (either deliberately or due to equipment failure) for months on end, the modern singlehander is in touch with his or her support team, family and fans several times a day. When the Italian sailor Simone Bianchetti took part in the 2002–2003 Around Alone race (the new name for the BOC Challenge), he spoke by satellite phone to his wife Inbar Meytsar every two to three hours, day and night. So important was this connection that for the six months he was at sea she scheduled her life around his, sleeping when he slept, and being available to talk whenever he was awake.

That's not to say the experience is any less tough or gruelling – modern technology imposes other demands, such as providing the media with daily updates to keep the sponsors happy, which the early singlehanders never even dreamed of. Moreover, email and satellite phones are of no use when the spinnaker's wrapped around your forestay, or when your cockpit's full of water, or when you've tripped over the side of the boat.

Psychologically, however, there is a world of difference between not hearing from your loved ones for months and being able to say 'I love you' on a daily (or hourly) basis. There has been frequent speculation that if Crowhurst had been able to talk to his wife in those final days (as he attempted, repeatedly but unsuccessfully, to do), he would probably not have taken his own life.

'The experience of modern single-handed sailors can't compare to that of skippers 40-50 years ago,' says Dr Neil Weston, professor of sports psychology at Portsmouth University. 'The boats are so different and their time away is so different. Nowadays, skippers sail around the world in less than a third the time Robin Knox-Johnston took in 1968. But they are still sleep-deprived and exhausted, and they still have to cope with the same sea and the same weather conditions. And they have a lot of data to take in. Whereas Sir Robin hardly knew where the other competitors in the Golden Globe were, nowadays skippers receive six-hourly race updates.'[1]

Dr Weston interviewed five skippers in the 2006–2007 Velux 5 Oceans Race (the rebranded Around Alone/BOC Challenge) and worked closely with British sailor Dee Caffari while she was taking part in the 2008–2009 Vendée Globe non-stop round-the-world race. He concluded that social support via a modern telecommunication system – known in the jargon as the 'stress-buffering hypothesis' – is one of the most effective ways modern singlehanded sailors cope with mental stress (or 'strain', as he would have it).

'This strategy was employed to deal with the isolation and loneliness associated with the activity, concerns around technical problems or possible threats, frustration over poor progress and when struggling

197

to deal with difficult environmental conditions,' he wrote in the book *Coping and Emotion in Sport*. 'Indeed, given the physically isolated and dangerous nature of SEOS [Solo Endurance Ocean Sailing], one could argue that social support is of greater importance in this type of sport than in safer land-based sports where there are few periods of sustained isolation and generally no threat to a performer's life.'[2]

One of the first sailors to use this approach to great effect was Ellen MacArthur, during her first circumnavigation in the 2000–2001 Vendée Globe race. She was in daily contact with her shore manager Mark Turner via email and satellite phone and used him as a sounding board for her emotional ups and downs, as well as for technical support. In return, her shore team filtered 10 emails per day from the thousands they received from fans and forwarded them to Ellen to keep her spirits up.

And her shore team wasn't above playing mind games with her in order to keep her going. Halfway across the Southern Ocean, after more than 50 days at sea and being faced with contrary winds that pushed her further and further south into the dangerous ice zone, Ellen reached her emotional low point, as she later recalled:

'It was more than just physical exhaustion; it was causing more pain inside than I had ever felt before. I clenched my teeth and threw my head down against the hard, wet floor and wept. I cried like a baby till I was so numb with the cold that the pain was dulled. Shivering and weak, I crawled into the cabin and slept in my waterproofs, curled up in a ball in the footwell by the engine.'[3]

To snap her out of it, Mark Turner told her a story he knew would enrage her. After her victory in a previous race, a rival skipper – who just happened to be ahead of her at that very moment – spread a rumour that she had received outside assistance, something that is strictly banned and would cause her to be eliminated from the race. The rumour was a lie, but Ellen was so incensed by the very suggestion that she redoubled her efforts to catch the offending skipper. It might not be what the experts had in mind when they coined the phrase 'stress-buffering', but it certainly had the desired effect.

Ellen was also one of the first to take sleep training seriously, and famously only slept in 20-minute periods for the entire 94-day voyage. Sleep deprivation is still the greatest challenge faced by singlehanded sailors. Too much sleep and they can't make the continuous adjustments needed for the boat to sail to its full potential; too little sleep and they risk making mistakes through exhaustion and therefore again not sailing the boat to its full potential.

Some of the most bewildering consequences of sleep deprivation for singlehanded sailors are the mental pirouettes the mind can perform after going days, weeks and even months without enough rest, including hallucinations, which can take many forms. For eight-times circumnavigator Dominique Wavre, it was all about his compass. 'My electricity cut out, and I had these little green lights to light up the compass,' he said. 'It looked like the eyes of a cat. I was convinced it was rubbing against my legs and asking for food. The next morning, my sandwich was in crumbs on the cockpit floor, from trying to feed it to the cat. Another time, I found myself in a field of cows...'[4]

Even top singlehanded sailors such as Jean Le Cam have their moments of psychosis. King Jean, as he is known, famously went missing during the 2009 Vendée Globe and was eventually found safe and sound in the upturned hull of his boat, drifting off Cape Horn. He finished second in the previous edition of the race, but only after some mind-bending moments. 'I was so exhausted I couldn't sleep,' he said. 'I thought I saw my sister on board. I gave her a big hug, and when I woke up, I realised it was a sail.'[5]

During the 2006–2007 Velux 5 Oceans race, which he went on to win, Swiss sailor Bernard Stamm was convinced someone was out to get him. It turned out it was just his anorak. He also had some strange observations about the angle of the sea. 'Sometimes it looks as if the sea is on a slope,' he said. 'It really feels like I'm going uphill, and that pisses me off because then I don't seem to be going so fast!'[6]

Short races are generally more dangerous than long races, when skippers can at least get into a regular rhythm. The legendary French singlehanded race the Solitaire du Figaro, for instance, in which 50 or more skippers compete in four legs of about 500 miles each, is famous for pushing sailors to the limit of endurance. Most of the skippers therefore receive training in sleep management before the event at a specialist centre in Port-La-Forêt in Britanny. Damien Davenne, one of the sleep coaches at the centre, explains the phenomenon:

'You can easily exit a dream when you wake up in the morning after a good night's sleep, but if you are forced to stay awake then dreams can become very intrusive. That's what's called a hallucination. It's a waking dream which turns into reality for someone who is sleep deprived. The distinction between reality and illusion becomes blurred. It all works fine if you sleep normally, because everything is set to protect the individual from their dreams. But if you prevent them sleeping, dreams – which are indispensable to life – take over everything, not just deep sleep but REM too.'[7]

Since its inception in 1970, the Figaro has provided a training ground for hundreds of aspiring solo sailors – as well as a rich source of material for sleep psychologists. Stories of hallucinations abound and have become part of the mythology of the race. For example, one sailor famously mistook his compass for a severed monkey's head trying to gobble him up, saying that the white compass lines became teeth, and the red compass light looked like blood.

Jeanne Grégoire, who has competed in the Figaro since 2002, has experienced several interesting apparitions. 'Once, I saw Cardinal Richelieu at the front of the boat, holding a crocodile in his arms,' she said. 'I knew it wasn't real, but I couldn't stop myself seeing it. Another time, I saw four old ladies in the cockpit. I couldn't let go the sheet. I couldn't do anything, except stare at these four old ladies having tea in my cockpit.'[8]

Likewise, Figaro sailor Véronique Loisel also had her pilot of the *Pinta* moment, but this time with another, more experienced competitor, as she later explained:

'One night I was explaining to Karen Lebovici how my boat worked. When I finished, I handed the helm over to her and went down below to have a nap. I was really quite cross when, a few seconds later, the pilot started beeping to show we were going off course. I thought to myself, "She's a bit daft that Karen; she might be famous, but if she can't steer a boat in calm weather then she can go to hell!" I was forced to come out again, and then I realised there was no-one at the helm.'[9]

While these experiences are amusing to read about, they can seriously affect the skippers' performances and, in extreme cases, endanger their lives. This was the case for one skipper who recalled seeing figures beckoning him into a harbour only to find, after he'd ignored them and anchored off instead, that there was nothing but rocks along that stretch of coast. Another skipper thought he had arrived in harbour and could even hear the cheer of the crowd. It was only after he tried to step ashore that he realised he was in mid-ocean. Only his harness saved him from leaving his boat and becoming another 'lost at sea' statistic.

✳   ✳   ✳

Fifty years after the original Golden Globe Race, a commemorative event was planned for 2018. The idea was to reintroduce the element of 'adventure' which the organisers (and Sir Robin Knox-Johnston himself) felt had vanished from the mainstream singlehanded round-the-world races. Only traditional boats 32–36ft long and designed before 1988 were allowed to enter, and competitors were not allowed to use any electronic devices, such as GPS, plotters, weatherfax or even autopilots (though a GPS in a sealed box was carried on each boat in case of emergency). Whereas the top modern singlehanders could expect to 'loop the loop' in less than 80 days, the organisers of the 2018 Golden Globe didn't expect anyone home sooner than 300 days after the start.

Susie Goodall was one of only two female skippers to enter the race. Although the 29-year-old British sailor had skippered yachts as far afield as Spitsbergen, Greenland and Iceland, she had never tackled a long-distance singlehanded passage until her qualifying voyage for the Golden Globe – a 7,500-mile round trip from Plymouth to Antigua and back – in February 2017. After an unexpectedly easy passage across the Bay of Biscay, things got interesting once she rounded Cape Finisterre, at the northeastern tip of Spain.

'Coming down the coast of Portugal I had a solid Force 6 gusting up to 8, and had my first real taste of serious sleep deprivation. I didn't sleep for two days because there was so much shipping around, and I had to hand steer because the self-steering had broken. I was just exhausted. I was approaching Lisbon at about midnight when this man appeared in front of me, and another sat next to me and took the helm. They were both wearing red coats, one had brown hair and the other blond hair. I didn't recognize either of them, but they looked Danish, or Scandinavian. The one at the helm said, "Don't worry, it's ok, we're here." It must have only been 10 seconds and, I thought oh my god, someone's on my boat, and started to freak out. I decided to make myself some coffee and try to stay awake. Then they just disappeared. It was so real, I didn't know what to make of it.'[10]

It was another classic Pilot of the *Pinta* hallucination, in which an exhausted sailor desperate for respite dreams up their own relief crew to take a watch while they have a snooze. In most cases, the outcome is positive – the sailor gets some rest, the boat stays on course, disaster is averted – though of course the sailors who get the 'rogue' pilot who steers their boat onto a reef may simply no longer be here to tell the tale. The main surprise for Susie was that it happened so soon – within her first ten days of sailing solo.

'I know hallucinations happen to a lot of solo sailors, but I wasn't expecting it so early,' she said. 'I think I'm going to have to embrace it, because they were clearly there to look after me!'[11]

On the vexed question of whether female sailors are a match for their male counterparts, Susie was clear that on a long-distance race such as the Golden Globe, it's all in the mind.

'I don't think it's an advantage or disadvantage being a woman,' she said. 'Yes, men are naturally stronger and it takes more physical training for me to reach the same physical strength, but at the end of the day a race like this is going to be a mental challenge. I can be just as strong as all the guys in the race, but if I'm not mentally fit then I won't stand a chance. That's the beauty of it: it's an even playing field, and when we're out on the water, we're all equal – we're all just sailors.'[12]

CHAPTER 19

DIVING DEEP

On 29 April 1993, Bill Vincent did something extraordinary. The 47-year-old carpenter from Bath calmly adjusted the spinnaker of the yacht he was sailing on, stepped up onto the guardrail at the back of boat, and dived into the sea. 'He did not jump, nor did he fall. The dive appeared to be a premeditated act,' said Adrian Rayson, who was steering the vessel at the time, at a subsequent inquiry. 'It was a perfectly executed dive.'[1]

Once in the water, Vincent started swimming away from the yacht. According to Rayson, he looked back once, but made no attempt to swim back or attract the crew's attention. He seemed to have absolutely no intention of being saved.

Vincent was taking part in the British Steel Challenge, a 28,000-mile yacht race in which 10 crews made up of a professional skipper and 13 amateurs raced 10 identical yachts around the world the 'wrong way' – ie against the prevailing winds and currents. The *Daily Mail* dubbed the race the 'Mid-life Crisis Challenge',[2] and some said it was foolish to send novices on such a dangerous route. But organiser Chay Blyth pressed ahead regardless, calling the event (which cost £14,850 per head) 'the toughest yacht race ever – an extraordinary adventure for ordinary people'.[3] Like many others, Vincent had seen a story about the race on the 10 o'clock news, and had immediately driven to London to sign up for it, despite never having sailed before.

Vincent was something of an oddball among the solicitors, teachers, doctors, insurance brokers, company directors and other professionals who made up the majority of the crews. A former member of a robbery gang, he had spent most of his youth in borstals and had been in and out of prison to pay for his crimes, until he met his wife Pauline. She had apparently turned his life around, and after he was released from prison, Vincent had been employed as an odd-job man at Bristol University, and the couple had got married and had two children. When he announced he was going to take part in the British Steel Challenge, his family was supportive, his wife taking a second job to help pay the entry fee, and his children donating part of their newspaper-round earnings.

And it certainly was the experience of a lifetime. Despite snagging on a buoy at the start of the race, *Heath Insured* flew down the Atlantic and, thanks to some unconventional routing, ended up in third place at the end of the first leg. Despite all his worldly possessions (including his clothes) being stolen during the stopover in Rio, Vincent seemed to enjoy himself and made many friends – including none other than the famous Great Train Robbery crook Ronnie Biggs, who came to Vincent's rescue after he had been robbed. On board *Heath Insured*, Vincent was a well-liked member of the crew, and became the unofficial ship's barber.

Heath Insured didn't fare so well on the next two legs of the race, however, finishing in sixth place on both occasions, but at least they managed to avoid dismasting, mutiny and major injury – all of which took place on some of the other boats. And, besides, there was plenty to enjoy apart from the racing. As they headed off from Hobart, on the third leg of the race, Rayson wrote: 'Nature has put on a glorious display tonight. The sky is alive with Southern lights with vast curtains of pastel-coloured hues adorning the heavens. Elsewhere, strong beams of blue pierce the sky. A trip to the Planetarium in London will never be the same again!'[4]

As they set off from Cape Town on the final leg of the race, up the Atlantic and home to England, most of the crew were in ebullient mood – except for Vincent, who had become strangely silent and withdrawn. 'Since leaving Cape Town, Bill Vincent had seemed prepossessed with a personal problem and appeared listless and depressed,'[5] Rayson later told the Department of Transport inquiry – though he didn't speculate about what might have been on his mind.

Even so, the events of 29 April caught everyone by surprise. Samantha Brewster, another crewmate, was sitting in the cockpit when she saw Vincent out of the corner of her eye as he made his dive. 'I turned round to look at him,' she said. 'He had his left foot on top of the pushpit and was stepping up. I yelled "Bill!" At the same time he dived over the stern and swam away.'[6]

The yacht's skipper, Adrian Donovan, heard her scream and rushed on deck. Within seconds, an emergency buoy had been thrown overboard to mark the spot where Vincent had jumped, but even though the crew tried to maintain visual contact with the buoy and Vincent, both were soon lost behind in the Atlantic swell. The crew quickly lowered the spinnaker (used only for downwind sailing) and headed back to the Man Overboard position given on their GPS. Two crew were hoisted up the mast and four other lookouts were posted at strategic positions on the boat, but despite having the exact coordinates of Vincent's last known position, there was no sign of him. By then, daylight was fading, but they carried on searching with torches throughout the night.

The next morning, 18 hours after Vincent had jumped overboard, the search was called off and *Heath Insured* continued on its way, arriving back in Southampton four weeks later. His body was never found.

What kind of mental turmoil prompted Vincent to do something so extreme? Was he profoundly depressed, as Rayson seems to imply, or was it a momentary aberration – a moment of madness? Yachting journalist Barry Pickthall, who covered the race, has his own theory. 'My feeling, and it is shared by some of his *Heath Insured* crewmates, was that Bill could not face going back to the humdrum of suburban life, and decided quite deliberately to end it all – at the height of the party.'[7] Or, to put it another way, he couldn't face settling for the Planetarium after seeing the stars in the southern sky.

It's a tragic but romantic notion, this idea of a man so in thrall with the sea that he would sacrifice everything not to leave it. It's Moitessier all over again, except that the famous French sailor had the good sense (and means) to sail on to Tahiti to avoid returning to the 'snake pit' and thereby reached his own nirvana. Stuck on someone else's boat with 13 other people, Vincent didn't have that option, and was bound to return to the 'snake pit' as the race came inexorably to an end. His only options were to accept being bound to that wheel, or to jump off it and escape. Tragically for the family and crew who were left to pick up the pieces, he chose to jump.

CHAPTER 20

CABIN FEVER

Nowhere to run, nowhere to hide. The same factors that make the Royal Navy less susceptible to mental illness in wartime (according to the official statistics) can make or break crews sailing in peacetime. Cooped up together with less personal space than prisoners in a cell, crews have to find ways to work together or risk endangering life and limb. For, once at sea, there is no escape from the physical constraints of the vessel, and failure to operate it successfully can mean going off course, losing a race or even being shipwrecked.

It's often been noted that the 'social density' of yachts is absurdly high, with six to eight people sharing a floor space of around 10–20m² (30–60ft²). That equates to about 2–3m² (6–10ft²) per person – or half the 4m² (13ft²) minimum specified by the EU for prisoners living in a multi-occupancy cell. Stuck in such a small space for days or weeks on end, often with virtual strangers, the chance that you'll invade other people's personal space is high. In stormy weather, when no one's had enough sleep and people are being thrown about the cramped living quarters, either dragging off wet clothing or putting slightly less wet clothing back on, it's easy for even the most mild-mannered person to feel claustrophobic and irritable.

Yachts, like prisons, are what sociologists describe as 'total institutions', where the lives of the crew are completely bound up with running the ship. There is minimal separation of personal and work roles, and even sleep is carried out within the confines of the common project. It's a self-contained world that operates regardless of almost any outside forces – apart from the weather. Given this extremely contained situation, crew structures on board ships and yachts have long been an area of fascination for anyone studying group dynamics and leadership issues.

In 2000, seven years after Bill Vincent had performed his extraordinary dive off the stern of *Heath Insured*, the BT Global Challenge (as the British Steel Challenge was by then called) became the subject of two academic studies in team management. In what was perhaps a sign of the times, both were concerned with how the leadership qualities of the 12 skippers – and in particular their emotional intelligence – affected the outcome of the race and how that could be applied to a business environment.

'Because the yachts were identical, the race provided a near-perfect setting for demonstrating the impact of people on performance,' the editors of *People Management* magazine commented. 'The gap between winning and losing was largely down to leadership and teamwork resulting in skilful navigation.'[1]

According to one study, the yachts' skippers, who were selected and paid for by the race organisers, were all 'highly emotionally intelligent'[2] – and indeed the more emotionally intelligent they were, the more successful they were in the race. This conclusion ties in with other studies that suggest that emotional intelligence is twice as important as IQ and technical skills in achieving success in a business environment.

On the other hand, skippers who held their distance from the rest of the crew (eg eating some meals separately) were generally more successful than those who 'were motivated by a need for close friendly relationships with others and for being popular'[3] (ie too needy). Showing vulnerability was seen as a positive trait, it seems, but not if it went too far.

The report also claimed that the yacht crews were generally less emotionally intelligent than the skippers, although they scored higher in interpersonal skills and conscientiousness. The most successful crew tended to have high IQs and be highly driven, rather than being emotionally intelligent. Given that the crew members had each paid £25,000 to take part in the race, however, they were effectively self-selecting and were likely to come from high-achieving and self-motivated backgrounds.

The skipper's mood, the report said, accounted for at least 50 per cent of the crew's mood. In other words, a grumpy skipper creates an unhappy crew.

As the race progressed, the intuitiveness of the more successful skippers and crews increased, while the emotional intelligence of the crews at the back of the fleet actually decreased. 'The atmosphere on the losing boats would very likely have been declining,' the report speculated, 'and the crew may have found they were getting on each other's nerves.'[4] As well they might, packed together at 17 people per 72ft boat (excluding the skipper), for 30,000 miles…

More instructively, one of the skippers is quoted as saying: 'When things were going well, then they acted as a team. When things did not go so well they acted as individuals.'[5]

The authors of the report included a helpful diagram that correlated leaderships skills with various parts of a yacht. Thus, emotional intelligence, self-belief, integrity, self-control and a sense of purpose were the vessel's ballast, essential for providing stability. Management skills were its mainsail, providing forward drive. Various leadership attributes, such as shared belief, were the foresails, providing extra thrust and with the ability to be changed to suit the prevailing conditions. Technical knowledge and leadership style were the vessel's helm, determining the direction of travel.

The key to preventing crew dissatisfaction, according to another study[6] conducted in the 1980s, was:

- a clear chain of command
- clear communication systems
- plenty of social interaction
- a co-operative attitude to problem solving
- awareness of each other's personal space
- the creation of private areas

✳   ✳   ✳

To find out what happens when these golden rules are ignored, you don't have to look any further than the yacht *Apollonia* and what is probably the most notorious case of dysfunctional crew dynamics in the annals of modern yachting.

Herbert Klein was a shipping agent from a town near Düsseldorf in Germany. A confident, carefree person, by the time he was in his mid-30s, Klein had saved enough to chuck in his desk job and set off on an adventure. He bought a 54ft wooden yacht called *Apollonia* and, together with his girlfriend Gabriele Humpert, decided to head to the

Caribbean to start a charter business. The trouble was, neither of them knew enough about sailing to sail the boat across the Atlantic on their own, so they were obliged to employ a skipper and crew to help them. By the time they reached the Canaries in summer 1981, their first crew had deserted them, and Klein was on the lookout for a new crew.

It so happened that Paul Termann and his girlfriend Dorothea Permin were on the quayside at Gran Canaria looking for a ride. Termann was a former electrician from East Germany who had escaped to the West in 1957 and had served in the German army as helicopter pilot. Back in civilian life, he became a train driver, first on long-distance trains and then on the Hamburg underground. As his professional horizons diminished, he became increasingly obsessed with sailing and took several evening classes in navigation and seamanship, though he never made any long voyages. By 1980 he too was ready for an adventure, and he and Permin accordingly signed up for a round-the-world voyage on a yacht as paying crew, setting off from Germany in spring 1981. They only got as far as the Canaries, however, before the owner ran out of money and chucked them off the boat without refunding their fares.

It would be hard to imagine two more different people than Termann and Klein: one brought up under the regimented strictures of communist East Germany, the other a lucky beneficiary of the West German 'economic miracle'. Yet, when they met on the quayside at a marina in Las Palmas, they quickly realised they might be of use to each other. So it was that, without checking their professional or personal backgrounds, Klein agreed to take Termann on as navigator and Permin as crew for the crossing to the Caribbean. He showed similar lack of judgement (or was he just over-optimistic?) when he recruited the last two members of the crew, Michael Wunsch and Dieter Giesen, through a newspaper advertisement back in Germany: one had no sailing experience whatsoever, and the other had only ever sailed on small boats on Lake Constance.

And so, in November 1981, *Apollonia* and her inexpert crew set off from the Canaries for a 3,000-mile journey across the Atlantic. It wasn't the first time a skipper had picked up an inexperienced crew on the quayside or from a newspaper ad – it's the kind of thing that happens on boats all the time and no doubt always will – but, as the voyage went on, it became clear there was a serious clash of personalities between the fun-loving Klein and the dour, serious-minded Termann. This wouldn't have mattered a jot had they been in a different situation, but stuck on board a small yacht, making a potentially hazardous ocean crossing, the pressure soon built up. The crux of the problem was that, despite having less experience, Klein was in a position of power as the owner and official skipper of the yacht, while Termann, who was far more knowledgeable, had to bow to Klein's decisions. Their different temperaments only aggravated this imbalance: Klein was out to have fun, while Termann was all too aware of the possible dangers and determined to tell everyone how things should be done.

The crew of the *Apollonia* soon split into two groups, with Klein and his girlfriend and the two new recruits on one side, and Termann and his girlfriend on the other. And there were countless opportunities for disagreement. For instance, Klein and his gang dived off the bow of the boat and pulled themselves back on board by means of a line streamed out from the stern; Termann said this was dangerous, and was then accused of being a coward. Termann found an improperly tied knot and delivered a sermon on boat safety; Klein and friends mocked him for being too pedantic and deliberately used knots where he asked them not to. Termann played Elvis; Klein and his crew played reggae. Halfway across the Atlantic, Klein's group celebrated with a bottle of champagne; Termann and Permin weren't invited to join them.

In many ways, the situation on board *Apollonia* perfectly reflected the two men's status in the world at large: the happy-go-lucky Klein was buoyed by a big circle of friends, while the more literal-minded Termann was marginalised and unpopular. Termann was no doubt fully aware of this disparity, and this continuing sense of failure can't have helped his state of mind. All the while, Klein continued to mock and humiliate him in front of the others, stoking the simmering rage.

The final straw was, as it so often is, a trivial matter. On the morning of 13 December, at the start of the 08.00 watch, Permin made breakfast for Termann and herself, without washing up the previous night's dishes. Klein told her off, and Termann intervened on her behalf. The slow build-up of anger from the previous 14 days finally exploded into all-out fury. Termann pulled out a gun and told the others he was taking over command of the yacht. 'You have only ten minutes left to live,'[6] he told Klein.

First, though, he made Klein sign some papers – either a bond for 25,000 Deutchmarks or a much-needed recommendation to help him get work in the future, it's not entirely clear which. Late in the afternoon, he then ordered the others to go on the foredeck and change the jib – which Klein took as a sign he was planning to kill them and sail short-handed. After helping to change the sail, Klein went down below and struck Termann over the head with a pump handle. Bloodied but still conscious, Termann grabbed the gun and fired wildly, first injuring Wunsch, one of the newspaper-ad crew, and then killing Klein's girlfriend. Klein tried to hide, but Termann and Permin hunted him down and shot him dead. They then threw both bodies over the side.

Four days later, *Apollonia* moored up in Bridgetown, Barbados, having completed her Atlantic crossing in a relatively speedy 18 days. Somehow, Termann's story about Klein and his girlfriend falling over the side in a storm was taken at face value by the authorities, despite clear evidence there had been no storm in that part of the Atlantic at that time. It wasn't until all four surviving crew were safely back in Germany that Wunsch and Giesen finally told the police what had really happened. At Termann's trial, provocation was given as his main defence – a kind of ocean-borne *crime passionnel* – but the court concluded he was not mentally ill and knew what he was doing when he committed the murders, thereby ruling out a sentence of manslaughter on the grounds of diminished responsibility. Instead, Termann received a double life sentence for the murders of Klein and Humpert, and 15 years for the attempted murder of Wunsch. His girlfriend Permin received three years for being an accessory to murder.

Despite the verdict, it's hard to imagine that Termann wasn't in some way mentally unbalanced when he committed the murders. He had a history of low self-esteem and possible depression that can be traced right back to his time in the armed forces, when his final report made reference to mood swings and an inability to cope with stress. It's the kind of low-level mental illness that in normal life might be cured by a course of Prozac or other antidepressant – not the sort of thing you would ever imagine leading to a double murder. As we have already seen, though, within the confines of a small yacht or ship, emotions tend to become magnified and distorted – not just

216

because of claustrophobia and lack of private space, but because of the nature of sailing.

Because, just as sailing increases our sense of being alive, it also heightens our mistakes. Small errors can make a big difference when sailing a boat across 3,000 miles of ocean – be it dropping a winch handle over the side, which means you have to 'sweat' the lines by hand, or steering slightly the wrong course, which can send you onto the rocks. It's a life-affirming but also stress-inducing environment not suited to those of a nervous disposition.

Would Termann and Klein have fallen out during a long road trip, or on a mountaineering expedition? Probably, but they would have always had the option to just walk away. Just having that option – which is simply not available sailing a boat across the Atlantic, apart from on a liferaft – would act as a release valve and bring a certain amount of perspective.

✳   ✳   ✳

There was severe disagreement among the crew of *Grimalkin* as they discussed whether or not to abandon ship on 14 August 1979. The yacht was one of 303 competitors in the legendary Fastnet Race, racing the 600 miles from Cowes, on the Isle of Wight, to the southern tip of Ireland and back. That year, a sudden and particularly vicious storm hit the fleet as they crossed the Irish Sea during the third day of the race. Many of the yachts, designed more for speed than to withstand heavy weather, were unable to cope with the extreme conditions, and soon Royal Navy helicopters were scouring the area trying to identify boats and rescue survivors. By the time it was all over, five boats had sunk, 15 crew had died, and 136 sailors had been rescued. It was the largest peacetime air-sea rescue operation ever mounted.

That morning, *Grimalkin*'s crew was in the thick of the storm, with force 12 winds and waves measuring 18–21m (60–70ft) relentlessly pounding their boat. They had taken down all their sails and were running before the wind under a bare mast, with ropes streamed from the back of the boat to slow her down. The six men were in survival mode, just trying to cope with the elements, completely oblivious to the direction in which they were heading or what might lie ahead of them. Yet, despite their best efforts, even with two of crew at the helm, the yacht was repeatedly knocked down – effectively a 90-degree capsize. Attached to the boat by their harnesses, the crew were tossed in and out of the cockpit like puppets, sometimes landing in the sea and being dragged along the side of the boat, sometimes landing on top of each other in the cockpit.

Below decks, the cabin was awash with water and all their belongings and equipment were being tossed around as if in a washing machine. The yacht's skipper, David Sheahan, had sent out a MAYDAY on the yacht's radio but had been cracked on the head by a tin of food when the boat was knocked down, and was suffering from concussion. A second member of the crew, Gerry Winks, was suffering from exposure and was barely conscious, while a third, Nick Ward, had a serious leg injury.

So it was the other three members of the crew, Dave, Mike and David's 17-year-old son Matt, who decided enough was enough. They would have to launch the lifeboat and abandon ship. It was a contentious decision because boarding a lifeboat in a storm is no guarantee of safety and is generally regarded as the very last resort, only to be undertaken when all efforts to save the mother ship have failed. The rule of thumb is never to step down into a lifeboat; only step up – in other words, the yacht should actually be sinking before you step off it. If a yacht is floating higher than the lifeboat, then it's generally regarded as a safer bet. Indeed, of the 24 yachts abandoned during the 1979 Fastnet, only five actually sank, while the others were all later recovered – including a yacht abandoned by three crew who died after their liferaft capsized and fell apart in the storm.

David and Gerry were too comatose to have a say in the matter of whether to abandon ship, and only Nick argued against doing so. In the end, the discussion was brought to an abrupt end as another enormous wave knocked the boat over again – this time into a full 180-degree capsize. All six men were trapped underwater, unable to breathe, for several minutes. Matt and Dave managed to wriggle free and surfaced next to the overturned boat. Mike freed both himself and David by cutting their harness straps with a knife.

When the boat eventually righted herself, Nick and Gerry were both slumped in the cockpit, apparently dead. A few feet away from the boat, face down in the water, was a body floating away. It was Matt's father, David Sheahan. With the wind still howling and enormous waves crashing over the boat, there was nothing Matt or anyone else could do to save him.

By now, Mike and Dave had launched the lifeboat and were urging Matt to get on board. With his beloved boat low in the water, his father lost over the side, and two crew in the cockpit seemingly dead, there was little reason for him to stay. He stepped down into the liferaft, into a different kind of hell, as the three men were spun round by the waves until a Royal Navy helicopter eventually picked them up.

But the men they left behind weren't dead, and the ordeal for one of them had only just begun. By the time Nick Ward regained consciousness, he had been thrown back in the water and was being towed by his harness, his head banging repeatedly against the side of the boat. When his calls for help went unanswered, he dragged himself back onto *Grimalkin*, only to find the boat deserted and the lifeboat gone. It was a devastating moment for the 23-year-old, as he tried to work out what had happened and where his crewmates could possibly be.

After a few minutes he realised he wasn't alone; another member of the crew, Gerry Winks, was floating by the side of the boat, still attached by his harness, right next to where Nick had been a few minutes before. Using the violent rolling of the boat to help him, he managed to winch the man back on board and perform mouth-to-mouth resuscitation. But it was to no avail, and after a few minutes, Gerry died.

Left alone to fend for himself, with the storm still raging and the boat gradually getting lower and lower in the water, it would have been easy for Nick to collapse under the strain. He did not, though, and what is remarkable about Nick's account of his ordeal is how he held it together, despite the worsening situation on the boat and his own deteriorating physical condition. He had many irrational moments during the subsequent 12 hours – not least talking continually to Gerry, as if he were still alive – but he also had an overwhelming urge to survive. Later, when asked how he found the mental strength to carry on, he would say it came from his experience as a child, when he had a brain haemorrhage and was partially paralysed. Through sheer determination, he had managed to retrain his brain to operate the muscles on the left side of his body, and over the course of several months, he had regained the use of his limbs (although he was left with lifelong epilepsy). He used similar methods to survive on *Grimalkin*, he said.

Nick's trauma would come later. It started in the hospital bed, when he was told that his crewmates had been picked up from the liferaft just an hour or so after they had left the boat. He later wrote:

'As the information filtered into my brain, I felt more alone than I had done at any time on *Grimalkin* with Gerry. I began to tremble. Although Pa continued talking, I tuned out – his words now indistinct as the realisation dawned on me. At the time my three crewmates had been rescued – 09.30 – Gerry was still alive. I was overcome with nausea. I felt emotionally sick. I told my family that was enough, please, no more.'[7]

The timing of Gerry's death is disputed by the other crew members, who insist the coroner's report indicates he was already dead by the time they boarded the liferaft – but, regardless of that, there can be no doubt that Nick was still alive at that time, and it's this sense of betrayal that haunts his narrative and, arguably, has haunted his life ever since.

He later described his feelings:

'For some time after Fastnet I experienced what would now be labelled as post-traumatic stress. The most common symptom was waking up in the middle of the night seeing images of Gerry and David. I also began experiencing more [epileptic] seizures, some of which were severe. Ma would knock on my door in the early morning to wake me for work and sometimes find me writhing, half asleep, in the middle of a fit. Most of all, no matter how hard I resisted, I could not help myself from being drawn back, in my sleep and in my waking, to Gerry.'[8]

Over the next few years, Nick made several attempts to come to terms with what happened on board *Grimalkin* that day – including, ultimately, writing a book about his experience. Strangely, though, neither he nor the other surviving members of the crew made any attempt to come together and talk through their experiences – apart from one meeting with Matt when the pair went to look at *Grimalkin*, which had been recovered and brought ashore in Waterford, in southern Ireland, damaged but essentially still sound.

Twenty-five years later, Nick revisited *Grimalkin*, by then fully restored and under new ownership, in Weymouth. While he was on board, he casually lifted the cover of the cockpit well, where the liferaft was usually stowed, and was shocked to see it was not there. The owner explained it had gone for a service, but Nick was immediately cast back to the last time he had found the liferaft missing:

'My heart missed a beat – and it all came flooding back: the noises, the braced knees, the effort to stay in one place long enough to breathe. All the moored yachts around me disappeared and I was back in the western approaches, back in the Irish Sea. I felt nausea, experienced a strange smell, almost an aura.'[9]

At the end of his narrative, Nick was at pains to say he felt no bitterness towards the rest of the crew and that he was at peace with what happened, yet his repeated returns to the circumstances of that fatal race and his constant circling around the question of why he was 'left for dead' suggest that, nearly 40 years on, he was still deeply troubled by it all. Perhaps some wounds are too deep to ever heal.

CHAPTER 21

THE SILENT KILLER

The sea is a very big, and uniquely lawless, place. Nearly 71 per cent of the earth's surface is covered by sea – that's 140 million square miles – or 37 times the size of the USA. Yet, despite its massive size, the only part of it that is owned by anyone is the 12-mile strip that runs around the shore of any coastal nation – and even then, foreign ships are allowed 'innocent passage' through these territorial waters. Countries can also claim commercial rights to the sea's resources for up to 200 miles from their coast, for the purposes of fishing, drilling for oil, etc, but they have no control over which ships cross these waters, or over what happens on board them.

Beyond that, it's the high seas. Terra nullius. The only laws that apply here are the rules enshrined in Part VII of the United Nations Convention on the Law of the Sea, which is mainly concerned with establishing free access to these areas: the freedom to navigate, to fish, to lay cables, to fly over, to carry out scientific research, and to make artificial islands. This liberty to navigate is enjoyed by increasing numbers of ships, as more and more cargo is carried around the world as a result of globalisation. It's estimated that 90 per cent of the world's trade is carried by ship, with the result that more than 100,000 cargo ships currently ply the ship's oceans, carrying produce and products to the developed world, and a great deal of unwanted waste the other way.

The rules governing the construction and management of ships are laid out by another arm of the UN, the International Maritime Organization (IMO), but it doesn't have the power to enforce these laws. That's left to member states, which in turn pass that power on to classification societies, such as Lloyd's Register in the UK, Det Norske Veritas (DNV) in Norway and the Registro Italiano Navale (RINA) in Italy. They in turn are funded by the shipowners, whose main concern is to keep those 100,000 ships running as cheaply as possible. If the conditions of one country are too onerous, the ship is simply re-registered in another country whose interpretation of the rules is more lenient.

Not only that, but many of the countries of registration aren't countries at all, but simply legal constructs that operate these so-called flags of convenience as a business. 'Liberia', for instance, is run by a company in Virginia, 'Honduras' is operated from New York, and 'Bahamas' is based in London. There are even ships registered in landlocked countries such as Bolivia, Moldova and Mongolia.

It's an anarchic, self-regulating scenario that is ripe for exploitation by unscrupulous shipowners whose own identity is often hidden behind deliberately inscrutable chains of offshore companies, and who are seemingly accountable to no one.

This is certainly madness of a kind, and it gives rise to another, more tragic kind of madness. With minimal regulation, the only thing that influences which of the 1.5 million seamen are chosen to operate these ships is who can do the job at the lowest price. As a result, Polish and Greek crews have gradually been replaced by ones from Asia, mainly from the Philippines, India, China and Indonesia. A third of all ships' crews now come from the Philippines, and they are not only cheap but do their jobs well and generally speak good English, the international language of the sea.

However, there's another more sinister reason Asian crew are so popular, and that is because they are deemed to be expendable. Seafaring is said to be the second most dangerous occupation in the world, after deep-sea fishing. Every year, 2,000 sailors are killed on cargo ships – from either falling over the side and being crushed against the dock, or being thrown against machinery, or simply being 'lost at sea' – yet hardly any of these deaths are ever reported in the western media. You can be sure if 2,000 European sailors were being killed every year, there would be uproar and pressure would pile up on shipowners to improve safety standards.

In addition to the loss of life, there are other hazards that just wouldn't be conceivable in other walks of life. In 2016 alone, pirates attacked 191 ships and took 151 crew hostage – a fact that went almost completely unnoticed in the mainstream media. Even at its peak in 2011, when Somali pirates held 736 hostages and 32 ships, the story only briefly made headlines before sinking out of the public consciousness. By contrast, when two Libyan terrorists hijacked an Afriqiyah Airways plane in December 2016 and took 118 passengers hostages, it was headline news around the world.

Conditions on many of these ships are basic to say the least. Until 2012, the official recommendation was that seamen shouldn't work more than 98 hours per week – more than double the EU limit – despite clear evidence that fatigue was endemic among ships' crews and that they were literally falling asleep on the job. Even when seamen are off work, there's little respite, as the living quarters on board most ships are more like a hospital or a prison than a home. Social interaction, especially on ships with crews of many different ethnic backgrounds, is limited. Free internet access is only now becoming universally available, and many crews still rely on the ship's skipper to send and receive emails.

The stresses of life at sea have a direct impact on seamen's mental health, as several reports have shown. A study of stress among seamen in the Dutch port of Rotterdam, for instance, observed that 'seamen have a lower life expectancy and more psychiatric illness, an increased risk for high cholesterol, for hypertension, neurosis, and stomach complaints, liver cirrhosis, suicide, and alcohol abuse'.[1] The reasons given include loneliness, homesickness, stress, burnout and conflicts between the ship's ranks. And, like their colleagues in the Royal Navy during World War II, the Dutch seamen's stress was often expressed as stomach complaints, which were notably more common among seamen than they were among the rest of the population.

With no resident doctor on board, when one of the crew goes 'off the deep end',[2] it's left to the rest of the crew to deal with the situation, until the ship gets back to port. And that could take several days or even weeks, as only the most extreme problem will persuade a ship's skipper to deviate from the vessel's strict timetable, for fear of losing his job. This has awful consequences, as witnessed by one chaplain from the Ministry to Seafarers in Vancouver who described a tragic scene he stumbled across while doing his rounds:

'I immediately noticed that there was something wrong during a recent ship visit when I met the first crew members. They looked nervous and there was a lot of commotion inside! Apparently, two crew members, the cook and a mechanic, had mentally "snapped".

'I was escorted to a room and there was one of the most pitiful sights I've ever seen. On a stretcher lay the cook all tied up while fearfully staring at the ceiling. He had needed to be restrained as he had become very aggressive, trying to hurt other crew members and throwing furniture through the mess room. They could not trust his behavior [sic], hence for the safety of the other crew members they had to tie him up. Similarly, the other crew member had been restrained in another area of the ship. Understandably, the captain was very nervous since this was his first voyage as captain and then to have two crew members snapping mentally. Not a good way to start your career.

'Both sick crew members would need medical attention. An hour later, in what looked like a Hollywood crime scene, they were taken via ambulance, along with fire truck and police escort to St Paul's Hospital [in Vancouver]. Their ship left the next day without them and eventually they were sent home to the Philippines… The next day it was business as usual at the Delta Port!' [Delta Port, in Vancouver, is Canada's largest container terminal.][3]

Not all cases of crew members who 'snap' have such a relatively happy ending. According to a report by the World Health Organization (WHO), seamen have the second-highest rate of suicide of all professions – second only to vets. Robert Iversen, a retired fishery biologist who served in the US Navy, has been campaigning for greater awareness of mental health issues on ships. He examined 20 separate studies into deaths at sea covering the years 1960–2009 and concluded that 1,011 of the 17,026 deaths reported were suicides – or a staggering 5.9 per cent. And that's not including the hundreds of sailors who disappeared at sea in unexplained circumstances, half of which are thought to be suicides.

Another study showed that from 1919 to 2005 (but excluding the World War II years), some 1,734 sailors committed suicide in the British Merchant Navy alone, while another 1,511 disappeared at sea. The same study looked in more detail at suicides in the years 1976–2005 and found that the vast majority (98 per cent) were men – the only women being two stewardesses from passenger ferries and an entertainer on a cruise ship. The main causes of death were jumping over the side (81 per cent) and hanging (15 per cent), while others cut their wrists, jumped from a height or asphyxiated themselves, and one drove a car into a dock. The suicide rate was much higher among the lower ranks, especially deck ratings (35 per cent) and catering crew (37 per cent), than it was among officers (2 per cent). And there was a notable increase on bigger ships, with vessels of 5,000 tons and over accounting for 72 per cent of suicides.

There was some good news, however, as the figures suggested that, after a peak in the 1960s, suicide rates among British seamen had reduced and were now more in line with the rest of the population. Even the peak in the 1960s reflected a general trend, as suicide rates in the UK as a whole peaked at that time.

The causes of suicide on modern merchant ships are similar wherever the crews come from. The primary reason is loneliness, as seamen are usually away from home for months at a time. The situation has worsened as the ships' turnover time in port has decreased. Whereas ships used to typically spend several days in port, unloading and then loading cargo, modern mechanisation and increased efficiency (notably with the advent of containers, or 'boxes') means it can all be done in a matter of hours. That means sailors' shore-leave time has dwindled and, in some cases, depending on their shift pattern, they may get no shore leave at all.

Other factors include work-related problems, such as not getting on with other members of the crew, disciplinary issues and work pressure, which altogether accounted for 30 per cent of suicides among British merchant seaman. As with sailors across the ages, domestic worries unrelated to work feature highly, with 13 per cent of suicides attributed to marital or girlfriend disputes, including impending divorces, and a further 9 per cent to other family problems. Nearly a third of the victims had had previous mental problems, including hallucinations and schizophrenia, sometimes related to excessive drinking.

Paradoxically, the reduction in shore leave has had one beneficial effect: less time ashore means seamen have less opportunity to get drunk, and alcohol abuse has fallen since the 1970s. This could also be explained by the increased use of Asian and other non-European crews, who do not have such a culture of drinking.

The multinational make-up of most modern crews can, however, also create problems and lead to bullying and intolerance. One ship's chaplain said: 'Chaplains and ship visitors often confront the clash of cultures and nationalities aboard ship. Certain nationalities should never be put together on the same ship. Racism and abuse are prevalent on many open registry ships [ie ships sailing under 'flags of convenience'] today.'[4]

But perhaps the biggest reason of all for the high rate of suicides among seamen is often overlooked: the easy availability of a means of killing oneself. Seamen are surrounded by sea 24 hours a day, and it only takes a moment to climb over a railing and jump in. Whereas in most walks of life the logistics of killing oneself operate as a delaying mechanism, allowing the person to calm down and reconsider, on board ship a moment of despair can quickly turn into an irreversible act. A similar explanation is given for the high suicide rate among vets, doctors and dentists, who all have ready access to supplies of potentially lethal drugs that they might be tempted to use against themselves. As the academic journal *Psychological Medicine* puts it: 'High occupational suicide rates are often linked to easy occupational access to a method of suicide.'[5]

A study of suicides among Polish seamen came to some surprising conclusions. It found that 50 of the 491 men who died on Polish merchant ships and deep-sea fishing boats between 1960 and 1999 had committed suicide – accounting for 10.2 per cent of deaths at sea. This compared with just 1.2 per cent of deaths among the male population in the same period in the country at large (only the male population was considered because the ships' crews were all male). Again, this excluded the large number of sailors missing at sea – accounting for 17 per cent of all deaths at sea – 5 per cent of which 'had not been explained sufficiently'.[6]

The report stated:

'One of the main features of this life is a strict social isolation, imposing limitations in satisfying the seafarer's physiological, psychological and sexual needs. They spend the whole time during the voyage within a closed, strongly hierarchical group of other crew members with a "paramilitary" organizational structure and they have limited possibilities of contact with the family. This situation leads to the inability of a person to manage stress.

'The pressure of such a situation in the marine environment seems particularly evident in the group of deep-sea fishermen, going for very long voyages (usually 4–6 months) under hard weather conditions, without calling at ports which offers a chance for recreation, having low living standards on their crowded trawlers-factory ships, and being exposed to high risk of work-related accidents and injuries.'[7]

Seamen working on smaller fishing boats, who didn't go so far afield and had regular contact with their families, suffered from negligible rates of suicide: only one case was recorded among a total of 177 deaths at sea in this group, or 0.6 per cent.

The report makes another important point when it says: 'It is possible that persons with concealed social integration problems deliberately choose the employment on sea-going ships.'[8] This echoes the research done by Ørnulv Ødegård into the high level of mental illness among Norwegian immigrants to the USA in the 1930s (see Chapter 8). He concluded that people who suffered from schizophrenia were less likely to integrate in their native countries and therefore were more likely to emigrate abroad. Likewise, the crews on merchant ships and deep-sea fishing boats are likely to be self-selecting and include a higher proportion of social misfits than the general population – including some with mental health issues.

There is, however, a glimmer of hope. The Maritime Labour Convention of 2006 set minimum standards for seamen's working hours, accommodation, recreation, food and medical care – including mental health care – which came into force in 2013. According to the convention, seamen should work a maximum of 72 hours per week – less than the previous recommended maximum of 98 hours, though still high. The convention also includes a clause requiring the authorities to address the issues relating to the 'physical and mental health effects of fatigue' and the 'effects of drug and alcohol dependency',[9] as well as a host of other measures to improve the domestic and personal aspects of life at sea.

As of 2016, 80 countries, representing 87 per cent of global shipping, had signed up to the convention, and even ships from non-signatory countries are expected to meet the standards when visiting ports in signatory countries. The catch is that certification is left up to the country of registration or an accredited body, and, as we have seen, not all shipping 'flags' operate to the highest standards. Provided that a ship has the right bits of paper, it's unlikely to be checked unless there are obvious signs of non-compliance – and by that time it might well be too late.

Nevertheless, the convention does signal a sea change in the industry's approach to the well-being and mental health of its lowest-paid workers. In June 2016, the Sailors' Society launched a new Wellness at Sea app for seafarers 'to combat issues such as fatigue, poor mental health and stress which affect seafarers on a daily basis and can be the difference between safe transit and a major incident'.[10] The app allows users to monitor their well-being in five key areas: social, emotional, physical, intellectual and spiritual. It even includes a copy of the Bible.

The Seafarers Hospital Society also launched an online counselling service in 2016, giving emotional and practical support to seafarers suffering from anxiety or depression and explicitly acknowledging the pressure this ocean-going workforce is under. 'One in four people experience a mental health problem in their lifetime and seafarers are no different – in fact they are probably under more pressure than most,'[11] said SHS secretary Peter Coulson.

And it's not just cargo ships that suffer from a high level of suicides and unexplained deaths. As the popularity and size of cruise ships grows year by year, so does the number of people lost overboard. The website www.cruisejunkie.com claims that 284 people went overboard on cruise ships between 2000 and 2016. Some of these people were saved, but most were not. The website suggests 214 people went missing in the 10 years from 2006 to 2015, an average of 21 people per year.

According to the American coastguard, most of these accidents happen at night. By law, high railings up to 1.15m (45in) high (about chest height on an average adult) have to be fitted on all open decks, making it virtually impossible for anyone to fall over by accident. Most cases of people falling overboard are therefore either a suicide attempt or a drunken prank gone wrong. Statistics suggest that the majority of victims are men, with an average age of 41 (young by cruise-ship standards), and that most of them tend to go overboard on the last night of a cruise.

A whole website, www.cruiseshipdeaths.com, is devoted to the subject, and lists the individual cases of hundreds of people who have died on cruise ships, either from natural causes or misadventure. These include 23 murders, 2 deaths from terrorist attacks, and 23 'suspicious' deaths. Perhaps most shocking, though, is the long list of 62 'overboard suicides', followed by 34 people who fell overboard for 'unknown' reasons and another 12 who fell overboard in 'suspicious' circumstances. Most of the 'suspicious' deaths involve alleged suicide cases that subsequent investigations suggest might have been murders.

Cruise-ship suicides certainly make for lurid headlines for news broadcasters, and include the man who was reported as having said that growing old was 'sh*t', before throwing himself off a ship in the Tasman Sea, and the man who 'jumped to his death from luxury cruise ship after anti-gay taunts from crew'.[12]

What these figures really reveal is the extent of lawlessness on ships on the high seas. Unless the incident takes place within a country's territorial waters (ie a mere 12 miles from the shore), the obligation to investigate wrongdoing on cruise ships and cargo ships alike falls on the country of registry. Given that cruise ships are usually at sea for weeks at a time and travel thousands of miles, by the time the authorities from these countries launch an investigation, any evidence has almost always vanished long ago – literally washed over the side into the deep blue sea.

It's a perfect set-up for unscrupulous predators to make use of to take advantage of vulnerable individuals – www.cruisejunkie.com lists more than 100 'publicly reported' cases of sexual assault on cruise ships in 2003–2007 alone – or even to commit homicide. One of the 'missing' passengers listed on www.cruiseshipdeaths.com was a man who won $10,000 in the ship's casino, only to mysteriously go missing later that night. His body was found washed up on a Greek island a few weeks later, without the $10,000.

The situation made headlines in 2011 when Rebecca Coriam disappeared from the cruise ship *Disney Wonder*. Since the incident took place in international waters between the USA and Mexico, the only person to investigate the incident was a single police officer from the Bahamas, where the ship was registered, who spent just one day on board. The fact that Coriam and the company that runs the ship were both British was irrelevant. No evidence of a crime was found – even though her credit card was used after she had disappeared – and the cruise company dismissed Coriam's death as suicide. Her family insists she was not suicidal.

Former Deputy Prime Minister John Prescott, himself a former ship's steward, told the BBC: 'People don't know whether she died or she was thrown over the side. What is so alarming is many people are going missing and nothing is being done about it.' He went on to say there was 'almost a conspiracy of silence' surrounding the case, and called for the law to be changed because Britain 'should be looking after our citizens'.[13]

✳   ✳   ✳

Another explanation for those mysterious disappearances at sea might be an age-old affliction dating back to the Age of Sail. Calenture was much discussed in the 19th century, when it was said to have led to the deaths of hundreds of European crews sailing in hot climates (see Chapter 3). The condition was said to occur mainly in the tropics, while ships were drifting in hot, windless conditions, causing crews to become delirious and attempt to jump into the sea, believing it was 'the green fields of home'.[14] Unless held down by their crewmates, they usually ended up jumping over the side and drowning.

The modern version of the condition appears to be no less potent. Again, it usually takes place on hot, windless days, after the ship has been out of sight of land for a week or more. Crews describe being alone, staring over the ship's side and feeling an overwhelming desire to jump over the side. Some claim they hear a voice telling them they can fly. One study found that 50 per cent of a ship's crew of 70 officers and ratings had experienced the condition, and they used words such as 'lured', 'hypnotically attracted', 'powerless to resist', 'supremely infallible' and 'joyously entranced'[15] to describe the experience. In most cases, the consequence of succumbing to the desire would have been certain death – an involuntary suicide that would be written off as yet another 'lost at sea'.

The condition can develop into a phobia. One man said he had experienced calenture on his first voyage at sea and had had to drag himself away from the ship's railing. On subsequent trips he avoided going to the edge of the ship while it was underway, in case he felt compelled to jump over the side again. Another sailor always insisted on having company with him whenever he went on deck to prevent himself 'being lured into the ocean'.[16]

An article in the sailing blog www.cruisemates.com describes the feelings experienced by victims of calenture:

'It isn't the cruise or the ship that enables the suicide – it is the water surrounding [the] ship. [...] The first time I boarded a cruise ship, I was in awe of the beauty and power of the open sea and the marvel of human engineering that enabled me to traverse and even thrive in one of the world's least hospitable environments, the open ocean, which covers three-fifths of our planet. I was filled with a rare combination of admiration and fear as any mortal faced with something so mighty feels. I instinctively knew my life would end if I yielded all self-control and put myself overboard.

'If you have already been on a ship you already know what I mean. There are certain sights that evoke this same terrible admiration in us; looking over the edge of the Grand Canyon, walking across the Golden Gate Bridge or going to the observation platform on the Empire State Building. I believe it is a normal human reaction to look at these sights and wonder what it would be like to fall. These are places where people who have severe, possibly uncontrollable thoughts of suicide should never go. If anyone I knew had attempted suicide in the last two years and he told me he was considering his first cruise, I would counsel him against it.'[17]

What's being portrayed is the 'oceanic feeling'[18] described by Freud in *Civilisation and Its Discontents*. It's a feeling of being at one with the world, with infinity. It's an impulse also experienced by high-altitude pilots, polar explorers and mountaineers, who are all exposed to unbounded non-human environments.

Inevitably, perhaps, some psychoanalysts have given it a sexual spin, relating this 'oceanic feeling' to the supposed sexual symbolism of the sea. 'To merge with the most procreative womb of all time is to secure wider sexual horizons,'[19] wrote Moussaieff Masson in 1980. Elsewhere, Otto Fenichel wrote in the 1944 edition of *Psychoanalytic Quarterly*: 'The person, experiencing himself in a landscape, does not simply feel love or hatred for the father-mountain, or the mother-ocean, but undergoes a kind of identification with them. He feels the "unio mystica" with the nature-parents.'[20]

Or, as a doctor based at the Port Health Centre in Hamburg put it: 'The sea can hold a morbid attraction for depressive individuals.'[21]

CHAPTER 22

HEALING WAVES

Paradoxically, while the sea can precipitate depression and mental illness in some people, for many others it has exactly the opposite effect. The healing power of the sea has been written about since ancient times, inspiring the Greek dramatist Euripides to write: 'The sea washes away the ills of humankind.'[1] It's been credited with improving circulation, stimulating the immune system, and curing a range of illnesses, such as asthma, eczema, psoriasis, osteoporosis, arthritis, and even tuberculosis. It's also been shown to cure depression, boost the libido and improve sleep (and no, the last two are not mutually exclusive!). Thalassotherapy (from the Greek 'thalassa' – ie the sea) is only the latest name for an idea that has been around for centuries.

There have been many attempts to dissect the beneficial effect of the sea, to explain the physical and psychological boost most people feel from swimming, sailing or simply going for a bracing walk at the seaside. One theory is that sea air is full of negative ions, which increase our body's ability to absorb oxygen, and therefore make us feel more energised. Negative ions are also thought to balance the levels of serotonin in the body, which has a major influence on our mental state. Some suggest the sound of breaking waves affects the wave patterns of the brain and makes us feel more relaxed, while others claim the colour of the sea – or possibly the twinkling pattern of the sun reflected on its surface – has an effect on the brain's operation.

And it turns out that those ancient Greeks were right: the sea really does heal our bodies, thanks to its rich chemical make-up. Its high levels of salt (3.5 per cent) and potassium (1.1 per cent) promote healing, which can improve skin complaints such as psoriasis, while its magnesium content (3.7 per cent) helps the skin retain moisture and become more flexible. Regular sea bathing has also been shown to alleviate allergies such as hay fever, whereby the sea acts as a 'saline douche' and keeps nasal passages clear of pollen. More generally, research has shown that people who live by the sea have healthier respiratory systems since their airways are purified by the antiseptic properties of salt.

A more radical explanation was offered by French doctor René Quinton, who discovered in the early 20th century that the chemical make-up of sea water is remarkably similar to that of blood – human and animal. He conducted experiments on fish, a lizard, a chicken, a rabbit, a dog, and even a human being, which proved they could absorb an astonishing amount of sea water into their bloodstream without any adverse affects. Quinton concluded that, as humans and animals originate from the sea, we have maintained the chemical connection with our ancestry. We came from the sea, and we remain part ocean no matter how landlocked our bodies have become.

In Britain, the sudden explosion in the popularity of swimming in the 18th century and the subsequent boom of coastal resorts such as Brighton and Blackpool can be largely attributed to the efforts of one man. Dr Richard Russell was convinced of the curative effects of sea water and in 1750 wrote a book, *A Dissertation on the Use of Sea Water in Diseases of the Glands*, which explained how it could be used to treat 'scurvy, jaundice, King's evil, leprosy and the Glandular Consumption',[2] among other illnesses. He claimed great success using potions that included ingredients such as cuttlefish bone, crabs' eyes, woodlice, vipers' flesh and syrup of violets, taken with pints of salt water.

Russell was a great advocate of 'cold bathing in the sea', particularly for scurvy, as he believed the sea water not only cleansed the skin but filtered through it and got rid of any accumulation of phlegm in the glands, 'and thus removes the inward cause of the disease, as well as the outward foulness of the skin'. He also recommended swimming to treat 'melancholy madness' (thought to be brought on by an excess of black bile), bites from mad dogs, and impotency 'arising from the immoderate use of venery'[3] (ie excessive sex).

Russell opened a shoreside surgery and health spa in Brighton in 1753, and soon had a steady stream of visitors imbibing his dubious concoctions and immersing themselves in the sea. This type of holiday by the sea was offered as an alternative to other types of health spa, popular since ancient times, with Russell arguing that sea water was healthier than fresh water. One of his patrons was none other than the Prince Regent, George IV, who built a holiday home in Brighton, the spectacular Royal Pavilion, which contributed greatly to the prosperity of the town as a seaside resort. In was only a matter of time before sea bathing spread around the British coast, and then further afield to other European countries to eventually become the global phenomenon it is today.

The concept was reinvented for the 21st century in the form of 'wild swimming', the proponents of which make great claims for its heath-promoting effects. And indeed there is plenty of evidence to support their assertions. Research suggests that immersing the body in cold water acts as a mild 'stressor' that triggers a rush of adrenalin and activates our immune system. The adrenalin makes us feel more 'alive' and acts as a natural painkiller, diverting our attention away from our aches and pains. Research by NASA has shown that regular swimming in cold water brings down blood pressure, reduces cholesterol levels, and encourages healthier distribution of fat. It also suggests that wild swimmers might have better sex lives, since splashing around in all that cold water apparently increases the levels of testosterone in men and oestrogen in women.

There are also more philosophical, less measurable reasons for taking time out from our everyday stresses and having some device-free time immersed in nature. Once in the water, instinct takes over; the body looks after itself and, in a rare moment of mind–body harmony, the mind is free to let go and observe the surroundings. To be in the moment. There's nothing much you can do about anything when you're swimming in a rocky creek or muddy pool, away from the usual stress triggers. It's a point made by John Jerome in his book *Blue Rooms*, when he writes: 'The thing about the ritual morning plunge, the entry into water that provides the small existential moment, is its total privacy. Swimming is between me and the water, nothing else. The moment the water encloses me, I am, gratefully, alone.'[4]

CHAPTER 23

TOUGH LOVE

'There, sailing the sea, we play every part of life: control, direction, effort, fate; and there we can test ourselves. All that concerns the sea is profound and final. The sea provides visions, darkness, revelations... The sea has taken me to itself whenever I sought it and given me relief from men. It has rendered remote the cares and wastes of the land; for of all creatures that breathe upon the earth we of mankind are the fullest of sorrow. But the sea shall comfort us, and assure us.'[1]
Hilaire Belloc

As the Age of Sail faded into a glorified, romantic memory, and ships were powered increasingly by steam and diesel, there was a sense that something had been lost with the increased mechanisation of seafaring. Modern life was becoming cushy, not only for the growing numbers of landlubbers stuck in office jobs, but for sailors too. The situation came to a head during World War II when Lawrence Holt, head of the Blue Funnel Line, observed that, contrary to expectations, older sailors coped better with extreme situations such as shipwrecks and survival in lifeboats than their younger counterparts.

He turned to German educator Kurt Hahn (founder of what would become known as the Duke of Edinburgh Award) for help. Hahn concluded that the younger sailors hadn't had enough life experience to give them the confidence to deal with extreme adversity. Not only that, but most of the older sailors had sound practical skills gained from serving on sailing ships before they were phased out. To bolster the younger sailors' confidence and mental resilience, therefore, Hahn created an outdoor training programme that included both nautical and land-based components. In effect, the courses reintroduced elements of danger, discomfort and unpredictability into otherwise cosseted lives. The idea was not only to toughen up the trainees physically and give them practical skills, but also to fortify them psychologically to cope with a survival situation.

The first Outward Bound courses took place in Aberdyfi in Wales in 1941, and an intrinsic part of the programme was a voyage out to sea on an old wooden ketch called the *Garibaldi*. The concept quickly spread to other countries around the world, and by 1975 more than 200 schools in the USA were running Outward Bound courses, with dozens of other organisations mimicking the approach. By the time the original Outward Bound Trust celebrated its 75th anniversary in 2016, it could boast that more than a million people had been through its programme. A whole new industry of outdoor adventure training had been born – all thanks to the need of the Merchant Navy to have more mentally prepared young seamen.

Sail training had long been used by navies to train young cadets, and huge archaic square-rigged training ships were still being built specifically for this purpose long after the warships themselves had been converted to steam and diesel. It seemed as if you couldn't call yourself a real sailor unless you had served your time climbing the rigging, furling and unfurling sails, and tying a long splice – even if none of this was any use once you joined your great diesel-powered warship. There was an unspoken agreement that it was character forming, and that the role of cadet training was as much to do with moulding the person as it was to do with learning practical skills.

None of this was available to the general public until the 1930s, when, just as the great sailing cargo ships were making their last commercial voyages – mostly transporting grain from Australia, or nitrate from Chile – a few pioneering individuals realised that these ships could be used to carry cargo of a different kind. One of these was the Australian sailor and author Alan Villiers, who in 1934 bought a defunct Danish school ship that he renamed the *Joseph Conrad* and, carrying only amateur paying crew, sailed round the world. Part of his crew was 'at risk' youth, whom he took on board free of charge, in the hope of improving their life prospects – thereby continuing a long tradition of social rehabilitation at sea. Irving and Electa Johnson did the same thing with their two training ships, both called *Yankee*, circumnavigating the world seven times in the space of 25 years, entirely with amateur crews.

However, the modern era of sail training was really born in 1956. That year, a handful of square-rigged ships took part in a race from Torbay, on the south coast of England, to Lisbon in Portugal. What was intended as a farewell tribute to the great leviathans of sail turned out to be their resurrection. The following year, the ships gathered again for another race, and the year after that for another race, and soon the Sail Training Association (now Sail Training International, or STI) was formed. As the value of sail training outside the usual naval establishment was recognised, old boats were restored and new boats

245

built, and the Tall Ships Race became an annual, multi-leg fixture, with ports competing to be among the stopover destinations. Nowadays, the race is regularly contested by more than 100 vessels – though not all of these are square-riggers, as smaller sail-training vessels have been allowed to join the fray – and, significantly, the winning boat isn't the one that wins the most races but the one whose crew 'has done most to help further international understanding and friendship during the races'.[2]

Much has been written about the ways in which sail training benefits young people's psychological welfare, although there has been little systematic research into *why* it is so effective. An attempt to quantify the experience was made by the R. Tucker Thompson Sail Training Trust, which operates an 85ft schooner in the Northland region of New Zealand – an area with chronic unemployment, low wages and low academic achievement. The parents and carers of 77 trainees were questioned before and after their children took part in a seven-day voyage on the ship. The response was overwhelming, with 81 per cent of parents/carers saying their child was more confident after the voyage, 68 per cent that they were getting on better with other students, and 58 per cent that they showed an improved attitude towards figures of authority (eg teachers). A resounding 98.7 per cent (ie all but one of the parents/carers) believed their child had benefited in some way from the voyage.

For some, the experience proved genuinely life-changing, as described by one parent:

'Before the voyage [my daughter] was afraid of heights and very afraid of boats and also would never eat fish or seafood. The voyage changed all of the above attitudes completely. In addition and more importantly the structure of the ship with Captain, first mate, crew – its regularity, organisation and reliability gave her an insight into her own nature and need for organisation and structure that has been instrumental in her later career choices and actually changed her whole attitude to herself. As soon as she returned she was inspired and away she went.'[3]

A similar survey of 300 trainees carried out by Edinburgh University on behalf of STI found that nearly 55 per cent of those taking part felt their confidence had improved, with the figure rising to 64 per cent among first-timers. Interestingly, while 40 per cent of trainees said they were worried about being seasick before the voyage, fewer than 15 per cent listed it as a negative experience after the voyage. On the other hand, while only 13 per cent were concerned about their physical discomfort before the voyage, nearly 22 per cent listed it as a negative afterwards – although, as the report tactfully puts it: 'It might however be argued that a degree of physical discomfort is a necessary part of the experience of seafaring and not one that trainees would necessarily benefit by being insulated from.'[4]

Another study looked at the relative merits of land-based adventure programmes compared with those that take place at sea, and came up with some surprising conclusions. For a start, it found that the smaller, more clearly delineated boundaries of a boat, compared with the bigger, more blurred boundaries of a campsite, were 'much more meaningful' for the trainees. Far from proving a source of frustration, the more limited area meant the trainees were more engaged in activities and less liable to go wandering off doing their own thing, as well as allowing the staff greater control over what was going on. In particular, the report highlighted the role of the saloon as the 'central hub',[5] where trainees and staff gathered several times a day for games, meals and discussions, and suggested it was far more effective in fostering a community spirit than the benches and tables provided by the campsite.

Moreover, far from finding the specialised language and unfamiliar procedures of sailing off-putting, the study found that trainees were more engaged on the training ship precisely because everything was a little bit different and they had to figure things out and couldn't take anything for granted. Even going to the 'heads' (not the 'loo') became an adventure, as they had to learn how to operate the manual pump in the right sequence. As a result, they were more easily persuaded to perform tasks they might normally try to avoid, due to their novelty value.

Sail training can be particularly effective at dealing with young offenders and children with behavioural problems, and several programmes have been set up specifically to cater for this group. The Trinity Sailing Foundation in the shabby-chic fishing port of Brixham, on the south coast of England, operates three sail-training vessels and has a long track record of dealing with both troubled and 'untroubled' kids, as Trinity Sailing's operations manager Ben Wheatley explained.

'Some of the kids don't respond well to the structure of sail training, but for others it can have a profound effect. The joke in sail training circles is that when you get the really "good" kids, who know how to sail and do everything they're told, you have an awesome time but they probably don't really need it. It's when you get the really tough kids, when you're up until 2am trying to get someone to bed and running around trying to find someone who's gone missing on shore, that's when you're really making a difference – that's what sail training is all about.

'Sail training isolates the kids from their normal surroundings. If they are camping onshore, they can still run away or get a taxi home, but on a boat that's not an option. The boundaries are more obvious; so if you tell someone not to sit on the rail because they might fall overboard, then that's very real. Most groups when they arrive have a predetermined pecking order: some are the bullies, some are quieter, some in between – but none has ever been sailing before, so they all start at the same level. And it's not always the ones you expect to who do well. Sometimes, the quiet one might be really good at helming and the brave one will go up the rigging, or the other way round, and they get respect for that. It changes the dynamic of the group, and that usually carries over when they get home.'[6]

Seasickness is the ultimate leveller, and some sail-training skippers faced with groups of particularly troublesome kids have been known to deliberately go out in bad weather to make them seasick. 'Because,' as Ben says, 'no one can be a bully when they're seasick.'[7]

Despite this, sometimes things don't go as planned, as he explains:

'Years ago, before I joined Trinity, I sailed on a voyage with a bunch of young offenders from Aberdeen to Glasgow, over the top of Scotland. They arrived in a Group 4 security van, and were quite hardcore. We were a bit naïve and didn't realise they were doing drugs, until one collapsed and had to be evacuated. Halfway round, they started getting quite agitated, and we had to work out how to deal with them. It's no good trying to pull rank with these kids, because they are used to challenging authority, that's what they do all the time. So we had to talk to them on their level, in a non-threatening way, and take a more unconventional approach. They were eventually taken off in handcuffs, after they threatened to knife one of the crew. I feel like we failed them, but we had to get them off for the sake of the other kids on board.'[8]

Ben had a more successful experience a few years later when he sailed with a mixed group of kids from several famous trouble spots – Israel and Palestine, Greece and Turkey, Catholic and Protestant Belfast – on a 12-day trip around southern England and northern France. The old rivalries soon flared up and there was much heated debate for the first few days, but by splitting the nationalities between different watches, the young people were forced to work together for the safety of the ship, as Ben recounted:

'One Israeli guy and a Palestinian guy who were sharing a cabin became friends after they discovered they both liked football and the same kind of music. By the end of the cruise, they were sharing music on their iPods and knocking a football around whenever they went ashore. It turned out they only lived three miles away from each, but on either side of the West Bank barrier, and neither had ever been to each other's neighbourhood. When they got home, the Israeli kid's mum told him she had a terminal illness, and he posted something about it on the sail training message board. A few days later there was a knock on his door and the Palestinian guy turned up with a bunch of flowers – he had gone through all the searches and queues to visit his friend. They kept in touch after that, and their families became friends too. They managed to overcome a millennium-long divide, thanks to a 12-day voyage at sea.'[9]

✳   ✳   ✳

One man who knows all about the therapeutic effects of the sea is Shaun Pascoe. A former commander of a medical emergency team in the Royal Air Force, he served in Chinook helicopters evacuating the wounded from war zones. During four sorties in Afghanistan, he moved 1,490 soldiers – a quarter of the 6,500 patients moved by Chinooks during the conflict. It was dangerous, high-stress work, and he was faced daily with scenes of horror that would be unimaginable to most people.

'After a while, the work took its toll,' he said. 'I experienced bursts of anger, dissociation, seeing things that weren't there, paranoia, flashbacks. I was displaying all the symptoms of post-traumatic stress disorder. But it was when I found myself in the corner of a room, rocking back and forth, not knowing how I'd got there, that I realised I needed help.'[10]

As a key member of a highly specialised military corps, Pascoe got the best treatment money could buy at the Maudsley Hospital in London. At the same time, he started studying for a sailing qualification, and immediately felt the benefits of being on the water. 'I wouldn't have engaged with the treatment without it,' he recalls. 'The treatment was hard: I'd go up to London once a week, and would be crying in the toilet on the way back. The only thing that kept me going was knowing a few days later I'd be out sailing with a few guys.'[11]

A year later, Pascoe was invalided our of the Loyal Air Force and used his resettlement money to set up a charity to help former armed forces personnel adjust to civilian life – through sailing. He called the organisation Turn to Starboard because, as the organisation's website puts it:

'When two boats are heading straight towards each other, they avoid collision by following a simple rule of sailing – turn to starboard (turn to the right). We use sailing to help Armed Forces personnel and their families make the right turn.'[12]

The response was extraordinary, as the project was immediately backed by influential organisations such as Help for Heroes and several leading Armed Forces charities. After just two years it was gifted a 91ft sail-training schooner (the former *Spirit of Fairbridge*, renamed the *Spirit of Falmouth*) by the Prince's Trust, and promptly embarked on a round-Britain voyage crewed entirely by military veterans. In the space of just four years, the charity had accrued £700,000 in assets, taken 767 people sailing, and built up a staff of 11 employees (mostly ex-military personnel).

'The effects of sailing are quite profound,' said Pascoe. 'You're taken away from land and reminded that there's a big wide world out there. And suddenly your problems become smaller.' He went on, 'On a practical level, you don't have a phone on you, no email, no car key in your pocket – nothing to remind you of your day-to-day worries. The impact can be really quite quick and obvious – to the extent of some of our clients crying when they get off the boat, because they're having to go back to it.'[13]

Part of the process is to provide vocational skills so the clients can get jobs at the end of the course – including skippering the *Spirit of Falmouth*, which is now entirely staffed by voluntary crew.

'A few years ago, you wouldn't get someone in the forces admitting to having mental health issues,' Pascoe adds. 'Now they'll put their hands up and talk about it, because they feel that's part of giving back, of helping other people with the same issues.'[14]

Former mental health worker Joseph Sabien took this approach a step further when he turned the boat itself into a mental health clinic. Sabien had hardly sailed at all when he set up the charity Sea Sanctuary with the intention of providing a genuine, medically approved treatment in a marine environment – something that had never been done before. Brought up in care, he had had his own mental health issues before training as a therapist and became convinced that something more compelling was needed than the 'clinical, sterile uninspiring model'[15] of standard NHS treatment. Although there was no real scientific data to support his thesis, he had noticed the therapeutic effects the sea had on many people and became convinced that its healing power could be harnessed in a systematic way to help people with mental health problems.

Sabien said:

'I still wanted to provide an evidence-based approach. It wasn't about going out and hugging masts, going heave-ho and hoping people would feel better at the end of it. It was about doing something within the marine environment, using the smells, the sounds, the sensory awareness, and combining it with something like mindfulness or cognitive behavioural therapy [CBT]. But the marine environment was key to recovery: the sky, the sea, the waves, the camaraderie, the sense of being around people again.'[16]

After an initial experiment on a 43ft wooden yacht, Sabien secured funding from the National Lottery to buy an 85ft sail-training ketch, which became the base from which a remarkable experiment took place. Groups of mentally ill adults, most of whom had never been sailing before, took part in a four-day cruise (really a potter around the bay and nearby creeks) that combined sail training and mental health training – with a professional skipper to do the sailing bit and a bona fide counsellor to do the mental health bit. Two support workers, who both knew how to sail, were also conscripted to help out as required in both departments.

From the outset, the programme meshed the two strands: sailing and mental health; body and brain. Safety procedures for the boat (bow and stern, port and starboard, 'mind the boom!') were delivered hand in hand with safety procedures for the person (personal boundaries, confidentiality, the 'buddy system'). Periods of navigating, during which the clients learned the basic principles of sailing (how to raise the sails, how to steer, how to drop anchor) alternated with periods at anchor, when clients learned about the principles of mindfulness and CBT, the two main methods used by the charity – such as the perils of negative thinking and automatic thinking, the benefits of mindful breathing, and techniques for personal anchoring (appropriately enough!).

And when the day was done, the clients enjoyed a hearty meal in the ship's saloon, chatted with their fellow crewmates and went on deck to commune with the stars, before heading to their bunks for a good night's sleep. 'And it's usually the best night's sleep they've had in years – not in weeks or days, but in years,' said Sabien. 'That can't just be attributed to the sea air; it's the whole experience.'[17]

He went on:

'And it's significant it's a wooden boat. No disrespect to the NHS, which I love, but patients often end up with plastic cups, stale biscuits, out-of-date posters on surgery walls, peeling paint – the whole message is "I'm not worth very much". We've taken that and flipped it on its head. We make sure we give people good food, good kit, good staff, so they're fully waterproofed, the boat's in good order, the varnish isn't peeling. The whole experience conveys to them that they are worth investing in. Would they get the same experience on a white plastic modern boat? I suspect not.'[18]

Even the constant work needed to maintain an old wooden boat can be turned to therapeutic effect, it seems, as explained by Sabien:

'There's something about looking after something, nurturing something, that can trigger an inner process. They see that, through a bit of work, they've turned something grey and damaged into something really beautiful. That can become a seed within people, subconsciously, that some things are worth investing in. Some people have very poor personal hygiene, for instance, and their nutrition isn't very good. You can see them reflecting, this is a small adjustment but it can have enormous effects on my wellbeing. And we're only looking at small steps, small adjustments.'[19]

The programme proved extremely effective, with clients showing an 80–84 per cent improvement in their well-being score after the 'intervention', as the cruises are called, and with 60–65 per cent still using the techniques they learned on board ship 12 months after taking part. Crucially to Sabien's vision of an 'evidence-based approach', the organisation became the first marine-based charity to receive the official backing and financial support of the NHS. As of 2016, Sea Sanctuary had taken 650 people sailing, some of them referred from bodies such as the NHS, the Devon and Cornwall Police Force, and the British Royal Legion, while others were self-referred and, in a few cases, self-funded.

✳   ✳   ✳

Dan Fielding is one of many deeply traumatised veterans who found respite through the Turn to Starboard scheme. He joined the Royal Marines when he was 17 and, during his 11 years in the forces, served in several trouble spots, including Sierra Leone (four times), Iraq and Northern Ireland. Despite being regularly faced with the carnage of war, he says he loved his job and describes his time with the Marines as the 'best time of my life' – until he was discharged due to a back injury in 2008. His account contains some harrowing scenes:

'You'd go over the line and find everything blown to bits. There were bodies everywhere, and people laying all over in different stages of being dead. It was not nice. I saw a lot of children maimed and hurt. It was absolutely awful, but you weren't focused on that. You were there to do a job; you were there to stop that happening, and you were focused on that. So there was a disconnect. You went out drinking with your mates who were doing the same thing, so it seemed normal. It was like a coping mechanism.

'It was leaving the Marines that was the down bit. Leaving it, and not doing it. Not fitting in. Not being part of that big family any more. I started a massive grieving process, first of all for the Marines and then, once that started, for everything else which I hadn't grieved for before. It was like a big overlay, like an acetate, over my life. All the images came flooding back. I'd be walking down the street and think, that's strange, the windows are open. Is someone going to shoot me? Or, all of a sudden the street would go quiet, and I'd become suspicious, when really everyone had just gone home for tea.

'Then the nightmares started. They were horrendous. I'd find myself in the back garden, chasing people over the back wall, acting it out, and then realise I was naked, and it was just a bottle of Coke, and all the neighbours were looking at me. When I had my daughter, I started thinking again of those children I'd seen, and how their fathers must have tried to save them. And, because I was injured, I worried if I'd be able to save my daughter if someone attacked us.

'I locked myself away and became a bit of a hermit, not washing, not looking after myself, not engaging. The only place I felt safe was on my boat. I'd always liked the sea and had sailed a bit when I was a kid, and crewed on a yacht. So when I was discharged I bought a 23ft sailing boat and sailed it around from the Bristol Channel. I didn't really understand about tides and went aground a few times, but I got home eventually. It was like my shed, and I was happy as Larry when I was on board. But unfortunately it sank during a storm.

'A friend's wife put me in touch with Turn to Starboard, and it took me three days to build up the bottle to go and see them. Once I got there, I immediately felt at home – more at home than in my own flat. Before I started, I thought being a Marine is the only thing I can do. If I can't do that, I'm useless. But when I started sailing, I thought, actually, I can do something else. And then I got good, and I thought I can do this well – better even than some others who have been doing it a lot longer than me. I'm not as useless as I think.

'Then I started taking sailing exams, and I gave myself the gift of allowing myself to potentially fail – because the Marines don't like failure, or a Freddie as they call it. But I passed my Day Skipper exam, then my Yachtmaster Theory and Offshore exams, then Cruising Instructor and Sailing Instructor. And now I'm a full-time instructor at Turn to Starboard – helping other people like me get through it.

'I don't think I'll ever get over my PTSD. I've learned how to manage it, but I'll never lose it. Sailing gives me a little respite. When I'm on a boat, I leave everything behind on land. The moment the engine's switched off, and the sail fills in with a kick, I get that amazing feeling; being pushed along by the wind, hanging there in the natural elements. It's what keeps me grounded – I couldn't be without it.'[20]

EPILOGUE

Who would have thought there were so many stories of madness at sea waiting to be told? Starting from doubting there would be enough material to fill this book, it soon became a case of what to leave out rather than what to put in. Time and space prevented me from visiting the archives at Bethlem Royal Hospital, which treated thousands of seamen throughout the 18th and 19th centuries, or the mental asylum at Great Yarmouth, which was run by and for the Royal Navy for most of the 19th century. There were literally hundreds of stories in local papers of seamen climbing the rigging, setting fire to their ships or murdering their crewmates in sea-induced frenzies. And don't get me started on those crazy singlehanded sailors, tripping on lack of sleep. It got to the point when it seemed that any singlehanded sailor who didn't have some kind of mental paroxysm just wasn't trying hard enough.

And then there were the dead-end 'leads' – stories shut down by a conspiracy of silence. My favourite was from a fellow journalist who told me about a skipper in a round-the-world race who was threatened with a knife by a disgruntled crew member. The skipper secretly put tranquillizers in a cup of coffee to calm the man down, but was then called on deck to sort out a problem. When he came back, he couldn't remember which cup he had spiked. He made a guess and the two of them sat in the saloon drinking coffee until, much to the skipper's relief, the other man eventually fell asleep. When I tried to contact the skipper to confirm the story, however, I was completely stonewalled. Another contact promised 'a fascinating story of alcohol abuse, mental illness and the toughness of a Southern Ocean Crossing',[1] but whenever I tried to Skype him to discuss it further he was mysteriously unavailable.

One race organiser tried to dissuade me from including a story on the grounds that it didn't fit the category of 'madness at sea' – even though the person concerned had committed suicide by deliberately jumping into the sea, which surely suggests a mental breakdown of some kind, however temporary.

The stigma of mental illness runs deep in our communal psyche, it seems, even in these supposedly enlightened times. Which makes it all the more remarkable that people such as Shaun Pascoe and Dan Fielding of Turn to Starboard – men who have witnessed horrors unimaginable to most of us and who have been emotionally scarred for life – can come forward and talk about their experiences with such candour. Their motivation is a desire to 'give something back'[2] (an expression they both used) so that others like them can come forward and experience the healing power of the sea.

For there is a wind of change, and an increased willingness to address these important issues. It's perhaps no coincidence that this book is being published in the same year that Prince Harry revealed he had to seek help to deal with his suppressed emotions after the death of his mother, Princess Diana, in 1997. The prince told the *Daily Telegraph* he 'shut down all his emotions' for nearly 20 years after losing his mother, and had come close to a complete breakdown 'on numerous occasions'.[3] He decided to speak about his experiences to encourage others to do the same and to help break the stigma around mental health issues.

As the preceding pages show, people going 'off the deep end' on the world's oceans is a common enough occurrence – be it in the rage of a psyched-up racing team or, increasingly, in the loneliness of long-haul cargo-ship crews. Yet, 200 years after Admiral Garrett said, 'A seaman who has lost his reason in the service of the Crown should receive the love and attention on a scale not less than a seaman who has lost a limb in the same cause,'[4] we still discriminate unfairly between physical and mental illness. If this book helps to stimulate discussion of these issues and encourages a broader acceptance of the lows as well as the highs of life at sea, then it will have been worth writing.

ACKNOWLEDGEMENTS

This book has been a long time in the making, so first, thanks to Janet Murphy at Bloomsbury for standing by the project through thick and thin. Thanks too to my editor Clara Jump for her encouragement, and to Lucy Doncaster for her precise yet discreet editing.

During my research, I was pleased to interview Neil Weston at Portsmouth University, Andrew Baines, curator of HMS *Victory*, Shaun Pascoe and Dan Fielding of Turn to Starboard, Joe Sabien of Sea Sanctuary, and Susie Goodall, a solo star in the making. Barry Pickthall shared some nuggets and allowed me to raid his library, and Dick Johnson had some bright ideas, as always. Thanks to all of them for their time and patience.

Thanks to Peter Coppack for his help with the Battle of Jutland section and to Dot Tose for the photo of her grandfather and great-uncle; also to Jean Strange for help tracking down a *Galatea* photo, and to Shirley Waring for sharing it.

Thanks too to Stephan Moitessier, Glynn Christian and James and Cath Bennet for helping with the family archives.

I am grateful to the Society of Authors for awarding me a grant which was very helpful in the book's early stages of development.

And of course to my wife Anna for helping to hone the idea in the first place and still managing to appear interested after four years of exposure.

ENDNOTES

DEDICATION
Emerson, RW, *English Traits*, Ticknor & Fields, Boston, 1866

INTRODUCTION
1   Szymańska, Kinga, Jaremin, Bogdan, and Rosik, Elżbieta, 'Suicides Among Polish Seamen and Fishermen During Work at Sea', *International Maritime Health*, Vol 57, 2006
2   Foucault, Michel, *Aesthetics, Method and Epistemology (Essential Works of Foucault, 1954–84)*, Penguin, London, 1998

CHAPTER 1
1   Stevenson, Anne, 'The sea is as near as we come to another world', from 'North Sea off Carnoustie', *Poems 1955–2005*, Bloodaxe Books, Hexham, Northumberland, 2005
2   Duppa, Richard, *Travels on the Continent, Sicily, and the Lipari Islands*, Longman, Rees, Orme & Co, 1829
3, 4 Victor, Prince Albert, Prince George of Wales, and Dalton, John N, *The cruise of Her Majesty's ship Bacchante, 1879–1882*, MacMillan & Co, 1886
5   Stockton, Richard, *Round-about Rambles in Lands of Fact and Fancy*, Scribner, Armstrong & Company, New York, 1872
6   www.shipsnostalgia.com/archive/index.php/t-18750.html
7   Stadler, Michael, *Psychology of Sailing*, Adlard Coles, London, 1987

CHAPTER 2
1   Pollock, Arthur William Alsager, 'Voyages of the Adventure and Beagle', *The United Service Journal*, Vol 35, 1841
2, 3, 4 Beals, HJ, *Four Travel Journals: The Americas, Antarctica and Africa, 1775–1874*, ed HJ Beals, Ashgate, London, 2007
5   Pigafetta, Antonio, *First Voyage Round the World by Magellan*, 1874

6   King, Phillip Parker, and FitzRoy, Robert, *Narrative of the Surveying Voyages of His Majesty's Ships Adventure and Beagle Between the Years 1826 and 1836*, 1839
7, 8 Beals, HJ, 2007
9   King and FitzRoy, 1839
10, 11, 12, 13 Letter to Admiralty Secretary John Wilson Croker by Phillip Parker King, 8 September 1828, www.rockvillepress.com/tierra/texts/kingletter.htm
14   King and FitzRoy, 1839
15   Letter to Croker, 1828
16   King and FitzRoy, 1839
17   Nichols, Peter, *Evolution's Captain*, Profile Books, London, 2003
18   King and FitzRoy, 1839
19   Taylor, James, *The Voyage of the Beagle*, Conway, London, 2008
20   Nichols, 2003
21, 22 Taylor, James, 2008
23, 24 beagleproject.wordpress.com/2012/02/26/coffee-talk-with-captain-fitzroy
25, 26, 27, 28 Taylor, James, 2008
29   darwinday.org/educate/oxforddebate
30   www.bbc.co.uk/news/magazine-32483678

CHAPTER 3

1   Bossier de Sauvages de Lacroix, François, *Dictionaires des Sciences Médicales*, 1771
2, 3 Falret, Jean-Pierre, *Du Délire*, 1839
4   Brown, Stephen, *Scurvy How a Surgeon, a Mariner, and a Gentleman Solved the Greatest Medical Mystery of the Age of Sail*, St Martin's Griffin, New York, 2003
5, 6 Walter, Richard, *Anson's Voyage Round the World*, Martin Hopkinson, London, 1928
7   Trotter, Thomas, *Observations on the Scurvy*, 1792
8   Melville, Herman, *Omoo*, Harper & Bros, 1847
9, 10 Stein, Glenn M, *Discovering the North-West Passage: The Four-Year Arctic Odyssey of HMS Investigator and the McClure Expedition*, McFarlane & Co, Jefferson, NC, 2015

CHAPTER 4

1, 2 Gartner, John D, *The Hypomanic Edge: The Link Between (A Little) Craziness and (A Lot of) Success in America*, Simon & Schuster, New York, 2005
3   Bergreen, Laurence, *Columbus: The Four Voyages, 1492–1504*, Penguin, New York, 2013

4   Granzotto, Gianni, *Christopher Columbus: The Dream and the Obsession*, Collins, London, 1986

5   Brock, Karen R, *Living with Bipolar Disorder: A Handbook for Patients and Their Families*, 2014, by permission of McFarland & Company Inc, Box 611, Jefferson NC 28640. www.mcfarlandpub.com

6, 7 Bligh, William, *Narrative of the Mutiny on the Bounty*, George Nicol, 1790

8   Christian, Glynn, *Fragile Paradise – The Discovery of Fletcher Christian, Bounty Mutineer*, Long Riders Guild Press, 2005

9   Description in Bligh's notebook, 1789, viewed online at National Library of Australia: www.nla.gov.au/apps/cdview/?pi=nla.ms-ms5393-2-s1-e

10   Dening, Greg, *Mr Bligh's Bad Language*, Cambridge University Press, Cambridge, 2010

11, 12, 13, 14 Druett, Joan, *In the Wake of Madness: The Murderous Voyage of the Whaleship Sharon*, Algonquin Books, Chapel Hill, 2004

CHAPTER 5

1   Blane, Sir Gilbert, *Statements of the Comparative Health of the British Navy From the Year 1779 to the Year 1814*, 1815

2   Lewis, Michael, *A Social History of the Navy 1793–1815*, George Allen & Unwin, London, 1960

3   Interview by the author with Andrew Baines, Curator, HMS *Victory*, www.hms-victory.com, March 2015

4   Adkins, Roy and Lesley, *Jack Tar: Life in Nelson's Navy*, Abacus, London, 2009

5–13 ADM 105/28, Report on Treatment of Naval Lunatics at Hoxton and Bedlam 1812–1813, National Archives

14   Jones, Edgar, and Greenberg, Neil, 'Royal Naval Psychiatry: Organization, Methods And Outcomes, 1900–1945', *The Mariner's Mirror*, Vol 92 No 2, May 2006

15   ADM 105/28, Report on Treatment of Naval Lunatics at Hoxton and Bedlam 1812–1813, National Archives

16–32 ADM 105/28, Reports on Individual Cases of Lunacy 1822–1832, and ADM 305/102, journal of lunatic asylum, 1830–1842, both National Archives

33, 34 Letter by 'Philanthropos' to the Presidents of Bethlem Hospital, *The Lancet*, Vol 1, 19 December 1840

35, 36, 37 ADM 105/28, Report on Condition of Lunatic Wards in Haslar Hospital 1824, National Archives

38, 39 ADM 305/102, journal of lunatic asylum, 1830–1842

✳ ENDNOTES

CHAPTER 6

1–8 Chase, Owen, *The Wreck of the Whaleship Essex*, Headline Books, 1999
9   Philbrick, Nathaniel, *In the Heart of the Sea: The Tragedy of the Whaleship Essex*, Penguin, New York, 2001

CHAPTER 7

1–5 Savigny, Jean Baptiste Henri and Corréeard, Alexandre, *Naufrage de la frégate La Méduse, faisant partie de l'expédition du Sénégal, en 1816*, Hoquet, 1817
6, 7, 8 *North Wales Chronicle*, 1 June 1872
9   Allen, William H, 'Thirst: Can Shipwrecked Men Survive if They Drink Seawater', *Natural History*, December 1956
10, 11 *Daily Mirror*, 19 May 1914
12, 13 Palmer, John, *Awful Shipwreck... Narrative of the Sufferings of the Crew of the Ship Francis Spaight, Etc*, 1837
14, 15 Leslie, Edward E, *Desperate Journeys, Abandoned Souls*, Houghton Mifflin, Boston, 1988
16 Simpson, AWB, *Cannibalism and the Common Law, The Story of the Tragic Last Voyage of the Mignonette and the Strange Legal Proceedings to Which it Gave Rise*, University of Chicago Press, Chicago, 1984

CHAPTER 8

1   Hastings, David, *Over the Mountains of the Sea: Life on the Migrant Ships 1870–1885*, Auckland University Press, Auckland, 2006
2–10 McCarthy, Angela, 'Migration and Madness at Sea: The Nineteenth- and Early Twentieth-century Voyage to New Zealand', *Social History of Medicine*, Vol 28, No 4, Nov 2015
11 Before the establishment of mental asylums in the mid-19th century, poor people with serious mental health issues were dealt with under the poor law, vagrancy law or criminal law
12 Fitton, Edward, *New Zealand: Its Present Condition, Prospects and Resources*, 1856
13 McCarthy, Angela, 2015
14 Smith, Michelle K, 'Did the Irish Famine Trigger Mental Illness in the Irish?', *Irish Central*, 16 December 2016
15–19 McCarthy, Angela, 2015
20, 21 Lindsay, W Lauder, 'Insanity in British Emigrants of the Middle and Upper Ranks', *Edinburgh Medical Journal*, Vol 15, 1869
22 Ødegård, Ørnulv, 'Emigration and Insanity: A Study of Mental Disease Among the Norwegian-born Population of Minnesota', *Acta Psychiatrica et Neurologia Supplementum*, Vol 4, 1932
23 McCarthy, Angela, 2015

24 Molina, Natalia, *How Race Is Made in America: Immigration, Citizenship, and the Historical Power of Racial Scripts*, University of California Press, Berkeley, 2014
25 Schrag, Peter, *Not Fit for Our Society: Nativism and Immigration*, University of California Press, Berkeley, 2010
26, 27 *Evening Standard*, 1858
28 *Roscommon Messenger*, 24 September 1859
29 *Belfast Weekly News*, 22 June 1889
30 *Belfast Telegraph*, 3 October 1873
31, 32 *Driffield Times*, 27 March 1909
33 *Aberdeen Evening Express*, 3 March 1890
34 Lindsay, W Lauder, 1869
35, 36 Leckie, Jacqueline, 'Lost Souls: Madness, Suicide, and Migration in Colonial Fiji until 1920', *Migration, Ethnicity, and Mental Health: International Perspectives, 1840–2010*, Routledge, Oxford, 2012
37–44 *Inverness Courier*, 2 June 1853

CHAPTER 9

1–6 *Louth and North Lincolnshire Advertiser*, 3 November 1866
7 'Loaded Down with Iniquity: The Sinking of the Evening Star', *Louisiana Cultural Vistas*, Fall 2015

CHAPTER 10

1 *Staffordshire Advertiser*, 19 January 1895
2, 3 *Shields Daily Gazette*, 5 September 1893
4 *Lincolnshire Echo*, 5 September 1895
5 *Shields Daily Gazette*, 7 December 1872
6 *Western Gazette*, 29 May 1891
7 *Falkirk Herald*, 18 August 1853
8 *Morpeth Herald*, 16 May 1874
9 Proceedings of the Old Bailey, James Cocks, James Gleaves, Edwin William Evans, John William Webster, Murder, 27 June 1887, ref t18870627-718 (available at www.oldbaileyonline.org)
10, 11 *Lancashire Evening Post*, 29 June 1909
12 *Sheffield Evening Telegraph*, 19 October 1893
13 *Portsmouth Evening News*, 5 March 1892
14 *Portland Guardian*, 9 May 1873
15 *South Australian Register*, August 1873
16, 17 *London Evening Standard*, 20 August 1844
18 *Morning Post*, 21 January 1841
19 *Sheffield Independent*, 31 March 1821
20 *Nottingham Evening Post*, 14 September 1915

21 *Bath Chronicle*, 25 January 1877
22, 23 *Grantham Journal*, 20 March 1875
24 *Nottingham Evening Post*, 22 September 1890
25 *Bell's Life*, 10 October 1830
26 *The Annual Register or A View of the History, Politics and Literature of the Year 1828*, 1829
27 *Manchester Courier*, 17 May 1913
28 www.sailors-society.org/about-us/our-history

CHAPTER 11

1–3 Strong, LAG, *Flying Angel: The Story of the Missions to Seamen*, Methuen, London, 1956

CHAPTER 12

1 Letter from Cpt Poland of HMS *Warspite*, to his brother, quoted in Coppack, Peter, *Tyneside and the Battle of Jutland*, Northumbria World War One Commemoration Project, 2016
2 Willis, Gunnery Petty Officer WJA, HMS *Calliope*, quoted in Coppack, Peter, 2016
3 'The Death Ride', www.royalnavy.mod.uk/news-and-latest-activity/features/jutland-100/battle-6-33pm
4, 5 Jones, Edgar, and Greenberg, Neil, 'Royal Naval Psychiatry: Organization, Methods and Outcomes, 1900–1945', *The Mariner's Mirror*, Vol 92 No 2, May 2006
6 *The Freud Encyclopedia: Theory, Therapy and Culture*, Taylor & Francis, London, 2002
7 Weidner, Carl, 'Traumatic Neurasthenia', *American Practitioner and News*, Vol 39, 1905
8 Coppack, Peter, 2016
9, 10, 11, 12 Jones, Edgar, and Greenberg, Neil, 2006
13, 14, 15 Jones, Edgar, 'The Gut War: Functional Somatic Disorders in the UK during the Second World War', *History of the Human Sciences*, December 2012
16 Monsarrat, Nicholas, *The Cruel Sea*, Penguin, London, 2009
17–22 Osmond, Humphry, 'Acute Illness at Sea – A Study of 50 Cases', *Journal of the Royal Naval Medical Service*, Vol 33, April 1947
23, 24 Anderson, EW, 'Lessons of War Psychiatry', *Journal of the Royal Naval Medical Service*, Vol 32, January 1946
25–31 Osmond, Humphry, 1947
32, 33 Dr Humphry Osmond obituary, *Telegraph*, 16 February 2004
34 Will, Otto Allen, 'The Psychotic Naval Prisoner', *Naval Medical Bulletin*, Vol 46, No5, May 1946

35, 36, 37 Boshes, LD, 'Psychiatry of the Naval Offender', *Hospital Corps Quarterly*, Vol 19, Issue 4, April 1946

CHAPTER 13

1   Bennett, GH, *Survivors: British Merchant Seamen in the Second World War*, Hambledon Continuum Press, an imprint of Bloomsbury Publishing Plc, London, 1999. © GH Bennett, reproduced with permission of Bloomsbury Publishing
2, 3 *Auckland Star*, 27 November 1944
4   Bennett, GH, 1999
5, 6 Lindemann, Hannes, *Alone at Sea*, Lindemann Press, 2013

CHAPTER 14

1, 2, 3, 4 Slocum, Joshua, *Sailing Alone Around the World*, Adlard Coles Nautical, London, 1996
5   Freud, Sigmund, *The Interpretation of Dreams*, Macmillan, New York, 1913
6, 7, 8 Spencer, Ann, *Alone At Sea: The Adventures of Joshua Slocum*, Doubleday Canada, Toronto, 1998
9, 10 Wolf, Geoffrey, *The Hard Way Around: The Passages of Joshua Slocum*, Alfred A Knopf, New York, 2010

CHAPTER 15

1,2 Knox-Johnston, Robin, *A World of My Own*, Cassell, London, 1969
3   Day, George, and McCormick, Herb, *Out There*, Seven Seas Press, Newport, 1983
4   Blagden, David, quoted by Page, Frank, 'Alone Against the Atlantic', *Observer*, 1980
5, 6, 7 Lewis, HE, Harries, JM, Lewis, DH, 'Voluntary Solitude: Studies of Men in a Singlehanded Transatlantic Sailing Race', *The Lancet*, 27 June 1964
8, 9 Howells, Valentine, *Sailing Into Solitude*, Landsker Publications, 2011
10   White, EB, and Thurber, James, *Is Sex Necessary? Or, Why You Feel the Way You Do*, Harper & Bros, 1929
11   Brown, Helen Gurley, *Sex and the Single Girl*, Bernard Geis Associates, New York, 1962
12   Berne, Eric, *Games People Play: The Psychology of Human Relationships*, Grove Press, New York, 1964
13   Harris, Thomas Anthony, *I'm OK – You're OK*, Harper & Row, New York, 1967
14   Reuben, David, *Everything You Wanted to Know About Sex (But Were Afraid To Ask)*, McKay, New York, 1969

15 Bach, Richard, *Jonathan Livingston Seagull*, Macmillan, New York, 1970
16–20 Bennet, Glin, 'Medical and Psychological Problems in the 1972 Singlehanded Transatlantic Yacht Race', *The Lancet*, 6 October 1973

CHAPTER 16

1   Verne, Jules, *Twenty Thousand Leagues Under the Sea*, 1870
2   Bennet, Glin, 'Psychological Breakdown at Sea: Hazards of Singlehanded Ocean Sailing', *British Journal of Medical Psychology*, Vol 47, Issue 3, September 1974
3, 4, 5, 6 Tomalin, Nicholas, and Hall, Ron, *The Strange Voyage of Donald Crowhurst*, Times Newspapers Ltd, London, 1970
7, 8 Bennet, Glin, 1974
9, 10 Moitessier, Bernard, *The Long Way*, Sheridan House, 1995
11 Centre Presse, Poitiers, 24 March 1969
12 *The Times*, March 1969
13 *The Times*, 23 June 1969
14 Laing, RD, *The Divided Self: An Existential Study in Sanity and Madness*, Penguin, London, 1960
15 Nichols, Peter, *A Voyage for Madmen*, Profile Books, London, 2001
16, 17, 18 Knox-Johnston, Robin, *A World of My Own*, Cassell, London, 1969

CHAPTER 17

1   Day, George, and McCormick, Herb, *Out There*, Seven Seas Press, 1983

CHAPTER 18

1   Interview by the author with Neil Weston, Department of Sport and Exercise Science, University of Portsmouth, www.port.ac.uk, 10 February 2014
2   Weston, Neil, *Coping and Emotion in Sport* (ed David Lavallee), Routledge, Oxford, 2011
3   MacArthur, Ellen, *Taking on the World*, Penguin Books, London, 2003. Copyright © Ellen MacArthur, 2003
4, 5, 6, 7 Musy, Isabelle, 'Vendée Globe: Hallucinations en Haute Mer', *Le Monde*, 13 December 2012
8   'Solitaire du Figaro: "Une course...hallucinante"', *Le Télégramme*, 29 July 2011
9   Loisel, Véronique, 'Les hallucinations en mer', 16 November 2010, veroniqueloisel.blogspot.com
10, 11, 12 Interview by the author with Susie Goodall, susiegoodall.co.uk, 19 April 2017

CHAPTER 19

1   MacDonald, Marianne, 'Yachtsman Lost at Sea "Dived from Race Boat"', *The Independent*, 29 May 1993
2, 3 'Chay Blyth Round-the-World Yacht Race Reunion', *Yachting World*, 15 January 2013
4   Pickthall, Barry, *No Guts – No Glory*, Carfax Publishing, Abingdon, 1993
5, 6 MacDonald, Marianne, 1993
7   Pickthall, Barry, email, 2 March 2017

CHAPTER 20

1   'Ocean's Twelve', *People Management*, 20 May 2002
2, 3, 4, 5 Dulewicz, Victor, and Higgs, Malcolm, 'Emotional Intelligence, Motivation and Personality: A Study of Leaders and Teams in a Round-the-World Yacht Race', Henley Management College, 2002
6   Alber, Von Alexander, 'Mord an Bord: "Du hast noch zehn Minuten zu leben"', *Westdeutsche Zeitung*, 20 December 2013
7, 8, 9 Ward, Nick, *Left For Dead*, Adlard Coles Nautical, an imprint of Bloomsbury Publishing Plc, London, 2007. © Nick Ward, reproduced by permission of Bloomsbury Publishing

CHAPTER 21

1   Agterberg, G, and Passchier, J, 'Stress Among Seamen', *Psychological Reports*, Vol 83, October 1998
2   Going off the deep end: 'To degenerate cognitively, to be in the process of having a mental breakdown, the process of going crazy' www.urbandictionary.com
3   Devries, Ernst, 'Seafarer Depression: Alone in a Wide, Wide Sea', Ministry to Seafarers, 2 February 2013, seafarerschaplain.blogspot.co.uk
4   Iversen, Robert TB, 'The Mental Health of Seafarers: A Brief Review', *International Maritime Health*, Vol 63, Issue 2, 2012
5   Roberts, SE, Jaremin, B, and Lloyd, K, 'High-risk Occupations for Suicide', *Psychological Medicine*, Vol 43, Issue 6, October 2012
6, 7, 8 Szymańska, Kinga, Jaremin, Bogdan, and Rosik, Elżbieta, 'Suicides Among Polish Seamen and Fishermen During Work at Sea', *International Maritime Health*, 2006, #57
9   Title 4, Regulation 4.3, Maritime Labour Convention 2006, www.mlc2006.com
10 'Society Launches Virtual Boaty McBoatface', www.sailors-society.org/about-us/press-room/boaty

11 'Seafarers Hospital Society Launches Free Online Mental Health and Wellbeing Service', seafarerswelfare.org, 12 September 2016

12 O'Reilly, Emma, and Evans, Natalie, 'Man "Jumped to his Death from Luxury Cruise Ship after Anti-gay Taunts from Crew"', *The Mirror*, 12 November 2015

13 'Vanished Disney Cruise Ship Worker Could Have Been "Murdered"', BBC News website, 30 October 2015, www.bbc.co.uk/news/uk-england-manchester-34659505

14 Lamb, Jonathan, *Scurvy: The Disease of Discovery*, Princeton University Press, Princeton, 2017

15, 16 Macleod, AD, 'Calenture: Missing at Sea?', *Psychology and Psychotherapy*, Vol 56, Issue 4, December 1983

17 Motter, Paul, 'Suicide, Even at Sea, Isn't Painless', www.cruisemates.com

18 Freud, Sigmund, *Civilisation and Its Discontents*, Penguin Classics, 2002

19 Masson, JM, *The Oceanic Feeling: The Origins of Religious Sentiment in Ancient India*, D Reidel, 1980

20 Fenichel, Otto, Psychoanalytic Quarterly, Vol XIII, June 1944

21 Low, Anthony, 'Seafarers and Passengers Who Disappear Without A Trace From Aboard Ships', *International Maritime Health*, Vol 57, 2006

CHAPTER 22

1 *The Complete Euripides: Volume II: Iphigenia in Tauris and Other Plays*, Oxford University Press, Oxford, 2010

2–3 Russell, Richard, *A Dissertation on the Use of Sea Water in Diseases of the Glands*, 1750

4 Jerome, John, *Blue Rooms: Ripples, Rivers, Pools, and Other Waters*, Henry Holt, 1997

CHAPTER 23

1 Extract from *The Cruise of the 'Nona'* by Hilaire Belloc, 1925, reprinted by permission of Peters Fraser & Dunlop (www.petersfraserdunlop.com) on behalf of the Estate of Hilaire Belloc

2 Race Trophies and Awards, www.sailtraininginternational.org

3 'Survey into the Effectiveness of R Tucker Thompson Sail Training Programmes' 2009–2013, © R Tucker Thompson Sail Training Trust, tucker.co.nz/youth-voyages/sail-training-survey

4 Allison, P, McCulloch, K, McLaughlin, P, Edwards, V, and Tett, L, 'The Characteristics and Value of the Sail Training Experience', University Of Edinburgh, June 2007

5   McCarthy, Luke, and Kotzee, Ben, 'Comparing Sail Training and Landbased Youth Development Activities: A Pilot Study', Dissertation for MSc in Youth Participation, 2011

6, 7, 8, 9 Interview by author with Ben Wheatley, Operations Director, Trinity Sailing Foundation, www.trinitysailing.org, 22 February 2017

10, 11 Interview by author with Squadron Leader Shaun Pascoe, Founder, Turn to Starboard, www.turntostarboard.co.uk, February 2017

12 'Who we are', www.turntostarboard.co.uk

13, 14 Interview with Shaun Pascoe, 2017

15–19 Interview by author with Joseph Sabien, CEO, Sea Sanctuary, www.seasanctuary.org.uk, 13 February 2017

20 Interview by author with Dan Fielding, Sailing Instructor, Turn to Starboard, www.turntostarboard.co.uk, February 2017

EPILOGUE

1   Private message

2   Interviews by author with Shaun Pascoe and Dan Fielding, Turn to Starboard, www.turntostarboard.co.uk, February 2017

3   Furness, Hannah, 'Prince Harry: I sought counselling after 20 years of not thinking about the death of my mother, Diana', *Daily Telegraph*, 19 April 2017

4   Jones, Edgar, 'The Gut War: Functional Somatic Disorders in the UK During the Second World War', *History of the Human Sciences*, December 2012

INDEX